THE COMPLETE GUIDE TO
MASONRY
& Stonework
Includes Decorative Concrete Treatments

Creative Publishing international

MINNEAPOLIS, MINNESOTA
www.creativepub.com

Contents

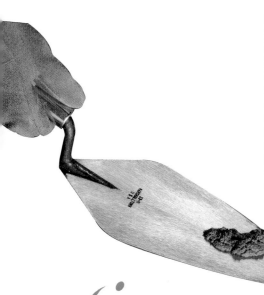

Creative Publishing
international

Printed by: R.R. Donnelley
10 9 8 7 6

President/CEO: Ken Fund

For Revised Edition:

Publisher: Bryan Trandem
Assistant Managing Editor: Tracy Stanley
Senior Editor: Mark Johanson
Senior Art Director: Dave Schelitzche
Page Layout: Joe Fahey
Creative Director, Photography: Tim Himsel
Lead Photographer: Steve Galvin
Additional Photographers: Andrea Rugg, Joel Schnell
Scene Shop Carpenter: Randy Austin
Additional Shop Carpenters: Sean Brennan, Glenn Austin
Photo Editor: Julie Caruso
Production Manager: Laura Hokkanen
Lead Editor: Thomas G. Lemmer

THE COMPLETE GUIDE TO MASONRY & Stonework
Created by: The Editors of Creative Publishing international,
Inc., in cooperation with Black & Decker. Black & Decker is a
trademark of The Black & Decker Corporation and is used under
license.

Stucco & Veneer

Natural Stone

Repair & Maintenance

Library of Congress
Cataloging-in-Publication Data

The Complete guide to masonry &
stonework : includes decorative concrete
treatments.

p. cm.
At head of title: Black & Decker.
Summary: "Features new projects for
building retaining walls with
tumbled concrete block, facing concrete
slabs and steps with natural
stone and ceramic tiles, creating outdoor
rock gardens, and easy methods
for casting concrete in forms to create
countertops, garden benches and
other accessories. Also provides new information on decorative concrete
finishes, including acid coloring, stamping,
and using cementitious
paints"--Provided by publisher.
ISBN-13: 978-1-58923-282-2 (softcover)
ISBN-10: 1-58923-282-8 (softcover)
1. Stonemasonry. I. Black & Decker Corporation (Towson, Md.).
TH5401.C655 2006
693'.1--dc22

2006017606

Other titles from Creative Publishing international
include:
*The Complete Guide to Home Wiring, The Com-
plete Guide to Home Plumbing, The Complete
Guide to Home Carpentry, The Complete Guide
to Decks, The Complete Guide to Painting & Dec-
orating, The Complete Guide To Bathrooms, The
Complete Guide to Kitchens, The Complete
Guide to Flooring, The Complete Guide to Roof-
ing & Siding, The Complete Guide to Landscape
Construction, The Complete Guide to Yard & Gar-
den Features, The Complete Guide to Creative
Landscapes, The Complete Guide to Windows &
Doors, The Complete Guide to Wood Storage
Projects, The Complete Guide to Easy Wood-
working Projects, The Complete Guide to Trim &
Finish Carpentry, The Complete Guide to Gaze-
bos & Arbors, The Complete Guide to Walls &
Ceilings, The Complete Guide to Ceramic &
Stone Tile, The Complete Guide to Choosing
Landscape Plants.*

Introduction

Masonry is a popular home building material for many reasons, including its beauty, versatility, and resistance to fire, earthquakes, and sound transmission. And let's not forget its remarkable durability. While few of us imagine that our homes will exist for centuries, when we choose masonry we're choosing a material that has precisely that capability. Some of the world's most venerable masonry structures—the Taj Mahal, the Egyptian Pyramids, the Colosseum in Rome, the Great Sphinx of Giza—have awed countless generations with their ability to withstand time.

Once upon a time, "masonry" was defined as the work product of a mason or stoneworker, but that definition no longer applies. These days, improved products and tools put many masonry projects well within the abilities of do-it-yourselfers. Within the pages of The Complete Guide to Masonry and Stonework, you'll find information on working with and making repairs to materials such as poured concrete, brick and block, stucco and natural stone.

Our goal is to help you understand the fundamentals of working with masonry so that you can design and carry out projects around your home. We recommend that you begin every major project by consulting a local building inspector about the regulations and requirements in your municipality. Pull all necessary permits and submit to all required inspections: when all is said and done, you and your family are well served by complying with these rules and regulations.

"Poured Concrete" (pages 14 to 97), introduces you to the tools, materials, and basic techniques necessary for pouring concrete, and then leads you—step-by-step— through basic projects, such as footings, sidewalks, steps, and slabs, and more sophisticated projects, such as a driveway and a cast concrete countertop.

"Brick and Block" (pages 100 to 165), presents the tools, materials, and basic techniques used when working with brick and block. The projects in this section include building concrete walls, block retaining walls, and pillars. You'll find both mortared and dry-set projects, as well as instructions on how to build steps with pre-cast forms.

"Stucco and Veneers" (pages 168 to 201), introduces you to the basic tools and techniques for installing masonry veneer, and then provides projects such as the application of stucco, surface-bonding cement, stone veneer and tiling over a concrete slab.

"Natural Stone" (pages 204 to 235), contains helpful advice on handling and building with cutstone, flagstone and other types of stone, showcasing their native beauty. Walls, walkways patios and more offer shining examples of the art of creative stonework.

"Repair and Maintenance" (pages 238 to 293), teaches you to maintain and repair concrete, brick and block, stucco, and stonework.

The Glossary (pages 294 and 295), provides definitions for many less well-known terms, and the Conversion Charts (pages 296 and 297) provides metric conversions for various units of measurement.

In The Complete Guide to Masonry and Stonework you'll find all the information you need to learn and enjoy the timeless craft of masonry.

Portfolio of Masonry & Stonework for the Home

In their raw state, concrete and rocks are about the most humble building materials you can find. But add some inspiration and a little hard work, and you'll be amazed at the feats that can be accomplished with these simple products. The projects featured on the following pages are just a sampling of the beauty of masonry.

Stucco (right) is a very popular and highly durable siding product that takes advantage of the many benefits of masonry materials.

Blocks, bricks, pavers and natural stone all find a home in this showcase-of-masonry landscape. Included are two retaining walls (one cut stone, one interlocking block with cast capstones), a concrete paver walkway and brick veneer, all interspersed with well-chosen landscape boulders.

Natural clay tile and a clay brick garden wall are separated by a border of light porcelain tiles to help enhance their complementary tones.

Cast stepping stones (right) allow landscapers to apply creative touches to the otherwise plain concrete gray tones: in this case, filling the gaps between stepping stones with crushed gravel.

Flagstone patios (below) are instantly recognizable and also highly regarded for their durability and the pleasing patterns that can be created by arranging shapes.

An outdoor kitchen is a perfect vehicle for incorporating masonry products into your yard. Here, stucco is used to clad the grilling work center that rests on a sprawling clay tile pool deck.

Dry-stacking stone is a venerable building technique that yields walls with unmatched natural appeal. While they require regular upkeep, the fact that the stones are not bonded together allows dry-stacked walls to move and shift during freeze/thaw cycles that can crumble a mortared wall.

Concrete pavers (above) come in many shapes and sizes that allow you to accomplish designs of virtually unlimited variety.

Cast concrete can be formed into a host of useful and decorative items for the garden, such as this planter cast in a 5-gallon bucket.

Poured concrete sidewalks don't need to be straight and uniform. Curves go a long way toward visually softening this rock-hard material.

Function is defined by arrangement when stacking and laying brick pavers (above). Laid flat, they're a patio or pool deck: stacked, they form a wall; and when you combine laid pavers and stacked pavers, you can create steps that match their surroundings exactly.

Brick veneer transforms these concrete column bases from ordinary to elegant.

Square and rectangular concrete pads (above) can be as soft and charming as any curved pathway when they are combined creatively.

The exposed aggregate squares in this concrete patio (right) take on the look of high-end landscape design because they are separated by a grid of brick pavers.

The massive presence of concrete is used to great design advantage in the cast concrete elements found in the patio and fireplace above. The simple lines and monochromatic tones are set off nicely by the greenery, giving the patio a distinct Eastern feeling.

Poured Concrete

Working with Concrete

Durable, versatile, and economical, poured concrete can be shaped and finished into a wide variety of surfaces and structures throughout your home and yard. Decorative surfaces and unique appearances can be produced with exposed aggregate, tints and stains, and special stamping tools.

Pouring footings or a foundation is the first step to many hardscape projects, such as fences, walls, sheds, and decks or gazebos, and is an excellent introduction to working with concrete. Pouring a small sidewalk or patio is a good way to learn about finishing concrete. It's best to save larger projects, such as driveways and large patios, until you are comfortable working with and finishing concrete, and have plenty of assistants on hand to help you.

Planning and preparation are the keys to successful concrete projects. Poured concrete yields the most durable and attractive final finish when it is poured at an air temperature between 50 and 80 degrees F and when the finishing steps are completed carefully in the order described in the following pages.

Good preparation means fewer delays at critical moments and leaves you free to focus on placing and smoothing the concrete—not on staking loose forms or locating misplaced tools. Before beginning to mix or pour the concrete, make sure the forms are sturdy enough to stand up to the weight and pressure that will be exerted on them and that they are staked and braced well. Forms that are taller than 4 or 5 inches should be tied with wire. The joints on the forms should be tight enough that the bleed water doesn't run through them.

One of the most difficult aspects of finishing concrete is recognizing when it's ready. Many people try to rush the process, with disappointing results. Wait until the bleed water disappears and the concrete has hardened somewhat before floating the surface. A good rule of thumb is when the footprints you leave are light enough that you can no longer identify the type of shoes you are wearing, the concrete is ready to be worked.

Components of Concrete

The basic ingredients of concrete are the same, whether the concrete is mixed from scratch, purchased premixed, or delivered by a ready-mix company. Portland cement is the bonding agent. It contains crushed lime, cement, and other bonding minerals. Sand and a combination of aggregates add volume and strength to the mix. Water activates the cement, then evaporates, allowing the concrete to dry into a solid mass. By varying the ratios of the ingredients, professionals can create concrete with special properties that are suited for specific situations.

Tools & Materials

Successfully pouring and finishing concrete depends in part on having the right tools. You will need special-purpose tools to help you prepare the site and then place, shape, and finish the concrete. It makes sense to purchase any tools you're sure to use again, but you will probably want to rent several of the specialty items, which are widely available at rental centers.

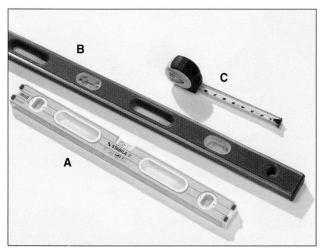

Layout and measuring tools for preparing jobsites and installing and levelling concrete forms include a 2-ft. level (A), a 4-ft. level (B) and tape measure (C).

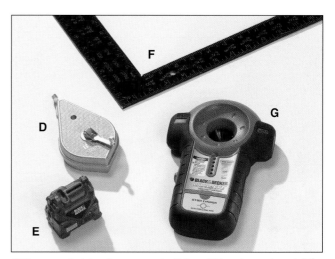

Other useful tools are a chalkline (D), a laser level (E), or a combination laser level and stud finder (G) and a carpenter's square.

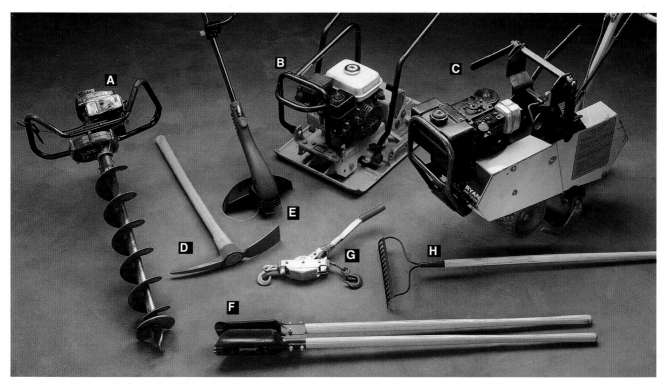

Landscaping tools for preparing sites for concrete projects include: power auger (A) for digging holes for posts or poles; power tamper (B) and power sod cutter (C) for driveway and other large-scale site preparation. Smaller landscaping tools, include: pick (D) for excavating hard or rocky soil; weed trimmer (E) for removing brush and weeds before digging; posthole digger (F) for when you have just a few holes to dig; come-along (G) for moving large rocks and other heavy objects without excessive lifting; and garden rake (H) for moving small amounts of soil and debris.

Safety tools and equipment include: particle masks, gloves, safety glasses, and tall rubber boots. Wear protective gear when handling dry or mixed concrete. These mixes are very alkaline and can burn eyes and skin.

Mixing and pouring tools include: masonry hoe and mortar box for mixing small amounts of concrete; garden hose and bucket for delivering and measuring water; and power mixer for mixing medium-sized (between $\frac{1}{2}$ and 1 cubic foot) loads of concrete.

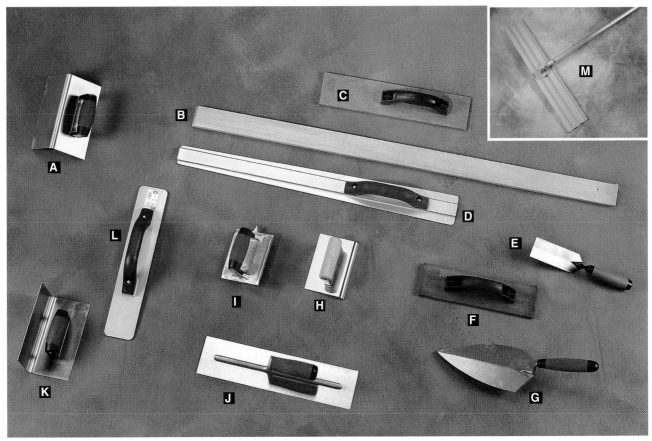

Finishing tools include: outside corner tool (A); screed board (B) for striking off placed concrete; long wood float (C); aluminum darby (D) for smoothing screeded concrete; square-end trowel (E) for finishing; standard-length wood float (F); mason's trowel (G); edger (H) for shaping and forming edges; groover (I) for forming control joints; a steel trowel (J); inside corner tool (K); magnesium float (L); and long-handled bull float (M) for smoothing large slabs.

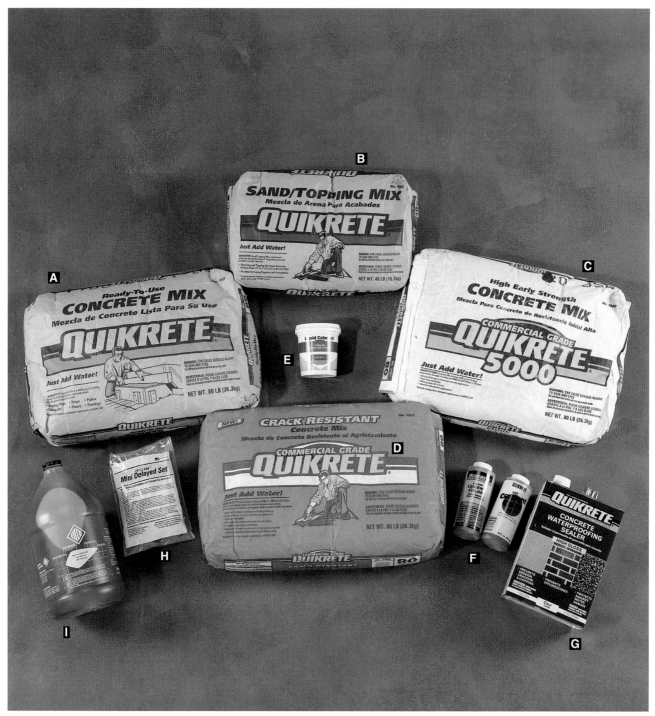

Concrete mix, usually sold in 40, 60 or 80-lb. bags, contains all the components of concrete. You simply add water, mix, and place the concrete. Several varieties are offered at most building centers. The most common are: general-purpose mix (A), which is the least expensive and is suitable for most do-it-yourself projects; sand mix (B) contains no mixed aggregate and is used for shallow pours, such as pouring overlays less than 2" thick (that's why it's sometimes called topping mix); high-early strength mix (C) contains agents that cause it to strengthen quickly, achieving 5000 psi after 28 days. This mix is particularly appropriate for patios, driveway aprons and con-

crete countertops. Other common bagged concrete varieties include fiber-reinforced, fast-setting and crack resistant (D).

Concrete additives include powdered colorant (E) and liquid pigments (F) that are added to the mix to produce vividly colored concrete; sealant (G) to promote curing by retaining water in freshly placed concrete. Less common admixtures used mostly by professionals (and therefore hard to find for DIYers) include retarder that slows down the cure time (H) and winter admixture (I) that reduces the time the concrete has to be protected from freezing.

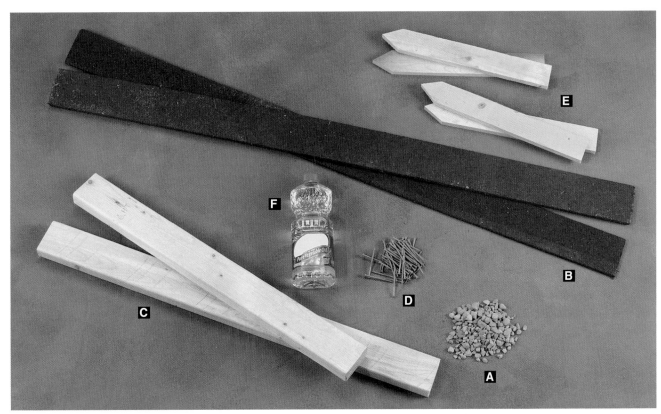

Materials for subbases and forms include: compactible gravel (A) to improve drainage beneath the poured concrete structure, asphalt-impregnated fiberboard (B) to keep concrete from bonding with adjoining structures, lumber (C) and 3" screws (D) for building forms, stakes (E) for holding the forms in place, and vegetable oil (F) or a commercial release agent to make it easier to remove the forms.

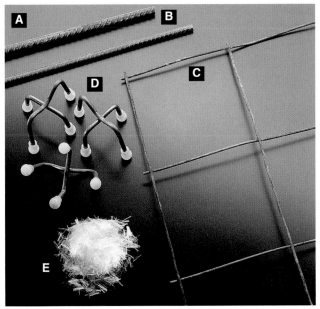

Reinforcement materials: Metal rebar (A & B), available in sizes ranging from #2 ($\frac{1}{8}$" diameter) to #5 ($\frac{5}{8}$" diameter) for reinforcing concrete slabs, like sidewalks, and in masonry walls. Wire mesh (C) (sometimes called re-mesh) is most common in 6 × 6" grids. For broad surfaces, like patios; bolsters (D) for suspending rebar and wire mesh; fiber additive (E) for strengthening small projects that receive little traffic.

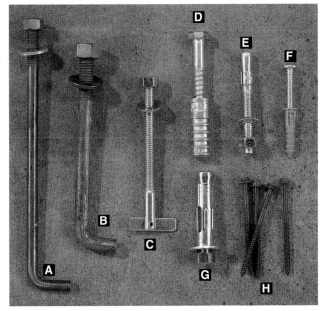

Masonry fasteners allow you to mount objects to concrete and other masonry surfaces. It is most effective to embed the fasteners in fresh concrete so that it cures around the hardware. Examples include: J-bolt with nuts and washers (A, B); removable T-anchor (C); metal sleeve anchor (D); compression sleeves (E, G); light-duty plastic anchor sleeve (F); self-tapping coated steel screws (H).

Planning Your Concrete Projects

There are two basic stages to planning and designing poured concrete projects. First, gather creative ideas to help plan an attractive, practical structure. Second, apply the basic standards of construction to create a structurally sound plan that complies with local building codes.

Begin by watching for good ideas wherever you go. As you drive or walk through neighborhoods, look for similar projects and observe detail and nuance. Once you've settled on a plan, test the layout by using a rope or hose to outline the proposed project areas. Remember that successful structures take into account size and scale, location, slope and drainage, reinforcement, material selection, and appearance. It's also advisable to take your own level of skills and experience into account, especially if you haven't worked with poured concrete often.

Finally, develop plan drawings for your project. If it's a simple project, quick sketches may be adequate. If permits will be necessary for your project, the building inspector is likely to request detailed plan drawings. (Always check with the local building department early in the planning process.) Either way, drawings help you recognize and avoid or deal with inherent challenges to your project.

Test project layouts before committing to your ideas. Use a rope or hose to outline the area, placing spacers where necessary to maintain accurate, even dimensions.

Make scaled plan drawings, using graph paper and drafting tools. Plan drawings help you eliminate design flaws and accurately estimate material requirements.

Estimating & Ordering Materials

Plan drawings are especially valuable when the time comes to estimate materials. With your drawing in hand, calculate the width and length of the project in feet, and then multiply the dimensions to get the square footage. Measure the thickness in feet (4 inches thick equals $\frac{1}{3}$ of a foot), then multiply the square footage times the thickness to the get the cubic footage. For example, 1 foot x 3 feet x $\frac{1}{3}$ foot = 1 cubic foot. Twenty-seven cubic feet equals one cubic yard.

Coverage rates for poured concrete are determined by the thickness of the slab. The same volume of concrete will yield less surface area if the thickness of the slab is increased.

With your estimates in hand, it's time to purchase mix or order concrete. For projects that require between half a cubic yard and one full cubic yard, plan to purchase ready-to-use mix and prepare the concrete in a power mixer. When purchasing the mix, you can estimate that one bag of concrete mix will produce about $\frac{1}{2}$ cubic foot of concrete.

If your estimate indicates that the project will require more than one cubic yard of concrete, order pre-mixed concrete and have it delivered to the project site.

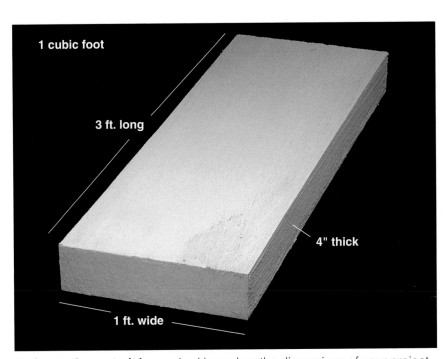

Estimate the materials required based on the dimensions of your project.

Concrete Coverage		
Volume	Slab Thickness	Surface Area
1 cu. yd.	2"	160 sq. ft.
1 cu. yd.	3"	110 sq. ft.
1 cu. yd.	4"	80 sq. ft
1 cu. yd.	5"	65 sq. ft.
1 cu. yd.	6"	55 sq. ft.
1 cu. yd.	8"	40 sq. ft.

This chart shows the relationship between slab thickness, surface area, and volume.

Ready-mix concrete delivered to your worksite is the only viable option for large pours, such as driveways or foundation walls. Professionals often hop right into the fresh mix, but as a DIYer try to stay out.

Ordering Ready-Mix Concrete

For large concrete jobs (one cubic yard or more), have ready-mix concrete delivered to the project site. Although ordering ready-mix concrete is more expensive than mixing it yourself, it saves time and insures uniform consistency throughout large projects.

In regions with severe climates, ready-mix concrete has another advantage: air-entrained concrete contains billions of microscopic air cells. These air cells provide tiny spaces where water can harmlessly expand as it freezes, which makes the concrete highly resistant to severe frost action and improves its workability and durability.

Ask friends and neighbors for referrals and try to select a reputable, reliable supplier. Before ordering the concrete, fully prepare the project site. When the site is ready, consult the supplier about how much and what type of concrete you need and schedule your delivery date. On the day before the scheduled pour, call the supplier to confirm the quantity and delivery time.

Before the day of the pour, prepare a clear delivery path to the project site. Decide where you want the truck to park and lay planks over the forms and subbase to make a path for the wheelbarrows or concrete hoppers. (If your driveway is asphalt or concrete that is cracked or damaged, have the truck park on the street to prevent further damage.)

When the truck arrives, ask the driver for a receipt. The receipt should indicate what time the concrete was mixed. If more than 90 minutes have elapsed since the concrete was mixed, do not accept the load.

Prepare the project site so everything is ready to go when the truck rolls up. The driver is seldom able to get access to the forms to pour the concrete directly into them, so be ready with your wheelbarrow brigade.

Good site preparation is one of the keys to a successful project. Patience and attention to detail when excavating, building forms, and establishing a subbase help ensure that your finished project is level and stable and will last for many years.

Basic Techniques

The first stage of any poured concrete project is the preparation of the project site. The basic steps are:

1) Lay out the project, using stakes and strings.

2) Clear the project area and remove the sod.

3) Excavate the site to allow for a subbase and footings (if necessary) and concrete.

4) Lay a subbase for drainage and stability and pour footings (if necessary).

5) Build and install reinforced wood forms.

Proper site preparation varies from project to project and site to site. Plan on a subbase of compactible gravel. Some projects require footings that extend past the frost line, while others, such as sidewalks, do not. Consult your local building inspector about the specific requirements of your project.

If your yard slopes more than 1 inch per foot, you may need to add or remove soil to level the surface; a landscape engineer or building inspector can advise you on how to prepare a sloping project site.

Everything You Need:

Tools: Rope, carpenter's square, hand maul, tape measure, mason's string, line level, spade, sod cutter, straightedge, level, wheelbarrow, shovel, hand tamper, circular saw, drill.

Materials: 2 × 4 lumber, 3" screws, compactible gravel, vegetable oil or commercial release agent.

SAFETY TIP

Contact your public utility company and have buried electric and gas lines marked before you begin to dig for this or any other project.

Tips for Preparing the Project Site

Measure the slope of the building site to determine if you need to do grading work before you start your project. First, drive stakes at each end of the project area. Attach a mason's string between the stakes and use a line level to set it at level. At each stake, measure from the string to the ground. The difference between the measurements (in inches) divided by the distance between stakes (in feet) will give you the slope (in inches per foot). If the slope is greater than 1" per foot, you may need to regrade the site.

Dig a test hole to the planned depth so you can evaluate the soil conditions and get a better idea of how easy the excavation will be. Sandy or loose soil may require amending; consult a landscape engineer.

Shown cut away

Compactible gravel subbase

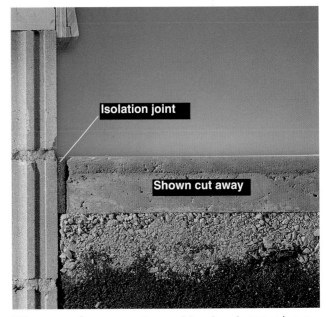

Isolation joint

Shown cut away

Add a compactible gravel subbase to provide a level, stable foundation for the concrete. The compactible gravel also improves drainage—an important consideration if you are building on soil that is high in clay content. For most building projects, pour a layer of compactible gravel about 5" thick, and use a tamper to compress it to 4".

When pouring concrete next to structures, glue a ½"-thick piece of asphalt-impregnated fiber board to the adjoining structure to keep the concrete from bonding with the structure. The board creates an isolation joint, allowing the structures to move independently, minimizing the risk of damage.

How to Lay Out & Excavate a Building Site

1 Lay out a rough project outline with a rope or hose. Use a carpenter's square to set perpendicular lines. To create the actual layout, begin by driving wood stakes near each corner of the rough layout. The goal is to arrange the stakes so they are outside the actual project area, but in alignment with the borders of the project. Where possible, use two stakes set back 1 ft. from each corner, so strings intersect to mark each corner (below). NOTE: In projects built next to permanent structures, the structure will define one project side.

2 Connect the stakes with mason's strings. The strings should follow the actual project outlines. To make sure the strings are square, use the 3-4-5 triangle method: measure and mark points 3 ft. out from one corner along one string, and 4 ft. out along the intersecting string at the corner. Measure between the points, and adjust the positions of the strings until the distance between the points is exactly 5 ft. A helper will make this easier.

3 Reset the stakes, if necessary, to conform to the positions of the squared strings. Check all corners with the 3-4-5 method, and adjust until the entire project area is exactly square. This can be a lengthy process with plenty of trial and error, but it is very important to the success of the project, especially if you plan to build on the concrete surface.

4 Attach a line level to one of the mason's strings to use as a reference. Adjust the string up or down as necessary until it is level. Adjust the other strings until they are level, making sure that intersecting strings contact one another (this ensures that they are all at the same height relative to ground level).

5 Most concrete surfaces should have a slight slope to direct water runoff, especially if they are near your house. To create a slope, shift the level mason's strings on opposite sides of the project downward on their stakes (the lower end should be farther away from the house). To create a standard slope of $\frac{1}{8}$" per foot, multiply the distance between the stakes on one side (in feet) by $\frac{1}{8}$. For example, if the stakes were 10 ft. apart, the result would be $\frac{10}{8}$ ($1\frac{1}{4}$"). You would move the strings down $1\frac{1}{4}$" on the stakes on the low ends.

6 Start excavating by removing the sod. Use a sod cutter if you wish to reuse the sod elsewhere in your yard (lay the sod as soon as possible). Otherwise, use a square-end spade to cut away sod. Strip off the sod at least 6" beyond the mason's strings to make room for 2 × 4 forms. You may need to remove the strings temporarily for this step.

7 Make a story pole as a guide for excavating the site. First, measure down to ground level from the high end of a slope line. Add $7\frac{1}{2}$" to that distance (4" for the subbase material and $3\frac{1}{2}$" for the concrete if you are using 2 × 4 forms). Mark the total distance on the story pole, measuring from one end. Remove soil from the site with a spade. Use the story pole to make sure the bottom of the site is consistent (the same distance from the slope line at all points) as you dig. Check points at the center of the site using a straightedge and a level placed on top of the soil.

8 Lay a subbase for the project (unless your project requires a frost footing). Pour a 5"-thick layer of compactible gravel in the project site, and tamp until the gravel is even and compressed to 4" in depth. NOTE: The subbase should extend at least 6" beyond the project outline.

1 A form is a frame, usually made from 2 × 4 lumber, laid around a project site to contain poured concrete and establish its thickness. Cut 2 × 4s to create a frame with inside dimensions equal to the total size of the project.

2 Use the mason's strings that outline the project as a reference for setting form boards in place. Starting with the longest form board, position the boards so the inside edges are directly below the strings.

3 Cut several pieces of 2 × 4 at least 12" long to use as stakes. Trim one end of each stake to a sharp point. Drive the stakes at 3-ft. intervals at the outside edges of the form boards, positioned to support any joints in the form boards.

4 Drive 3" deck screws through the stakes and into the form board on one side. Set a level so it spans the staked side of the form and the opposite form board, and use the level as a guide as you stake the second form board so it is level with the first. For large projects, use the mason's strings as the primary guide for setting the height of all form boards.

5 Once the forms are staked and leveled, drive 3" deck screws at the corners. Coat the insides of the forms with vegetable oil or a commercial release agent so concrete won't bond to them. TIP: Tack nails to the outsides of the forms to mark locations for control joints at intervals roughly 1½ times the slab's width (but no more than 30 times its thickness).

Variations for Building Forms

Use plywood (top left) for building taller forms for projects like concrete steps. Gang-cut plywood form sides, and brace with 2 × 4 arms attached to stakes and 2 × 4 cleats at the sides. **Use the earth as a form (bottom left)** when building footings for poured concrete building projects. Use standard wood forms for the tops of footings for building with brick or block, when the footing will be visible. **Create curves (above, right)** with ⅛" hardboard attached at the inside corners of a form frame. Drive support stakes behind the curved form.

Tips for Laying Metal Reinforcement

Cut rebar with a reciprocating saw that is equipped with a metal-cutting blade (cutting rebar with a hacksaw can take 5 to 10 minutes per cut). Use bolt cutters to cut wire mesh.

Overlap joints in rebar by at least 12", then bind the ends together with heavy-gauge wire. Overlap seams in wire mesh reinforcement by 12".

Leave at least 1" of clearance between the forms and the edges or ends of metal reinforcement. Use bolsters or small chunks of concrete to raise wire mesh reinforcement off the subbase, but make sure it is at least 2" below the tops of the forms.

Drainage
swale

Avoiding Drainage Problems

If your yard slopes in the direction of a planned masonry project, or if the soil drains poorly, take steps to avoid problems in the future. You can eliminate small slopes by filling in low-lying areas with fresh soil. If you're pouring a slab in a poorly drained area, protect the bottom of the slab by covering the ground with 6 mil polyethylene sheeting. For large low-lying areas, dig a drainage swale that will direct water toward a runoff area.

Everything You Need:

Tools: Garden stakes, shovel, hand tamper.

Materials: Fresh soil, 6 mil polyethylene sheeting, landscape fabric, coarse gravel, perforated drain pipe, splash block.

Standing water damages masonry, particularly if large quantities of water are allowed to permeate the base. Soil drainage is the key to preventing damage. In large low-lying areas, you can improve drainage by creating a shallow ditch, called a drainage swale, to carry runoff away from masonry. In some cases, more modest remedies, such as filler soil (below left) and rolled polyethylene (below right) are helpful.

Drainage Tips

Fill small low-lying areas by top-dressing them with soil. Spread the new soil evenly, then tamp it with a hand tamper and add soil as needed to fill the area.

A layer of polyethylene at the bottom of a site for a walk or driveway can protect the slab from the damaging effects of moisture.

How to Make a Drainage Swale

1 Use stakes to mark a route that will direct water toward a runoff area. The outlet must be lower than any point in the problem area. Remove the sod along the route and set it in the shade—you can re-lay it when the swale is completed.

2 Dig a 6"-deep trench, shaping the trench so it slopes gradually downward toward the outlet, and the sides and bottom are smooth.

3 Complete the swale by laying sod into the trench, then watering the area thoroughly to check the drainage.

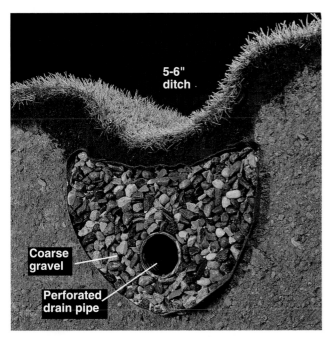

5-6" ditch

Coarse gravel

Perforated drain pipe

Splash block

OPTION: For severe drainage problems, dig a 2-ft.-deep swale angled slightly downward to the outlet point. Line the swale with landscape fabric. Spread a 2" layer of coarse gravel or river rock in the bottom of the swale, then lay perforated drain pipe over the gravel. Cover the pipe with a 5" layer of gravel, then wrap the landscape fabric over the top of the gravel. Cover the swale with soil and fresh sod (left). Set a splash block at the outlet to distribute the runoff and prevent erosion (right).

Too dry

Correct

Too wet

Mixing Concrete

A good mixture is crucial to any successful concrete project. Properly mixed concrete is damp enough to form in your hand when you squeeze, and dry enough to hold its shape. If the mixture is too dry, the aggregate will be difficult to work, and will not smooth out easily to produce an even, finished appearance. A wet mixture will slide off the trowel, and may cause cracking and other defects in the finished surface.

When mixing concrete on-site, purchase bags of dry pre-mixed concrete and simply add water. Follow the instructions carefully and take note of exactly how much water you add so the concrete will be uniform from one batch to the next. Never mix less than a full bag, however, since key ingredients may have settled to the bottom.

For smaller projects, mix the concrete in a wheelbarrow or mortar box. For larger projects, rent or buy a power mixer. Be aware that most power mixers should not be filled more than half full.

When mixing concrete, the more water you add, the weaker the concrete will become. If you need "slippery" concrete to get into the corners of a form (for example" add latex bonding agent or acrylic fortifier instead of water. Mix the concrete only until all of the dry ingredients are moistened; don't overwork it.

It is not always necessary to premix concrete when setting posts for projects such as fences, mailboxes, lamps, and swing sets. Special dry mixes are designed to be particularly easy to use: simply pour the mix into a prepared hole and add water according to the package directions.

Everything You Need:

Tools: Power mixer, wheelbarrow or mortar box, hoe, 5-gallon bucket, gloves, particle mask, safety glasses.

Materials: Concrete mix, water, additives as desired.

How to Mix Concrete by Hand

1 Empty premixed concrete bags into a mortar box or wheelbarrow. Form a hollow in the mound of dry mix, then pour water into the hollow. Start with one gallon of clean tap water per 60-lb. bag.

2 Work with a hoe, continuing to add water until a good consistency is achieved. Clear out any dry pockets from the corners. Do not overwork the mix. Also, keep track of how much water you use in the first batch so you will have a reliable recipe for subsequent batches.

How to Mix Concrete with a Power Mixer

1 Fill a bucket with 1 gallon of water for each 60-lb. bag of concrete you will use in the batch (for most power mixers, 3 bags is workable). Pour in half the water. Before you start power-mixing, review the operating instructions carefully.

2 Add all of the dry ingredients, then mix for one minute. Pour in water as needed until the proper consistency is achieved, and mix for three minutes. Pivot the mixing drum to empty the concrete into a wheelbarrow. Rinse out the drum immediately.

Placing Concrete

Placing concrete involves pouring it into forms, then leveling and smoothing it with special masonry tools. Once the surface is smooth and level, control joints are cut and the edges are rounded. Special attention to detail in these steps will result in a professional appearance. NOTE: If you plan to add a special finish, read "Finishing & Curing Concrete" (pages 38 and 39) before you begin your project.

Everything You Need:

Tools: Wheelbarrow, hoe, spade, hammer, mason's trowel, float, groover, edger.

Materials: Concrete, 2 × 4 lumber, mixing container, water.

Start pouring concrete at the farthest point from the concrete source, and work your way back.

Tips for Pouring Concrete

Do not overload your wheelbarrow. Experiment with sand or dry mix to find a comfortable, controllable volume. This also helps you get a feel for how many wheelbarrow loads it will take to complete your project.

Lay planks over the forms to make a ramp for the wheelbarrow. Avoid disturbing the building site by using ramp supports. Make sure you have a flat, stable surface between the concrete source and the forms.

How to Place Concrete

1 Load the wheelbarrow with fresh concrete. Make sure you have a clear path from the source to the site. Always load wheelbarrows from the front; loading wheelbarrows from the side can cause tipping.

2 Pour concrete in evenly spaced loads (each load is called a "pod"). Start at the end farthest from the concrete source, and pour so the top of the pod is a few inches above the top of the forms. Do not pour too close to the forms. NOTE: If you are using a ramp, stay clear of the end of the ramp.

3 Continue to place concrete pods next to preceding pods, working away from the first pod. Do not pour more concrete than you can tool at one time. Keep an eye on the concrete to make sure it does not harden before you can start tooling.

4 Distribute concrete evenly in the project area, using a masonry hoe. Work the concrete with a hoe until it is fairly flat, and the surface is slightly above the top of the forms. Remove excess concrete with a shovel.

(continued next page)

5 Immediately work the blade of a spade between the inside edges of the form and the concrete to remove trapped air bubbles that can weaken the concrete.

6 Rap the forms with a hammer or the blade of the shovel to help settle the concrete. This also draws finer aggregates in the concrete against the forms, creating a smoother surface on the sides. This is especially important when building steps.

7 Use a screed board—a straight piece of 2 × 4 long enough to rest on opposite forms—to remove the excess concrete before bleed water appears. Move the screed board in a sawing motion from left to right, and keep the screed flat as you work. If screeding leaves any valleys in the surface, add fresh concrete in the low areas and screed to level.

8 Cut control joints at marked locations (step 10, page 52) with a mason's trowel, using a straight 2 × 4 as a guide. Control joints are designed to control where the slab cracks in the future, as natural heaving and settling occur. Without control joints, a slab may develop a jagged, disfiguring crack.

9 Wait until bleed water disappears (see box), then float in an arcing motion, with the leading edge of the tool up. Stop floating as soon as the surface is smooth.

Understanding Bleed Water

Timing is key to an attractive concrete finish. When concrete is poured, the heavy materials gradually sink, leaving a thin layer of water—known as *bleed water*—on the surface. To achieve an attractive finish, it's important to let bleed water dry before proceeding with other steps. Follow these rules to avoid problems:

- Settle and screed the concrete and add control joints (steps 5 through 8) immediately after pouring and before bleed water appears. Otherwise, crazing, spalling, and other flaws are likely.
- Let bleed water dry before floating or edging. Concrete should be hard enough that foot pressure leaves no more than a ¼"-deep impression.
- Do not overfloat the concrete; it may cause bleed water to reappear. Stop floating (step 9) if a sheen appears, and resume when it is gone.

Note: Bleed water does not appear with air-entrained concrete, which is used in regions where temperatures often fall below freezing.

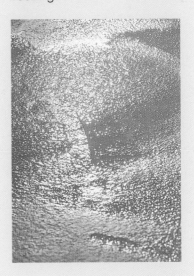

10 Once any bleed water has dried, draw a groover across the precut control joints (step 8), using a straight 2 × 4 as a guide. You may need to make several passes to create a smooth control joint.

11 Shape concrete with an edging tool between the forms and the concrete to create a smooth, finished appearance. You may need to make several passes. Use a wood float to smooth out any marks left by the groover or edger.

Exposed aggregate. Sometimes called "seeding," applying decorative aggregate to a fresh concrete surface creates an attractive effect with many design options. The photo above shows what various aggregates look like when they are used for an exposed-aggregate surface.

Broomed finish. Tool the concrete, then drag a broom across it. Wait until concrete is firm to the touch to achieve a finer texture and a more weather-resistant surface.

Finishing & Curing Concrete

Finishing and curing are critical final steps in a concrete project. They ensure that concrete reaches its maximum strength and remains free of defects that harm its appearance. There are many theories on the best way to cure concrete. In general, a good rule is to keep concrete damp and covered with plastic for at least a week.

A decorative finish dresses up concrete's appearance. Exposed-aggregate finishes are common on walkways and patios. Brooming is a good option for improved traction. Stamping patterns is a popular way to create surfaces that imitate brick and other materials. Look around your neighborhood for other examples of creative finishes. After concrete has fully cured, it should be treated with an appropriate concrete sealer.

Everything You Need:

Tools: Broom, wheelbarrow, shovel, magnesium float, groover, edger, hose, coarse brush.

Materials: Plastic sheeting, "seeding" aggregate, water.

How to Cure Concrete

Keep concrete covered and damp for at least a week to maximize strength and to minimize surface defects. Lift the plastic occasionally and wet the surface so the concrete cures slowly.

How to Create an Exposed-aggregate Finish

1 Place the concrete. After smoothing the surface with a screed board, let any bleed water disappear, then spread clean, washed aggregate evenly with a shovel or by hand. Spread smaller aggregate (up to 1" in diameter) in a single layer; for larger aggregate, maintain a separation between stones that is roughly equal to the size of one stone.

2 Pat the aggregate down with the screed board, then float the surface with a magnesium float until a thin layer of concrete covers the stones. Do not overfloat. If bleed water appears, stop floating and let it dry before completing the step. If you are seeding a large area, cover it with plastic to keep the concrete from hardening too quickly.

3 Cut control joints and tool the edges. Let concrete set for 30 to 60 minutes, then mist a section of the surface and scrub with a brush to remove the concrete covering the aggregate. If brushing dislodges some of the stones, reset them and try again later. When you can scrub without dislodging stones, mist and scrub the entire surface to expose the aggregate. Rinse clean. Do not let the concrete dry too long, or it will be difficult to scrub off.

4 After the concrete has cured for one week, remove the covering and rinse the surface with a hose. If a residue remains, try scrubbing it clean. If scrubbing is ineffective, wash the surface with a muriatic acid solution, then rinse immediately and thoroughly with water. OPTION: After three weeks, apply exposed-aggregate sealer.

Fast-setting concrete requires no mixing, making it ideal for setting posts. Just fill the post hole with the dry concrete mix, then add water. If you plan to work or shape the top of the footing, premix the concrete, but act quickly—some concrete blends will set in as little as 20 minutes.

Setting Posts in Concrete

Whether it's supporting a fence, a mailbox, or a basketball hoop, a post will stand solid and straight for many years if you anchor it in concrete. Concrete post footings are easy to pour, and they protect wood and metal posts from rusting and rotting.

Posts that support structures, such as a deck, generally must be supported by footings that extend below the frost line. Check with your local building inspector for footing requirements for your project.

Everything You Need:

Tools: Shovel, clamshell digger, digging bar, hand tamper, saw, drill, maul, level, trowel.

Materials: Gravel, concrete mix, post lumber, 2 × 4 lumber, screws, wood sealer (for wood posts).

Tips for Setting Posts

To discourage rot, use cedar, redwood, or pressure-treated pine for wood posts. Seal cut ends with a wood sealer before setting the posts in concrete. Shape the tops of posts or attach post caps to prevent water from settling and promoting rot.

To brace metal posts, fashion a 2 × 4 collar. Assemble the collar around the middle of the post, using 3" deck screws. Use shims to hold the collar in place. Plumb the post, and attach braces to two adjacent sides of the collar.

How to Set a Post in Concrete

1 Dig a hole that is three times wider than the post width (or diameter) and as deep as ⅓ the post length, plus 6". Use a clamshell digger for most of the digging and a digging bar to dislodge rocks and loosen compacted soil.

2 Pour 6" of loose gravel into the bottom of the hole to ensure proper drainage. Tamp the gravel, using a hand tamper or wood post.

3 Set the post in the hole. Attach 2 × 4 braces to two adjacent faces of the post. Check for plumb, then drive a stake into the ground near the end of each brace, and attach the ends of the braces to the stakes.

4 Fill the hole 4" below ground level with fast-setting concrete. Check the post again to make sure it is plumb, then add the recommended amount of water. When it's dry, cover the footing with soil or sod.

OPTION: For added protection against rot, premix the concrete and overfill the hole slightly. Using a trowel, quickly shape the concrete to form a crown that will shed water away from the post.

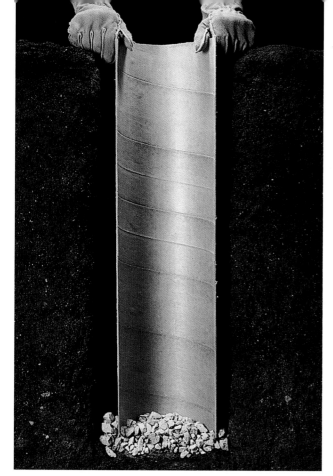

To install tube forms for concrete piers, dig holes with a clamshell digger or power auger. Pour 2" to 3" of loose gravel in the bottom for drainage, then cut and insert the tube, leaving about 2" of tube above ground level. Pack soil around tubes to hold them in place.

Concrete Piers

Concrete pier footings support the weight of outdoor structures, such as decks and pergolas. Check local codes to determine the size and depth of pier footings required in your area. In cold climates, footings must be deeper than the soil frost line.

To help protect posts from water damage, each footing should be poured so that it is 2" above ground level. Tube-shaped forms let you extend the footings above ground level.

As an alternative to inserting J-bolts into wet concrete, you can use masonry anchors, or install anchor bolts with an epoxy designed for masonry installations.

Before digging, consult local utilities for location of any underground electrical, telephone, or water lines that might interfere with footings.

Everything You Need

Tools: power auger or clamshell posthole digger, tape measure, pruning saw, shovel, reciprocating saw or handsaw, torpedo level, hoe, trowel, shovel, old toothbrush, plumb bob, utility knife, wheelbarrow.

Materials: 8" concrete tube forms, portland cement, sand, gravel, J-bolts, scrap 2 × 4.

How to Pour Concrete Piers

1 Install tube forms (above) and mix concrete. Pour concrete slowly into the tube, guiding concrete from the wheelbarrow with a shovel. Fill about half of the form. Use a long stick to tamp the concrete, filling any air gaps in the footing. Then finish pouring and tamping concrete into the form.

2 Level the concrete by pulling a 2 × 4 across the top of the tube form, using a sawing motion. Add concrete to any low spots.

3 Insert a J-bolt at an angle at the center of the footing, lowering it slowly and wiggling it slightly to eliminate any air gaps. Set the J-bolt so ¾" to 1" is exposed above the concrete. Brush away any wet concrete on the bolt threads with an old toothbrush.

4 Use a torpedo level to make sure the J-bolt is plumb. If necessary, adjust the bolt and repack concrete. Let concrete cure, then cut away exposed portion of tube with a utility knife.

How to Install Anchor Bolts with Epoxy

1 After pier has cured at least 48 hours, locate the bolt locations. Drill a hole for the threaded rod, using a hammer drill and masonry bit sized to match the diameter of rod. Use a speed square to align the drill vertically, set the depth gauge so the rod will protrude ¾" to 1" above the pier. After drilling, clean out debris in hole using a shop vac.

2 Wrap masking tape around ¾" to 1" of rod for reference. Inject epoxy into hole, using the mixing syringe provided by the manufacture. Use enough epoxy so a small amount is forced from the hole when the rod is fully inserted. Insert the rod immediately; epoxy begins to harden as soon as it is injected. Check the height of the rod, then allow the epoxy to cure for 16 to 24 hours. If necessary, trim the rod using a reciprocating saw with a metal cutting blade.

Footings are required by Building Code for concrete, stone, brick, and block structures that adjoin other permanent structures or that exceed the height specified by local codes. Frost footings extend 8" to 12" below the frost line. Slab footings, which are typically 8" thick, may be recommended for low, freestanding structures built using mortar or poured concrete. Before starting your project, ask a building inspector about footing recommendations and requirements for your area.

Poured Footings for Freestanding Walls

Footings provide a stable, level base for brick, block, stone, and poured concrete structures. They distribute the weight of the structure evenly, prevent sinking, and keep structures from moving during seasonal freeze-thaw cycles.

The required depth of a footing is usually determined by the *frost line*, which varies by region. The frost line is the point nearest ground level where the soil does not freeze. In colder climates, it is likely to be 48" or deeper. Frost footings (footings designed to keep structures from moving during freezing temperatures) should extend 12" below the frost line for the area. Your local building inspector can tell you the frost line depth for your area.

Everything You Need:

Tools: Rope, carpenter's square, hand maul, tape measure, mason's string, line level, spade, sod cutter, straightedge, level, wheelbarrow, shovel, hand tamper, circular saw, reciprocating saw, float, drill.

Materials: concrete mix, water, #3 rebar, 16-gauge wire 2 × 4 lumber, 3" screws, compactible gravel, vegetable oil or commercial release agent.

Tips for Planning:

• Describe the proposed structure to your local building inspector to find out whether it requires a footing, and whether the footing needs reinforcement. In some cases, 8"-thick slab footings can be used, as long as the subbase provides plenty of drainage.

• Keep footings separate from adjoining structures by installing an isolation board (page 25).

• For smaller poured concrete projects, consider pouring the footing and the structure as one unit.

• A multi-wall project such as a barbecue may require a floating footing (page 140).

44

Options for Forming Footings

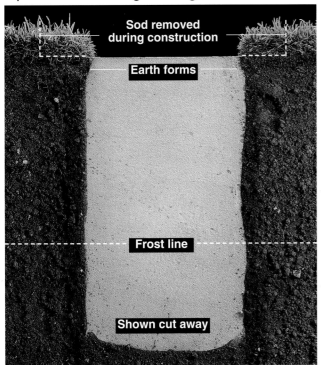

For poured concrete, use the earth as a form. Strip sod from around the project area, then strike off the concrete with a screed board resting on the earth at the edges of the top of the trench.

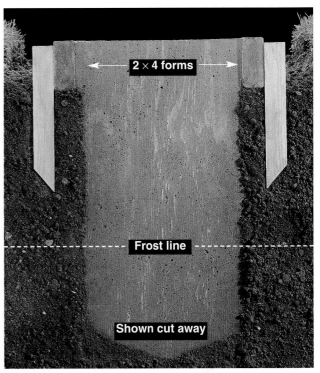

For brick, block, and stone, build level, recessed wood forms. Rest the screed board on the frames when you strike off the concrete to create a flat, even surface for stacking masonry units.

Tips for Building Footings

Make footings twice as wide as the wall or structure they will support. They also should extend at least 12" past the ends of the project area.

Add tie-rods if you will be pouring concrete over the footing. After the concrete sets up, press 12" sections of rebar 6" into the concrete. The tie-rods will anchor the footing to the structure it supports.

How to Pour a Footing

1 Make a rough outline of the footing, using a rope or hose. Outline the project area with stakes and mason's string (page 26).

2 Strip away sod 6" outside the project area on all sides, then excavate the trench for the footing to a depth 12" below the frost line.

3 Build and install a 2 × 4 form frame for the footing, aligning it with the mason's strings. Stake the form in place, and adjust to level.

VARIATION: If your project abuts another structure, such as a house foundation, slip a piece of asphalt-impregnated fiber board into the trench to create an isolation joint between the footing and the structure. Use a few dabs of construction adhesive to hold it in place.

4 Make two #3 rebar grids to reinforce the footing. For each grid, cut two pieces of #3 rebar 8" shorter than the length of the footing, and two pieces 4" shorter than the depth of the footing. Bind the pieces together with 16-gauge wire, forming a rectangle. Set the rebar grids upright in the trench, leaving 4" of space between the grids and the walls of the trench. Coat the inside edge of the form with vegetable oil or commercial release agent.

5 Mix and pour concrete, so it reaches the tops of the forms (pages 34 to 36). Screed the surface, using a 2 × 4. Float the concrete until it is smooth and level.

6 Cure the concrete for one week before you build on the footing. Remove the forms and backfill around the edges of the footing.

Sidewalks

Pouring a concrete walkway is one of the most practical projects you can master as a homeowner. Once you've excavated and poured a walkway, you can confidently take on larger concrete projects, such as patios and driveways.

Poured concrete sidewalls are practical and extremely durable. A frost footing is not required, but you will need to remove sod and excavate the site. The depth of the excavation varies from project to project and depends on the thickness of the masonry material, plus the thickness of the sand or compactible grave gravel subbase. The subbase provides a more stable surface than the soil itself and an opportunity for water to run off so it does not pool directly under the walkway.

For more information on these steps, and the most effective techniques, consult the "Planning Your Concrete Project" and "Basic Techniques" sections on pages 20 to 39.

Everything You Need:

Tools: Line level, hammer, shovel, sod cutter, wheelbarrow, tamper, drill, level, screed board, straightedge, mason's string, mason's float, mason's trowel, edger, groover, stiff-bristle broom.

Materials: Garden stakes, rebar, bolsters, 2 × 4 lumber, 2½" and 3" screws, concrete mix, concrete sealer, isolation board, compactible gravel, construction adhesive, nails.

Tips for Building a Concrete Sidewalk

Use a sod cutter to strip grass from your pathway site. Available at most rental centers, sod cutters excavate to a very even depth. The cut sod can be replanted in other parts of your lawn.

Install stakes and strings when laying out straight walkways, and measure from the strings to ensure straight sides and uniform excavation depth.

Options for Directing Water off Walkways

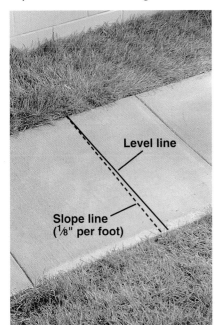

Level line

Slope line
(⅛" per foot)

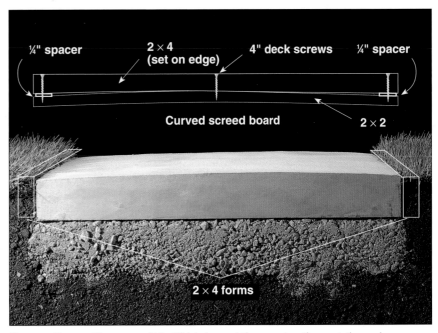

¼" spacer   2 × 4
(set on edge)   4" deck screws   ¼" spacer

Curved screed board   2 × 2

2 × 4 forms

Slope walkways away from the house to prevent water damage to the foundation or basement. Outline the location of the walkway with level mason's strings, then lower the outer string to create a slope of ⅛" per foot (see page 27).

Crown the walkway so it is ¼" higher at the center than at the edges. This will prevent water from pooling on the surface. To make the crown, construct a curved screed board by cutting a 2 × 2 and a 2 × 4 long enough to rest on the walkway forms. Butt them together edge to edge and insert a ¼" spacer between them at each end. Attach the parts with 4" deck screws driven at the center and the edges. The 2 × 2 will be drawn up at the center, creating a curved edge. Screed the concrete with the curved edge of the screed board facing down.

How to Build a Concrete Sidewalk

1 Select a rough layout, including any turns. Stake out the location and connect the stakes with mason's strings. Set the slope, if needed. Remove sod between and 6" beyond the lines, then excavate the site with a spade to a depth 4" greater than the thickness of the concrete walkway, following the slope lines to maintain consistent depth.

2 Pour a 5" layer of compactible gravel as a subbase for the walkway. Tamp the subbase until it compacts to an even 4" thick layer.

3 Build and install 2 × 4 forms set on edge (page 28). Miter-cut the ends at angled joints. Position them so the inside edges are lined up with the strings. Attach the forms with 3" deck screws, then drive 2 × 4 stakes next to the forms at 3-ft. intervals. Attach the stakes to the forms with 2½" deck screws. Use a level to make sure forms are level or set to achieve the desired slope. Drive stakes at each side of angled joints.

4 Glue an isolation board to the steps, house foundation, or other permanent structures that adjoin the walkway, using construction adhesive.

OPTION: Reinforce the walkway with #3 steel rebar. For a 3-ft.-wide walkway, lay two sections of rebar spaced evenly inside the project area. Use bolsters to support the rebar (make sure rebar is at least 2" below the tops of the forms). Bend rebar to follow any angles or curves, and overlap pieces at joints by 12". Mark locations for control joints (to be cut with a groover later) by tacking nails to the outside faces of the forms, spaced roughly at 3-ft. intervals.

5 Mix, then pour concrete into the project area. Use a masonry hoe to spread it evenly within the forms.

6 After pouring all of the concrete, run a spade along the inside edges of the form, then rap the outside edges of the forms with a hammer to help settle the concrete.

(continued next page)

7 Build a curved screed board (page 49) and use it to form a crown when you smooth out the concrete. NOTE: A helper makes this easier.

8 Smooth the surface with a float. Cut control joints at marked locations using a trowel and a straightedge. Let the concrete dry until any bleed water disappears.

9 Shape the edges of the concrete by running an edger along the forms. Smooth out any marks created by the edger, using a float. Lift the leading edge of the edger and float slightly as you work.

10 Once any bleed water has disappeared, draw a groover along the control joints, using a straight 2 × 4 as a guide. Use a float to smooth out any tool marks.

11 Create a textured, non-skid surface by drawing a clean, stiff-bristled broom across the surface. If you choose a simulated flagstone or brick paver finish, see pages 76-77. Avoid overlapping broom marks.

12 Cover the sidewalk with plastic sheeting and let the concrete cure for one week. Periodically lift the plastic and wet the surface so the concrete cures slowly.

13 Remove the forms, then backfill the space at the sides of the walkway with dirt or sod. Seal the concrete, if desired, according to the manufacturer's directions (INSET).

Landing depth
minimum = door + 12"

Riser height

6" - 8"

Tread depth

10" - 12"

Overall rise

Overall run

New concrete steps give a fresh, clean appearance to your house. And if your old steps are unstable, replacing them with concrete steps that have a non-skid surface will create a safer living environment.

Steps & Landings

Designing steps requires some calculations and some trial and error. As long as the design meets safety guidelines, you can adjust elements such as the landing depth and the dimensions of the steps. Sketching your plan on paper will make the job easier.

Before demolishing your old steps, measure them to see if they meet safety guidelines. If so, you can use them as a reference for your new steps. If not, start from scratch so your new steps do not repeat any design errors.

For steps with more than two risers, you'll need to install a handrail. Ask a building inspector about other requirements.

Everything You Need:

Tools: Tape measure, sledge hammer, shovel, drill, reciprocating saw, level, mason's string, hand tamper, mallet, concrete mixing tools, jig saw, clamps, ruler or framing square, float, step edger, broom,

Materials: 2 × 4 lumber, steel rebar grid, wire, bolsters, construction adhesive, compactible gravel, fill material, exterior-grade ¾" plywood, 2" deck screws, isolation board, #3 rebar, stakes, latex caulk, vegetable oil or commercial release agent.

How to Design Steps

1 Attach a mason's string to the house foundation, 1" below the bottom of the door threshold. Drive a stake where you want the base of the bottom step to fall. Attach the other end of the string to the stake and use a line level to level it. Measure the length of the string—this distance is the overall depth, or *run*, of the steps.

2 Measure down from the string to the bottom of the stake to determine the overall height, or *rise*, of the steps. Divide the overall rise by the estimated number of steps. The rise of each step should be between 6" and 8". For example, if the overall rise is 21" and you plan to build three steps, the rise of each step would be 7" (21 divided by 3), which falls within the recommended safety range for riser height.

3 Measure the width of your door and add at least 12"; this number is the minimum depth you should plan for the landing area of the steps. The landing depth plus the depth of each step should fit within the overall run of the steps. If necessary, you can increase the overall run by moving the stake at the planned base of the steps away from the house, or by increasing the depth of the landing.

4 Sketch a detailed plan for the steps, keeping these guidelines in mind: each step should be 10" to 12" deep, with a riser height between 6" and 8", and the landing should be at least 12" deeper than the swing radius (width) of your door. Adjust the parts of the steps as needed, but stay within the given ranges. Creating a final sketch will take time, but it is worth doing carefully.

How to Build Concrete Steps

1 Remove or demolish existing steps; if the old steps are concrete, set aside the rubble to use as fill material for the new steps. Wear protective gear, including eye protection and gloves, when demolishing concrete.

2 Dig 12"-wide trenches to the required depth for footings. Locate the trenches perpendicular to the foundation, spaced so the footings will extend 3" beyond the outside edges of the steps. Install steel rebar grids (page 29) for reinforcement. Affix isolation boards to the foundation wall inside each trench, using a few dabs of construction adhesive.

3 Mix the concrete and pour the footings. Level and smooth the concrete with a screed board. You do not need to float the surface afterwards.

4 When bleed water disappears, insert 12" sections of rebar 6" into the concrete, spaced at 12" intervals and centered side to side. Leave 1 ft. of clear space at each end.

5 Let the footings cure for two days, then excavate the area between them to 4" deep. Pour in a 5"-thick layer of compactible gravel subbase and tamp until it is level with the footings.

6 Transfer the measurements for the side forms from your working sketch onto ¾" exterior-grade plywood. Cut out the forms along the cutting lines, using a jig saw. Save time by clamping two pieces of plywood together and cutting both side forms at the same time. Add a ⅛" per foot back-to-front slope to the landing part of the form.

7 Cut form boards for the risers to fit between the side forms. Bevel the bottom edges of the boards when cutting to create clearance for the float at the back edges of the steps. Attach the riser forms to the side forms with 2" deck screws.

8 Cut a 2 × 4 to make a center support for the riser forms. Use 2" deck screws to attach 2 × 4 cleats to the riser forms, then attach the support to the cleats. Check to make sure all corners are square.

9 Cut an isolation board and glue it to the house foundation at the back of the project area. Set the form onto the footings, flush against the isolation board. Add 2 × 4 bracing arms to the sides of the form, attaching them to cleats on the sides and to stakes driven into the ground.

(continued next page)

How to Build Concrete Steps (continued)

10 Fill the form with clean fill (broken concrete or rubble). Stack the fill carefully, keeping it 6" away from the sides, back, and top edges of the form. Shovel smaller fragments onto the pile to fill the void areas.

11 Lay pieces of #3 metal rebar on top of the fill at 12" intervals, and attach them to bolsters with wire to keep them from moving when the concrete is poured. Keep rebar at least 2" below the top of the forms. Mist the forms and the rubble with water.

12 Coat the forms with vegetable oil or a commercial release agent, then mist them with water so concrete won't stick to the forms. Mix concrete and pour steps one at a time, beginning at the bottom. Settle and smooth the concrete with a screed board. Press a piece of #3 rebar 1" down into the "nose" of each tread for reinforcement.

13 Float the steps, working the front edge of the float underneath the beveled edge at the bottom of each riser form.

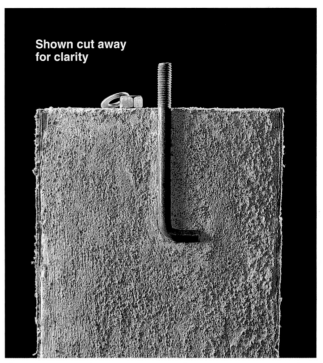

Shown cut away for clarity

14 Pour concrete into the forms for the remaining steps and the landing. Press rebar into the nose of each step. Keep an eye on the poured concrete as you work, and stop to float any concrete as soon as the bleed water disappears.

OPTION: For railings with mounting plates that attach to sunken J-bolts, install the bolts before the concrete sets (page 43). Otherwise, choose railings with surface-mounted hardware (see step 16) that can be attached after the steps are completed.

Mounting plate

15 Once the concrete sets, shape the steps and landing with a step edger. Float the surface. Sweep with a stiff-bristled broom for maximum traction.

16 Remove the forms as soon as the surface is firm to the touch, usually within several hours. Smooth rough edges with a float. Add concrete to fill any holes. If forms are removed later, more patching may be required. Backfill the area around the base of the steps, and seal the concrete. Install a railing.

8"-thick perimeter

Welded wire mesh

3½"-thick slab

Plywood form

4" compacted gravel

Slab Foundations

The slab foundation commonly used for sheds is called a slab-on-grade foundation. This combines a 3½"- to 4"-thick floor slab with an 8"- to 12"-thick perimeter footing that provides extra support for the walls of the building. The whole foundation can be poured at one time using a simple wood form.

Because they sit above ground, slab-on-grade foundations are susceptible to frost heave and in cold-weather climates are suitable only for detached buildings. Specific design requirements also vary by locality, so check with the local building department regarding the depth of the slab, the metal reinforcement required, the type and amount of gravel required for the subbase, and whether a plastic or other type of moisture barrier is needed under the slab.

The slab shown in this project has a 3½"-thick interior with an 8"-wide × 8"-deep footing along the perimeter. The top of the slab sits 4" above ground level, or grade. There is a 4"-thick layer of compacted gravel underneath the slab and the concrete is reinforced internally with a layer of 6 × 6" 10/10 welded wire mesh (WWM). (In some areas, you may be required to add rebar in the foundation perimeter—check the local code.) After the concrete is poured and finished, 8"-long J-bolts are set into the slab along the edges. These are used later to anchor the wall framing to the slab.

A slab for a shed requires a lot of concrete. Considering the amount involved, you'll probably want to order ready-mix concrete delivered by truck to the site (most companies have a one yard minimum). Order air-entrained concrete, which will hold up best, and tell the mixing company that you're using it for an exterior slab. An alternative for smaller slabs is to rent a concrete trailer from a rental center or landscaping company. They fill the trailer with one yard of mixed concrete and you tow it home.

If you've never worked with concrete, finishing a large slab can be a challenging introduction, and you might want some experienced help with the pour.

Estimating Concrete

Calculate the amount of concrete needed for a slab of this design using this formula:

Width × Length × Depth, in feet (of main slab)

Multiply by 1.5 (for footing edge and spillage)

Divide by 27 (to convert to cubic yards).

Example—for a 12 × 12-ft. × 3½" slab:

12 × 12 × .29 (3½") = 41.76

41.76 × 1.5 = 62.64

62.64 ÷ 27 = 2.32 cubic yards

Everything You Need:

Tools: Basic tools (page 16-19), circular saw, drill, mason's line, sledgehammer, line level, framing square, shovel, wheelbarrow, rented plate compactor, bolt cutters, bull float, hand-held concrete float.

Materials: Concrete edger, compactible gravel, 2 × 3 & 2 × 4 lumber, 1¼" & 2½" deck screws, ¾" A-C plywood, 8d nails, 6 × 6" 10/10 welded wire mesh, 1½" brick pavers, 8" J-bolts, 2"-thick rigid foam insulation.

How to Build a Concrete Slab Foundation

1 Set up stakes or batter boards (a 2 × 4 cross-piece fastened to two 2 × 4 stakes) with mason's lines to represent the outer dimensions of the slab, and excavate the site (pages 26 to 28). For the footing portion along the perimeter, dig a trench that is 8" wide × 8" deep. Add a 4" layer of compactible gravel over the entire excavation and rake it level. Compact the gravel thoroughly, using a rented plate compactor.

2 Cut 8" wide strips from exterior plywood, using a table saw or a circular saw with a straightedge. Cut the strips to length to create the sides of the form—the form's inner dimensions must equal the outer dimensions of the slab. Cut two sides 1½-in. longer so they can overlay the remaining two sides. Assemble the form by fastening the corners together with 2½-in. screws and check the inner dimensions. Note: For sides longer than 8 feet, join two strips with a mending plate made from scrap plywood; fasten the plate to the backsides of the strips with 1¼" deck screws.

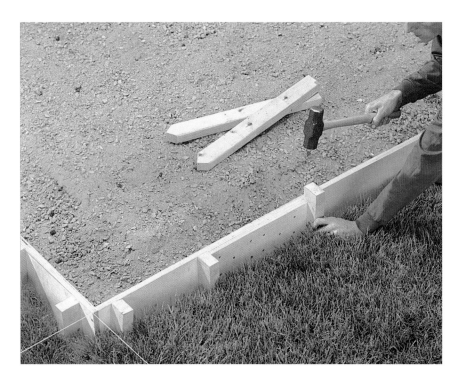

3 Cut 18"-long, 2 × 3 stakes—one for every linear foot of form, plus one extra stake for each corner. Place the form in the trench, align it with the mason's lines, and drive stakes against the form near the end of each side, driving down to 3" above grade. Using the mason's lines, position the form 4" above grade by shimming beneath it with stones or by removing stones. Measure the diagonals of the form to check for square and to make sure that the top edge is level. Drive stakes below the top of the form every 12", then secure the form with two deck screws driven into each stake. As you work, check with a string line to make sure the form sides are aligned.

(continued next page)

4 Lay out rows of 6 × 6" 10/10 welded wire mesh so their ends are 1" to 2" from the insides of the forms. Cut the mesh with bolt cutters or heavy pliers, standing on the unrolled mesh so it doesn't spring back when cut. Overlay rows by 6" and tie together with tie wire. Prop the mesh with metal bolsters or 1½" brick pavers.

5 Starting at one end, fill the form with concrete (pages 35 to 37). Stab the shovel into the concrete to eliminate air pockets, and to settle it around the wire mesh and along the forms. As the form fills, have two helpers screed the concrete, using a straight 2 × 4 that spans the form. Throw shovelfuls of concrete ahead of the screed board to fill low spots—the goal is to make the surface flat and level, if not smooth. Rap the outsides of the form with a hammer to settle concrete along the inside faces of the form.

6 After screeding, make one pass with a bull float to smooth the surface. Add small amounts of concrete to fill low spots created by floating, then smooth with the float. Set 8" J-bolts into the concrete 1¾" from the outside edges of the slab. The bolts should be plumb and protrude 2½" from the slab surface. After setting each bolt, smooth the concrete around the bolt, using a magnesium or wood concrete float.

7 Let the concrete dry until bleed water disappears and the surface appears dull. Pressure-test the concrete for firmness by stepping on it: if your foot sinks ¼" or less, the concrete is ready—float the concrete with a hand-held magnesium or wood float. If you can't reach the entire slab, lay 2"-thick rigid foam insulation over the concrete and kneel on the surface. Work back to smooth any impressions. Use an edge tool to shape the slab edges. Let the concrete cure for 24 hours, then strip the forms. Wait an additional 24 hours before building on the slab. NOTE: Air-entrained concrete may have very little bleed water, so it's best to rely on the pressure test.

Patio Slab Resurfacing

Patio tile is most frequently applied over a concrete subbase—either an existing concrete patio, or a new concrete slab. A third option, which we show you on the following pages, is to pour a new tile subbase over an existing concrete patio. This option involves far less work and expense than removing an old patio and pouring a new slab. And it ensures that your new tiled patio will not develop the same problems that may be present in the existing concrete surface. See page 196 to help you determine the best method for preparing an existing concrete patio for tile.

See the photographs below to help you determine the best method for preparing your existing concrete patio slab. To resurface a concrete sidewalk, see pages 254 to 255.

Everything You Need:

Tools: Basic hand tools, shovel, maul, straightedge, aviation snips, masonry hoe, mortar box, hand tamper, magnesium float, concrete edger, utility knife, margin trowel.

Materials: 30# building paper, plastic sheeting, 2 × 4 and 2 × 2 lumber, 2½" and 3" deck screws, ⅜" stucco lath, roofing cement.

New subbase

Old patio

Tips for Evaluating Concrete Surfaces

A good surface is free from any major cracks or badly flaking concrete (called spalling). You can apply patio tile directly over a concrete surface that is in good condition if it has control joints.

A fair surface may exhibit minor cracking and spalling, but has no major cracks or badly deteriorated spots. Install a new concrete subbase over a surface in fair condition before laying patio tile.

A poor surface contains deep or large cracks, broken, sunken or heaved concrete, or extensive spalling. If you have this kind of surface, remove the concrete completely and replace it with a new concrete slab before you lay patio tile.

63

How to Install a Subbase for Patio Tile

1 Dig a trench at least 6" wide, and no more than 4" deep, around the patio to create room for 2 × 4 forms. Clean dirt and debris from the exposed sides of the patio. Cut and fit 2 × 4 frames around the patio, joining the ends with 3" deck screws. Cut wood stakes from 2 × 4s and drive them next to the forms, at 2-ft. intervals.

2 Adjust the form height: set stucco lath on the surface, then set a 2 × 2 spacer on top of the lath (their combined thickness equals the thickness of the subbase). Adjust the form boards so the tops are level with the 2 × 2, and screw the stakes to the forms with 2½" deck screws.

3 Remove the 2 × 2 spacers and stucco lath, then lay strips of 30# building paper over the patio surface, overlapping seams by 6", to create a *bond-breaker* for the new surface. Crease the building paper at the edges and corners, making sure the paper extends past the tops of the forms. Make a small cut in the paper at each corner for easier folding.

4 Lay strips of stucco lath over the building-paper bond-breaker, overlapping seams by 1". Keep the lath 1" away from forms and the wall. Use aviation snips to cut the stucco lath (wear heavy gloves when handling metal).

5 Build temporary 2 × 2 forms to divide the project into working sections and provide rests for the screed board used to level and smooth the fresh concrete. Make the sections narrow enough that you can reach across the entire section (3-ft. to 4-ft. sections are comfortable for most people). Screw the ends of the 2 × 2s to the form boards so the tops are level.

6 Mix dry floor-mix concrete with water in a mortar box, blending with a masonry hoe, according to the manufacturer's directions, or use a power mixer.

NOTE: The mixture should be very dry when prepared so it can be pressed down into the voids in the stucco lath with a tamper.

7 Fill one working section with floor-mix concrete, up to the tops of the forms. Tamp the concrete thoroughly with a lightweight tamper to help force it into the voids in the lath and into corners. The lightweight tamper shown above is made from a 12" × 12" piece of ¾" plywood, with a 2 × 4 handle attached.

(continued next page)

How to Install a Subbase for Patio Tile (continued)

8 Level off the surface of the concrete by dragging a straight 2 × 4 screed board across the top, with the ends riding on the forms. Move the 2 × 4 in a sawing motion as you progress, creating a level surface and filling any voids in the concrete. If voids or hollows remain, add more concrete and smooth it off.

9 Use a magnesium float to smooth the surface of the concrete. Applying very light pressure, move the float back and forth in an arching motion, tipping the lead edge up slightly to avoid gouging the surface.

10 Pour and smooth out the next working section, repeating steps 7 to 9. After floating this section, remove the 2 × 2 temporary form between the two sections. Fill the void left behind with fresh concrete. Float the fresh concrete with the magnesium float until the concrete is smooth and level and blends into the working section on each side. Pour and finish the remaining working sections one at a time, using the same techniques.

11 Let the concrete dry until pressing the surface with your finger does not leave a mark. Cut contours around all edges of the subbase with a concrete edger. Tip the lead edge of the edger up slightly to avoid gouging the surface. Smooth out any marks left by the edger using a float.

12 Cover the concrete with sheets of plastic, and cure for at least three days (see manufacturer's directions for recommended curing time). Weight down the edges of the sheeting. After curing is compete, remove the plastic and disassemble and remove the forms.

13 Trim off the building paper around the sides of the patio using a utility knife. Apply roofing cement to the exposed sides of the patio, using a trowel or putty knife to fill and seal the seam between the old and new surfaces. After the roofing cement dries, shovel dirt or ground cover back into the trench around the patio.

Find the slope of your current driveway by dividing the length in feet (the horizontal distance from the apron to the curb) by the vertical drop in inches. This tells you how many inches per foot the new driveway should slope. It's easiest to use a water level to measure the vertical drop. Joints cut in the driveway's surface or created with strips of felt placed between sections of the driveway reduce damage from cracking and buckling. A crowned surface encourages water to run off to the sides.

Driveways

Pouring a driveway is a lot like pouring a patio or walk, but on a larger scale. It's particularly useful to divide the driveway into sections that you can pour one at a time. A wood divider is removed after each section is firm and repositioned to pour the next section. For driveways wider than 10 feet, a control joint is added down the center to keep cracks from spreading. Driveways up to 10 feet wide are simplest because you can pour fiber-reinforced concrete directly over the subbase without additional reinforcement. (Check with your building inspector regarding local requirements.) For a larger slab, add metal reinforcement, using the approach used for a walkway (page 29).

Pay attention to drainage conditions when planning your driveway. Soil that drains poorly can damage a slab. If drainage is poor, line your

Everything You Need:

Tools: Level, water level, mason's string, screed board, mallet, wheelbarrow, circular saw, drill, broom, coarse brush, hand float, concrete edger and groover, darby, shovel, wheelbarrow, hoe, spade, hammer, trowel, edger, bucket, measuring tape, hand tamper or power tamper.

Materials: Stakes, 2 × 4 and 1 × 2 lumber, crushed stone, fiber-reinforced concrete mix, 4"-wide bituminous felt, 2" deck screws, vegetable oil or commercial release agent, 6 mil plastic sheeting.

site with polyethylene sheeting before pouring. It is critical to establish a gradual slope and a crowned surface so water runs off the driveway. NOTE: It's important to handle bleed water carefully as you pour a driveway. Review the section on bleed water (page 37) before beginning your project.

How to Lay Out a Driveway Slab

Laying Out the Site

A proper layout is key to determining how well your driveway functions. Start by calculating the amount of drop per foot on the site (page 172). You need this number so you can maintain a gradual slope as you excavate. Plan to excavate an area 10" wider than the slab. This allows room for stakes and forms that will hold the concrete in place. How deep you need to dig depends on the thickness of the slab and the subbase, typically 4" each. (Check with your building inspector. Building Codes in some areas call for a 6" slab—in that case, you'll need 2 × 6s instead of 2 × 4s for forms.) Use beveled 12" 1 × 2 stakes and mason's strings to mark the edges of the site. Set the stakes at a consistent height so you can use them to check the depth of the excavated site.

8" (minimum depth)

1 Excavate the site (pages 76 to 78), using stakes and mason's strings to establish the proper slope. You may have to remove the stakes temporarily to smooth the bottom of the site with a 2 × 4 and pack the soil with a tamper.

2 Pour a 4" layer of crushed stone as a subbase. Screed with a long 2 × 4, then tamp the stone. You can make small adjustments to the slope of the site, as required, by adjusting the thickness of the subbase.

3½"

3 Drive stakes at the corners of the site, 3½" in from each side. Connect the stakes on each side with mason's strings. Use a water level (inset, right) to check that the strings are set to the correct slope. Adjust the stakes as necessary.

4 Position 2 × 4 forms inside the strings with the tops level with the strings. Plant stakes every 2 ft. outside the forms, with the tops slightly lower than the tops of the forms. Drive deck screws through the stakes and into the forms. Where forms meet (above), secure them to a single 1 × 4 stake.

(continued next page)

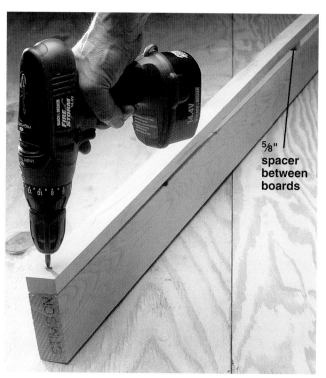

OPTION: Use 1 × 4s to create forms for turns in the driveway. Saw parallel ½"-deep kerfs in one side of each board, and bend the boards to form the proper curves. Attach the curved forms inside the stakes. Backfill beneath all of the forms.

5 Construct a divider equal in length to the width of the slab. Set a 1 × 2 on the edge of a 2 × 4; place a ⅝" × 1½" wood spacer midway between them, flush with the edges. Attach the two pieces with 2" deck screws so the screw heads sink below the surface. The curved top of the divider will form the crown of the driveway as you screed.

6 Position the divider roughly 6 ft. from the top of the driveway. Drive screws through the forms and into the divider to hold it in place temporarily. Place a felt isolation strip against the divider. Prop the strip in place temporarily with bricks. NOTE: If your site drains poorly, add a layer of polyethylene over the bottom of the site as a vapor barrier.

7 Coat the dividers and forms with vegetable oil or commercial release agent so concrete won't bond to their surfaces as it cures. Mix fiber-reinforced concrete for one section of the slab at a time, using a power mixer, or order concrete from a ready-mix supplier. If you use ready-mix, have helpers on hand so you can pour the concrete as soon as it arrives.

How to Pour a Driveway Slab

1 Pour pods of concrete (pages 34 to 37) into the first section, digging into the concrete with a shovel to eliminate air pockets. Remove the brick props inside the site once there is sufficient concrete in place to prop up the felt isolation strip.

2 Screed the concrete from side to side, using a 2 × 4 resting on the driveway apron and the crowned divider. Raise the leading edge of the board slightly as you move it across the concrete. Add concrete to any low spots. Re-screed if necessary.

3 Float the surface with a darby, then let the surface cure for 2-4 hours, or until it is solid enough to support your weight. NOTE: For a slab wider than 10 ft., cut a control joint down the slab's center line.

4 Use an edger along the inside of the forms to create smooth edges. Remove the divider and screw it in place alongside a felt strip to pour the next section. Screw the divider in place and prop it with bricks.

5 Finish the surface as desired as each section hardens. Cover the sections with polyethylene sheeting, misting daily with water for two weeks. Remove the forms and seal the concrete.

Coloring Concrete

There are a variety of products available for creating colored concrete. Adding a dry coloring dye or a liquid agent to the concrete mix will produce consistent results throughout the concrete itself, although matching colors between separate batches can be tricky. For best results, measure materials carefully. If you're blending your own concrete mix, use white Portland cement to achieve more vibrant colors.

Dry pigment colors only the surface of poured concrete. It is easy to work with—simply dust the powder over the concrete prior to final floating, then finish with a magnesium float. To create a more consistent, uniform appearance, apply the powder in two coats, using the second to touch up any soft or light areas. Or you can apply the pigment dust unevenly on purpose to create a variety of interesting effects.

Regardless of which coloring agent you use, make sure to follow the manufacturer's recommendations to get the best results.

Liquid coloring agents are mixed with water and then added to dry concrete mix. This produces consistent coloring throughout the entire batch of mixed concrete. If you're mixing larger quantities of concrete, measure coloring agents carefully to help match color between batches.

How to Apply a Surface Tinting Pigment

1 Following the manufacturer's instructions, dust the powdered pigment over the concrete surface evenly, sifting the pigment through your fingers. Save about a third of the product for a second coat.

2 Float the concrete surface using a magnesium float. After floating, dust the remaining powder over bare or light spots, then float again. Avoid over-working the concrete with the float, as that may cause bleed water to rise and dilute the color.

Acid Staining

Acid staining is a popular option for creating unique concrete surfaces—both interior and exterior. The penetrating acid reacts with the concrete to produce a range of somewhat unpredictable effects. Because of many factors, such as the content of the concrete mix and the amount of moisture in it, determining exactly what the finished surface will look like can be tricky. If you're after consistency or predictability, acid staining may not be for you. But if you're more adventurous, acid staining provides a one-of-a-kind concrete floor.

Each acid stain manufacturer has its own recommendations for how long concrete must cure before applying their products. But in general, the more water present in the concrete, the more intense the color. If working indoors, make sure the area is well ventilated and wear a respirator with a cartridge rated to protect against acid vapors. See the resources list on page 298 to find more information on acid staining.

It is important that acid stain be applied to concrete that has been thoroughly cleaned and allowed to dry. Inspect the surface as it dries, noting areas that are discolored or that dry unevenly—these areas will most likely take stain differently, as will patched or repaired concrete.

Everything You Need:

Tools: plastic bucket, large brush with acid-resistant bristles, heavy rubber gloves, goggles, pump sprayer.

Materials: Acid stain, water, clean rags, water-based concrete sealer.

How to Acid Stain Concrete

1 After the concrete surface has been thoroughly cleaned and dried, dilute the stain with water, according to the manufacturer's instructions. Use a paintbrush with acid-resistant bristles to apply stain as evenly as possible, working systematically to work it into the surface. Minimize brush strokes.

2 After the entire surface is covered with stain, let it absorb according to the directions, then wipe up any excess stain using clean, dry rags. Discard rags that become saturated to avoid redistributing stain. After the stain is wiped up, rinse the surface with plenty of clean water.

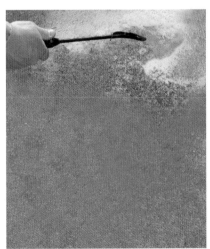

3 Allow the stain to dry for a few days (or as directed), then apply a water-based concrete sealer, using a brush, roller, or, for faster results, a hand-pump sprayer.

Simulating Flagstones

Carving joints in a concrete walk is an easy way to simulate the look of natural flagstones and add interest to an otherwise undistinguished path. By tinting the concrete before pouring it and carving the joints, you can create a walk that resembles a tightly-laid flagstone path, hence the name *false flagstone* often given to this age-old finishing technique.

Start by studying some flagstone paths in your neighborhood and sketching on paper the look you want to recreate. This way, you can also get an idea of the color to aim for when tinting the concrete mix. Keep in mind the color of your house and landscaping, and experiment with tint until you find a complementary hue.

Give a freshly poured concrete walk the appearance of a natural flagstone path by pressing lines into the surface after floating, then refloating the surface for a durable finish.

Everything You Need:

Tools: Jointing tool or curved ¾" copper pipe, screed board, magnesium float.

Materials: 2 × 4 lumber, concrete mix, colorant, concrete sealer.

How to Simulate Flagstones in a Concrete Walkway

1 Pour concrete into forms according to the basic walk-building technique, and smooth the surface with a screed board and then a magnesium float.

2 Cut shallow lines in the concrete, using a jointing tool or a curved copper pipe. Refloat the surface, and remove the forms once the concrete has cured. Protect the surface with clear concrete sealer.

Simulating Brick Pavers

An alternative to the simulated-flagstone technique is to pour your walk in sections, using a patterned mold to create either a brick paver or stepping stone effect. You won't need to set up forms for this project—the mold shapes the concrete as you place it. Once you've staked out your site and poured a subbase, you can go right to placing the concrete in the mold. But you will need to take extra care each time you place the mold to make sure the walk follows the path you intended. As with the "false flagstone" project, you may want to tint the concrete before pouring to recreate the tones of natural stone or pavers.

Turn to the related sections for directions on excavating your site, and estimating, mixing and pouring concrete. For maximum traction, finish the surface by using a brooming technique.

Everything You Need:

Tools: Trowels, concrete mold, shovel, broom.

Materials: Concrete mix, tint, isolation board, compactible gravel, concrete sealer, mason's sand, mortar.

Pour fresh concrete into plastic molds to create slabs with the appearance of neatly arrayed brick pavers. Molds are available for creating "bricks" or "stones" of various shapes and sizes.

How to Use Concrete Paving Molds

1 Place the mold at the start of your prepared site. Fill each mold cavity, and smooth the surface flush with the top of the mold, using a trowel. Let the bleed water dry, and then lift the mold and set it aside.

2 Smooth the edges of the concrete with a trowel. To pour subsequent sections, place the mold with the same orientation or rotate it ¼ turn. Continue to place and fill the mold until you reach the end of the walk. In the final placement, fill as many cavities as required to reach the walk's edge. Wait a week, then apply clear concrete sealer. OPTION: Finish the walk by filling the joints with sand or dry mortar.

Stamped Concrete Finishes

Stamped concrete can emulate the appearance of expensive imported stones or just about any other paver, but at a much lower cost.

Stamped finishes can bring interesting texture to ordinary concrete sidewalks, patios, and driveways. Stamping mats are available in a variety of textures and patterns, and can be rented at most equipment rental centers and concrete supply stores.

As you plan your concrete project, also plan the layout of the stamping mats to help maintain a consistent pattern across the project. For best results, mark a reference line at or near the center of the project and align the first mat with it. Align the subsequent mats with the first, working outward toward the ends of the project. Plan for long seams to fall across the project rather then along the length of it to avoid misaligned seams. You may have to hand-finish textures at corners, along sides, or near other obstructions using specialty stamps or an aluminum chisel.

The stamping pads should be pressed into slightly stiff concrete to a depth of about 1". Professionals typically use enough pads to cover the entire project area. For DIYers, it probably makes more sense to have one or two pads and reuse them.

Professional grade

DIY friendly

Stamping mats can be pressed onto fresh concrete, as with the professional-grade mats in the larger photo above (these are fairly expensive). DIY-oriented stamping mats are cheaper and feature fewer options. The DIY mats are usually open grids, so they can be used as either stamp pads or molds.

Everything You Need:

Tools: Tools for mixing and pouring concrete, textured stamping mats, hand tamp, aluminum chisel, pressure washer.

Materials: Materials for mixing, pouring and coloring concrete, powder release agent.

How to Stamp a Concrete Surface

1 Pour a concrete slab and mark a reference line for the first mat at or near the center of the form. When the bleed water disappears from the surface, toss powder release agent across the surface, in the amount specified in the manufacturer's instructions.

2 Align the first stamping mat with the reference line on the form, following your layout plan. Once the mat is placed, do not adjust it. Carefully step onto the mat or use a hand tamp to embed the stamp into the concrete.

3 Butt the second pad against the first, so the seams are flush and aligned. Embed the mat into the concrete, then place a third mat, maintaining the continuous pattern. Remove and reuse mats. When the project area is wider than the stamping pads, complete rows across the width before stamping lengthwise.

4 After the concrete has cured for three days, remove left over release agent from the surface using a pressure washer with a wide-fan spray—work in smooth, even strokes no more than 24" from the surface. Allow the concrete to cure fully for an additional week, then apply an acrylic concrete sealer, according the manufacturer's instructions. Remove the forms and backfill.

Exposed-Aggregate Patio

An exposed-aggregate patio project relies on basic site-preparation and concrete-pouring techniques, and adds an attractive finish.

Everything You Need:

Tools: Shovel, rope or hose, mason's string, tape measure, hand tamper, level, drill, wheelbarrow, masonry hoe, hammer, screed board, mason's trowel, edger, magnesium float, stiff-bristle brush, hose and spray attachment, paint roller.

Materials: 2½" and 4" deck screws, stakes, compactible gravel, pressure-treated 2 × 4s, reinforcing mesh, bolsters, small aggregate, concrete mix, plastic sheeting, exposed-aggregate sealer.

A concrete slab project becomes an attractive patio when divided by wood forms and seeded with stones. The forms replace control joints and a gravel subbase provides stability and drainage. Refer to the section on laying out and excavating your site before starting your project.

How to Build an Exposed-aggregate Patio

1 Prepare the building site by removing any existing building materials, like sidewalks or landing areas.

2 Lay out the rough position of the patio using a rope or hose, then mark the exact layout with stakes and mason's strings. Measure the diagonals to make sure the project area is square. Establish a ⅛" per ft. slope away from the house.

3 Remove sod and excavate the project area to a consistent depth, using mason's strings and a story pole as reference.

4 Create a subbase for the patio by pouring a 5"-thick layer of compactible gravel, then tamping until it is even and 4" thick.

5 Cut pressure-treated 2 × 4 boards to build a permanent form frame that outlines the entire patio site. Lay the boards in place, using the mason's strings as guides. Fasten the ends together with 2½" galvanized deck screws. Temporarily stake the forms at 2-ft. intervals. Set a straight 2 × 4 across the side forms, and set a level on top of the 2 × 4 to check the side forms for level.

Half-length form boards

Full-length form board

6 Cut and install pressure-treated 2 × 4s to divide the square into quadrants: cut one piece full length, and attach two one-half length pieces to it with screws driven toenail style. Drive 4" deck screws partway into the forms every 12" at inside locations. The portions that stick out will act as tie rods between the poured concrete and the permanent forms. TIP: Protect the tops of the permanent forms by covering them with masking tape.

(continued next page)

How to Build an Exposed-aggregate Patio (continued)

7 Cut reinforcing wire mesh to fit inside each quadrant, leaving 1" clearance on all sides. Mix concrete and pour the quadrants one at a time, starting with the one located farthest from the concrete source. Use a masonry hoe to spread the concrete evenly in the forms.

8 Settle the concrete by sliding a spade along the inside edges of the forms and rapping the outer edges with a hammer. Smooth off the concrete using a straight 2 × 4 as a screed board. Let any bleed water disappear before continuing.

9 After screeding the surface, cover the concrete with a full layer of aggregate seeds. Use a magnesium float to embed the aggregate completely into the concrete.

10 Tool the edges of the quadrant with an edger, then use a float to smooth any marks left behind. TIP: If you plan to pour more quadrants immediately, cover the seeded concrete with plastic so it does not set up too quickly.

11 Pour the remaining quadrants, repeating steps 7 to 10. Check poured quadrants periodically; uncover the quadrants once any bleed water has evaporated.

12 Mist the concrete surface with water and scrub the surface with a stiff-bristled brush to expose the aggregate. Remove the protective tape from the forms, then re-cover the quadrants with plastic and let the concrete cure for a week.

13 After the concrete has cured, rinse and scrub the aggregate again to clean off any remaining residue. TIP: Use diluted muriatic acid to wash off stubborn concrete residue. Read manufacturer's instructions for mixing ratios and safety precautions.

14 Once the patio has cured for three weeks, seal the surface with exposed-aggregate sealer. Reapply sealer annually, following manufacturer's recommendations.

Hardworking, or fun and fanciful, cast concrete objects are easy and inexpensive to make and offer a great opportunity for you to showcase your creativity. Casting small objects is also a great way to use up extra concrete.

Casting with Concrete

Casting decorative objects for the home and yard is an entertaining and creative exercise in handling concrete. Locating and making forms is a creative challenge itself, and the specific nature of the objects you eventually cast is often dictated by the potential you see in everyday objects that you encounter.

The best forms for casting are rigid or semirigid, with a slick surface and the ability to contain water. Plastic and rubber objects are ideal, but you can really use just about any material, especially if you use it for a single casting and are not concerned about breaking it when you release the cast object. Some examples of useful "found" forms include 5-gallon plastic buckets (insert a smaller bucket or a tube to cast a large concrete pot); trash can lids (pavers); nesting plastic bowls (pots and planters); or any sphere shapes, such as a basketball, that can be split in two (decorative orbs, bowls).

Making your owns forms is another fun exercise in creativity. Melamine-coated particleboard is a great material for this job because it holds its shape and the concrete will not stick to the surface. When combined with other materials, such as the metal flashing used to form the patio tabletop in this chapter, your casting options are practically unlimited.

For more complex and sophisticated castings, you can buy reusable forms in a very wide array of shapes and sizes. Garden benches, birdbaths, landscape edging, pavers, and statuary are just some of the objects you can cast with a couple bags of concrete and a purchased form. The best source for concrete casting forms is the Internet.

One of the best reasons to cast your own decorative and functional objects from concrete is that you can customize the finished look by coloring the concrete or using creative surface treatments, such as the footsteps in the pavers seen above.

Concrete Forms

Many objects can be used as forms for casting concrete. Semi-rigid items, like plastic bowls and buckets, are ideal because they require no special preparation, often include embossed shapes or designs, and are usually easy to strip from the cast object.

Constructed forms can cast items of practically any size or shape. For flat items, like tabletops and stepping stones, melamine-coated particleboard is a good choice because the melamine side does not require a release agent. Wood should be treated with a release agent like nonstick cooking spray.

Concrete For Casting

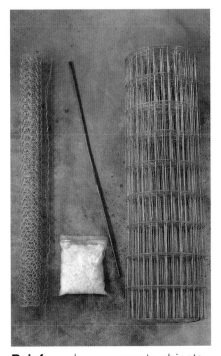

Bagged concrete with fiber reinforcement blended in at the plant is well-suited for larger castings that are likely to undergo stress (e.g., stepping stones and tabletops). For small items, use sand mix. In both cases, add acrylic fortifier to make the mixture more slippery without decreasing strength. A coloring agent (liquid or dry) adds new design possibilities.

Reinforce large concrete objects. Metal rods and mesh can be used, but keep them away from edges. Add synthetic reinforcing fibers if not included in your mix.

Garden Column

Prefabricated concrete casting forms give you the ability to make objects for your yard and garden that rival the best (and very expensive) artwork pieces sold at garden centers. Garden benches and birdbaths are among the most popular, but you can locate an array of forms for just about any objects you can imagine.

Because most of the objects cast with ready-made forms feature grooves, flutes or complex patterns, you'll have the best luck if you use a relatively wet mixture of concrete with small or sand-only aggregate. Adding latex bonding agent or acrylic fortifier also makes the concrete more slippery so it can conform to odd shapes more readily, but these agents do not reduce concrete strength, as adding more water does.

If your cast project will be placed outdoors, apply a penetrating concrete sealer about a week after the casting.

Everything You Need:

Tools: Shovel, mortar box, concrete forms.

Materials: Bagged concrete mix (fiber reinforced), nonstick cooking spray, acrylic fortifier.

This classical concrete column is cast using a simple plastic form purchased from an Internet supplier (see Resources). It can be used to support many garden items, including a display pedestal, a birdbath or a sundial.

Prefabricated casting forms typically are made from rugged PVC so they may be reused many times. You can mix and match the forms to create different objects. The forms above include a column form with grapevine or fluted insert, two different pedestal shapes, and an optional birdbath top

How to Cast a Garden Column

1 Choose a column form insert (optional) and slide it into the column form as a liner so the edges meet neatly. Tape the column together at the seam. Coat the insides of all form parts with a very light mist of nonstick cooking spray as a release agent.

2 Choose a sturdy, level work surface. Set the column form upright on a small piece of scrap plywood. Tape down the form with duct tape, keeping the tape clear of the form top. Mix a batch of fiber-reinforced concrete with an acrylic fortifier and shovel it into the forms. Rap the forms with a stick to settle the concrete and strike off the excess with a screed. Run additional tape "hold-downs" over the top of the column form to secure it to the plywood scrap tightly enough that the concrete will not run out from the bottom.

3 Set another scrap of plywood onto the top of the column form and weight it down. Let the parts dry for two days and then release them from the forms. Wash and rinse the parts to remove dusty residue.

4 Apply exterior landscape adhesive to the top of the base pedestal and set the column end into the adhesive so the column is centered. Bond the top pedestal in the same manner. Apply penetrating sealant. If it is not nearby, transport the column and pedestals to the location before bonding the parts.

Patio Table Top

Casting concrete is a good way to produce some types of replacement parts, such as a new top for this old iron patio table base. To make the form for this project a strip of galvanized roll flashing is inserted inside a ring of finish nails to create a circular shape. Larger tabletops should have rebar or rewire reinforcement, but this 24"-dia. top is small enough that fiber reinforcement strands are sufficient.

Everything You Need:

Tools: Aviator snips, hammer, caulk gun, magnesium float, pencil, drill/driver, rubber mallet, hammer.

Materials: Reinforced concrete mix, acrylic fortifier, concrete colorant, galvanized metal roll flashing, 6d nails, caulk, duct tape, melamine-coated particleboard, tabletop hardware.

This round patio table top was cast with fiber-reinforced concrete tinted yellow. It is a much simpler version of the kitchen island countertop cast on pages 90 to 97. By casting your own top, you can custom fit any table base you may have.

How to Cast a Round Table Top

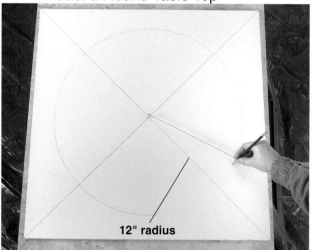

12" radius

1 Cut a piece of ¾" melamine (or just about any other sheet stock) to 30" x 30" and drive a small nail in the exact center. Tie string to the nail and tie a pencil to the other end, exactly 12" away form the nail. Pull the string tight and use this "compass" to draw a 12" radius (24" diameter) circle.

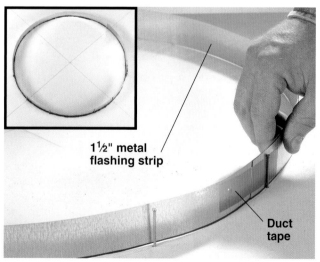

1½" metal flashing strip

Duct tape

2 Drive 6d finish nails on the circle line at 6" intervals. Keep the nails perpendicular. Cut a 1½" wide by 80"-long strip of galvanized (not aluminum) flashing, using aviator snips. Fit the flashing inside the circle with the cut edge down (factory edge up). Let the flashing spring out inside the circle and adjust so the circle is even. Tape the ends of the flashing with duct tape on the outside of the form.

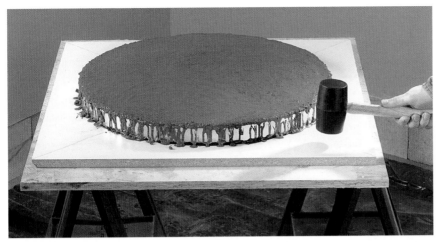

3 Caulk liberally around the outside edge of the flashing where it meets the base. After the caulk dries, fill the form with a relatively stiff mix of fiber-reinforced concrete. Add acrylic fortifier and pigment (if desired) to the water before mixing the concrete. Pound the form base gently with a rubber mallet to settle the concrete. Also, work a stick around the edges of the concrete form to help settle the concrete and make sure there are no voids.

4 Strike off the the top of the concrete with a wood screed and fill any voids or dips in the surface with fresh concrete. Let the concrete set up until the bleed water that rises to the surface evaporates. Then, float the surface with a steel or magnesium float to create a smooth, hard surface. Do not overwork the float, however, as this will draw aggregate to the surface and weaken the pour.

5 Let the concrete cure for at least two days, then remove the flashing and release the table tops. Grind and polish if you wish (see page 97). Then, attach the top to the table base. The table base shown here has screwholes in the bearing ring, so we marked the screw locations on the underside of the tabletop and then drilled holes for screw anchors. Seal the surface.

A deck bowl is cast using two nesting mixing bowls. This technique can be used with plastic bowls and buckets and planters of all sizes. Larger containers should be split in half and taped back together so you can extract the cast object more easily. We used sand mix with acrylic fortifier and black concrete pigment for this deck bowl.

Sand casting is a great way to use up the leftovers from a larger poured concrete project. To make this birdbath, you simply pile up some coarse wet sand and pour the leftover concrete onto the pile. Birds love the rough texture of the concrete surface.

1 Fill the larger nesting bowl about halfway with concrete. Then lower the smaller bowl down into the concrete. The concrete should just overflow slightly when the tops of the two bowls are level. Add more concrete if necessary.

1 Pile coarse sand about 10" to 12" high and 24" diameter at the bottom of the pile. Dampen the sand. Gently pour concrete over the top of the pile. There should be enough to trickle down to the ground all around. The concrete should be about 2" thick.

2 Place a piece of scrap wood on top of the bowls and weight it down with heavy object, like a full gallon can of paint. Rap the sides of the bowl with a stick to vibrate and settle the concrete. Add more if necessary. Let the concrete dry for a day, then remove the form.

2 Let the concrete dry overnight, then simply pull it off the sand pile and see how it turned out. Hose the sand off. Locate a suitable base (the metal legs from an old chiminea are used here) or set the birdbath on the ground.

Any everyday object that can hold moisture is potentially a concrete form. To make this decorative garden accent, we simply split an old basketball in two and filled the halves. Then we adhered the halves together. Clusters of orbs in various sizes look appealing. Or apply a decorative painted finish (for indoor use, try a metallic paint like copper).

Make your own stepping stones to inject some creativity into your garden. If you make a couple every weekend over the winter, by spring you'll be ready to install your new garden path.

1 Find an old basketball (thrift shops are a good source) and cut it in half along an equatorial line using scissors or a utility knife. Rinse out the inside, then fill each half to the top with concrete. Set the forms in a sandbox so they won't roll around.

1 Make a form large enough to cast two 1½" x 16" x 16" pavers at once. Two pavers can be cast with one 60-pound bag of concrete, plus casting two at a time helps you keep the left/right numbers equal.

2 Rap the forms repeatedly with a stick to settle the concrete, then strike off the excess by dragging a screed across the tops in a back-and-forth motion. When dried, remove from the forms and adhere the two halves together with concrete adhesive, filling gaps.

2 Fill the form with concrete, vibrate a strike off the excess concrete. Once the bleed water disappears, press one shoe about 1/8" into the concrete surface of each stepping stone. Remove the shoes once the concrete is dry to the touch.

Concrete countertops have many pluses and few minuses. They are durable, heat resistant, and relatively inexpensive. But most of all, they are highly attractive and a great fit with contemporary styles.

Kitchen Island Countertop

Once used exclusively for outdoor building projects, concrete has expanded its range to become a premier material for indoor construction as well. Still utilized mostly to cast countertops and vanity tops, concrete is continually finding new applications inside the home, including fireplace hearths, floors and even furnishings. Along with remarkable strength and extreme durability, concrete has charm and appeal unlike any other building material.

A concrete countertop may be cast in place or formed offsite and installed like a natural stone countertop. For a number of reasons, casting offsite makes more sense for most of us. In addition to keeping the mess and dust out of your living spaces, working in a garage or even outdoors lets you cast the countertops with the finished surface face-down in the form. This way, if you do a careful job building the form, you can keep the grinding and polishing to a bare minimum. In some cases, you may even be able to

simply remove the countertop from the form, flip it over and install it essentially as-is.

Thorough planning and careful form construction are the keys to a successful concrete countertop project. One of the first issues to tackle is weight: concrete weighs about 140 pounds per

Everything You Need:

Tools: Tape measure, pencil, table saw or circular saw, jigsaw, drill and right angle drill guide, level, carpenter's square, re-bar bender, reciprocating saw with metal cutting blade, aviation snips, pliers, concrete mixer, 5-gal. buckets, shovel, wheelbarrow, wooden float, variable speed angle grinder with grinding pads, belt sander, automotive buffer.

Materials: See photo, next page.

cubic foot (roughly 25 pounds per square foot for a 2" thick countertop). Most floors should be able to support a heavy countertop, but be sure to inspect floor joists and framing, especially in older homes, to determine if any reinforcement is needed. If you are unsure, consult a building professional, your local building inspector's office or a structural engineer.

The weight of the concrete is also a factor when it comes to cabinetry. Typical base cabinets should be reinforced at the back and across the top with ½". or ¾" plywood. Reinforcing cabinetry may increase the overall dimensions, which can cause problems with modular units or in areas with limited space.

After you design your project and determine the actual dimensions, you'll need to estimate the amount of concrete you'll need. Concrete is measured by volume in cubic feet; multiply the length by the wide and then by the thickness of the finished countertop for volume in cubic inches, then divide the sum by 1728 for cubic feet. For example, a countertop that will be 48-in.-long × 24-in.-wide × 3½-in.-thick will require 2⅓-cu.-ft. of mixed concrete (48 × 24 × 3.5 / 1728 = 2⅓).

The best way to achieve consistent results when mixing concrete is to use premixed materials. One 60-lb. bag. of premixed high-strength concrete equals ½-cu.-ft. of mixed concrete. A number of online concrete outlets also offer a virtual rainbow of dry-mix color pigments that are formulated with a water reducer admixture. Water reducers limit the amounts of water need the concrete mix uses to help produce a stronger mix and a smoother finished produce. See the page 298.

As you mix the concrete materials, blend all dry ingredients thoroughly in a motorized mixer for five minutes prior to adding liquid ingredients. Do not mix the concrete until the form is com-

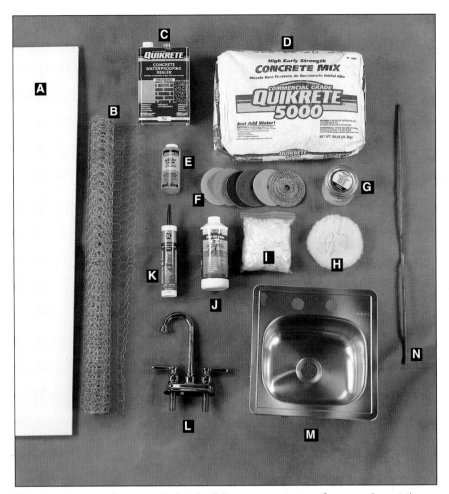

The basic supplies needed to build your countertop form and cast the countertop include: (A) Melamine coated particleboard for constructing the form; (B) poultry netting or welded wire for reinforcement; (C) concrete sealer (product shown is adequate, but for better protection look for a sealer that has both penetrating and film-forming properties); (D) high/early bagged concrete mix rated for 5,000 p.s.i.; (E) coloring agent (liquid or powder); (F) grinding pads (shown are 5" diamond pads ranging from 50 grit to 1,500 grit for grinding and polishing); (G) paste wax; (H) buffing bonnet for polisher; (I) fiber reinforcement (nylon); (J) acrylic fortifier, latex bonding agent (or water reducing admixture if you can locate it); (K) black or colored silicone caulk; (L) faucet set if installing sink; (M) sink (self rimming shown); (N) No. 3 rebar (⅜").

pletely built, with any sink or faucet knockouts and the reinforcement in place. For best results, mix the concrete in a single batch with a power mixer. Because the mixing container on power mixtures should never be more than half full (one-third full on some models) you'll need a relatively large mixer for all but the smallest countertops. For the island countertop projects shown here, a tow-behind nine cubic foot mixer was rented (yet another good reason for casting your countertop offsite). Once your casting is done, let the concrete cure for at least a week before you strip off the forms.

How to Cast a Concrete Countertop

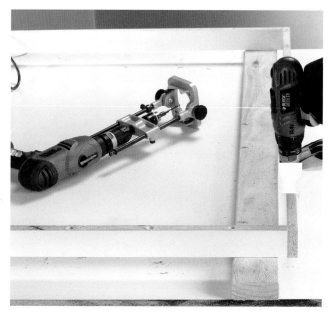

1 Cut ¾" melamine-coated particleboard into 2¼"-wide strips to make the form sides. Cut the sides to length (33½" and 41½" as shown here) and drill two countersunk pilot holes ⅜" in from the ends of the front and back form sides. Assemble the strips into a frame by driving a 2" coarse wallboard screws at each pilot hole and into the mating ends of the end form strips.

2 Mount a power drill in a right-angle drill guide (or use a drill press) and drill ¼"-dia. pilot holes for 3" deck screws at 6" intervals all the way through the tops of the form sides. Countersink the holes so the screw heads are recessed slightly from the surface.

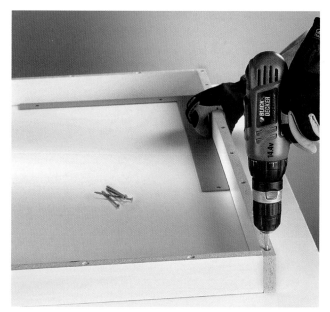

3 Center the form frame on the base, which should have the melamine side facing up. Test the corners with a carpenter's square to make sure they're square. Drive one 3½" deck screw per form side, near the middle. The screwheads should be slightly below the top edges if the forms. Check for square again, and continue driving the 3½" screws at 6" intervals through the pilot holes. Check for square frequently-the stress easily can pull the frame out of joint.

4 Make the sink knockout (if you're installing a sink). The sink we used requires a 14⅜" square cutout with corners that are rounded at a 1½" radius. Cut three pieces of ¾"-thick MDF to 14⅜" square, using a table saw if possible. With a compass, mark 1½"-radius curves at each corner for trimming. Make the trim cuts with a jigsaw (only if you stack and cut all three at once). Cut just outside the trim line and sand up to it with a pad sander for a smooth curve.

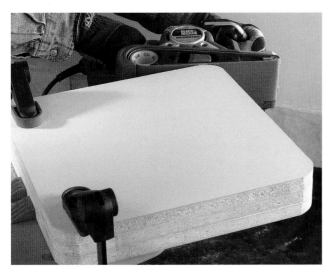

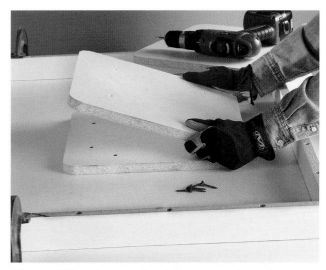

5 Use the rounded knockout blank as a template for marking and cutting the other two blanks to match. Clamp the three blanks together and sand the edges smooth and even. A belt sander on a stationary sanding station or an oscillating spindle sander works great for this. If you are strong and steady handed, you can freehand the corners with a portable belt sander. Don't over-sand—this will cause the sink knockout to be too small.

6 Install the sink knockout. Because gluing the faces together can add height to the knockout (and cause the concrete finishing tools to bang into it when they ride on the form tops), attach each blank directly to the layer below it, using countersunk screws. Keep the edges aligned perfectly, especially if you're planning to install an undermount sink.

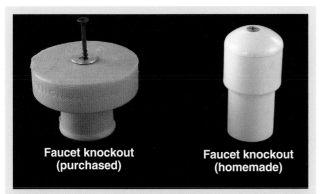

Faucet knockout (purchased)   **Faucet knockout (homemade)**

OPTION: If your sink faucet will not be mounted on the sink deck, you'll need to add knockouts for the faucet hole or holes, according to the requirements of the faucet manufacturer (one reason you should buy your sink and faucet before making your form). You can order knockouts from a concrete countertop supplies distributor, or you can create them with PVC plumbing pipe that has an outside diameter equal to the required faucet hole size. To anchor the PVC knockout, cover one end with a cap made for that size tubing. Drill a guide hole through the center of the cap so you can secure it with a screw. Before securing, position the knockout next to a form side and compare the heights. If the knockout is taller, trim the uncapped end so the lengths match.

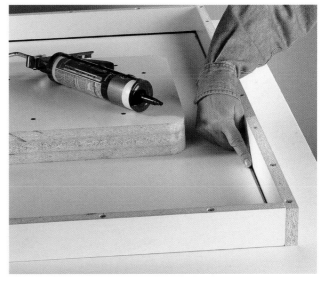

7 Seal any exposed edges with fast-drying polyurethane varnish, and then caulk the form once the varnish is dry. Run a very thin bead of colored silicone caulk (the coloring allows you to see where the caulk has been laid on the white melamine) in all the seams and then smooth carefully with a fingertip. In addition to keeping the wet concrete from seeping into gaps in the form, the caulk will create a slight roundover on the edges of the concrete. The more smoothly you caulk, the less grinding you'll have to do later. If you will be installing an undermount sink, also caulk around the sink knockout.

(continued next page)

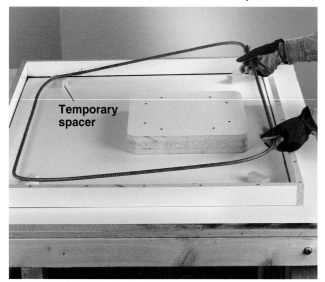

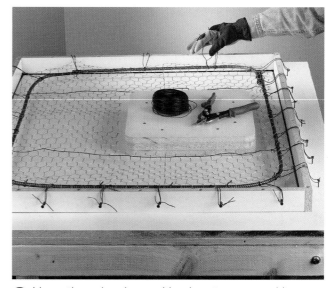

8 Add reinforcement to the form. For thicker castings, bend #3 (⅜") rebar to fit around the perimeter of the form, using a rebar bender. The rebar needs to be at least 1" away from all edges (including knockouts) and 1" away from the top surface. Metal reinforcement can telegraph through concrete if it is too close to the visible surfaces. Tie the ends of the rebar with wire and set it in the form on temporary 1" spacers.

9 Hang the rebar loop with wires to suspend it, keeping it far enough away from the concrete surface without using spacers. Drive a few screws into the outside faces of the form sides, near the top, use wire ties to hang the rebar. Once all of the ties are in place you may remove the temporary spacers. For extra insurance, add another reinforcing material, such as wire poultry netting, over the rebar and tie them together.

Temporary spacer

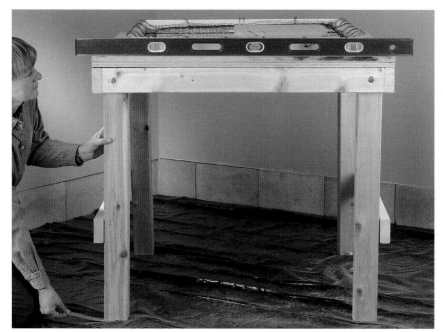

TIP: To keep the form from moving during the all-important pouring, finishing and curing stages, attach or clamp the sacrificial plywood worktop to the actual top. Check for level and insert shims between the worktop and the benchtop if needed. When possible, drive screws up through the benchtop and into the worktop to hold it steady. Otherwise, use c-clamps and check them regularly to make sure they're tight. If you're concerned about mess, slip a sheet of 3-mil plastic on the floor.

10 Add all of the dry ingredients into a concrete mixer that's large enough to do the whole pour. The dry ingredients include high/early concrete mix rated to 5,000 p.s.i., and synthetic fiber reinforcement. If you are using dry pigment, also add this now. Run the mixer for several minutes to thoroughly blend the dry ingredients.

11 Blend the wet ingredients (water plus any liquid concrete colorant and a water reducer or acrylic fortifier) in a bucket and, with the mixer running, add them slowly to the dry ingredients. Add more water as necessary until the concrete is thoroughly hydrated, but still stiff.

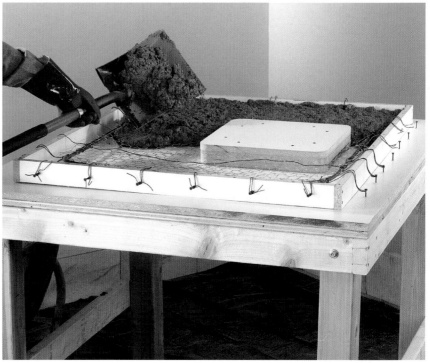

12 Fill the countertop form, making sure to pack the concrete into corners and press it through the reinforcement. Overfill the form slightly.

13 Vibrate the form vigorously as you work to settle concrete into all the voids. You can rent a concrete vibrator for this purpose, or simply strike the form repeatedly with a rubber mallet. If you have a helper and a sturdy floor and worktable, lift up and down on the ends of the table, bouncing it on the floor to cause vibrations (this is a very effective method if you can manage it safely). Make sure the table remains level when you're through.

14 Strike off excess concrete from the form using a 2x4 drawn along the tops of the forms in a sawing motion. If voids are created, pack them with fresh concrete and re-strike. Do not overwork the concrete

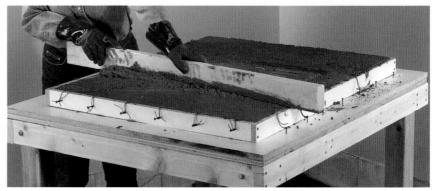

(continued next page)

15 Once you are certain you won't need to vibrate the form any further, snip the wire ties holding the rebar loop and embed the cut ends attached to the rebar below the concrete surface.

16 Smooth the surface of the concrete with a metal screeding tool, such as a length of angle iron or square metal tubing. Work slowly with a sawing motion, allowing the bleed water to fill in behind the screed. Since this surface will be the underside of the countertop, no further tooling is required. Cover with sheet plastic and allow the concrete to dry and cure undisturbed for a full week.

17 Remove the plastic covering and then unscrew and remove the forms. Do not pry against the fresh concrete. In most cases, you'll need to cut apart the sink knockout to prevent damaging the countertop when removing it. Drill a starter hole and then carefully cut up to the edge of the knockout. Cut the knockout into chunks until you can remove it all (INSET). The edges of the concrete will be fragile, so be very careful.

18 With a helper or two (or three), flip the countertop so the finished surface is exposed. Be extremely careful. The best technique is to roll the countertop onto an edge, position a couple 2 x 4 sleepers beneath it (insulation board works very well), and then gently lower it onto the sleepers.

OPTION: To expose the aggregate and create a very polished surface that resembles natural stone, grind the surface. Use a series of increasingly fine diamond-wheel grinding pads (50-grit, then 100, 200 and 400) mounted on a shock-protected 5" angle grinder (variable speed). This is messy work, and can go on for hours to get the desired result. Rinse the surface regularly with clean water and make sure it stays wet during grinding. For a gleaming surface, mount still finer pads (up to 1,500 grit) on the grinder and wet-polish.

19 Clean and seal the concrete with several coats of quality silicone-based concrete sealer (one with penetrating and film-forming agents). For extra protection and a renewable finish, apply a coat of paste wax after the last coat of sealer dries.

20 Undermount or self-rimming, the sink is easier to install before the countertop is mounted on the cabinet. Attach the sink according to the manufacturer's directions. Self-rimming sinks likely will require some modifications to the mounting hardware (or at least you'll need to buy some extra-long screws) to accommodate the thickness of the countertop.

21 Make sure the island cabinet is adequately reinforced and that as much plumbing as possible has been taken care of, then apply a thick bead of panel adhesive or silicone adhesive to the tops of the cabinets and stretchers. With at least one helper, lower the countertop onto the base and position it where you wish. Let the adhesive dry overnight before completing the sink hookup.

Brick & Block

Working with Brick and Block

Working with brick and block is a satisfying process: with each unit that is added, the project grows and its appearance improves. Whether you're building a block retaining wall, a brick barbeque, or paving a walk with mortared brick, you're sure to enjoy the project as well as its results.

Brick and block provide a sense of balance as well as color and texture to your home and landscape. Structures built with these materials are attractive, durable, and low maintenance.

Careful planning and a thoughtful design will help you build a project that makes sense for your home, your yard, and your budget. Projects are simpler to build if you create a design that limits the number of masonry units that must be cut.

Brick and decorative block colors, styles, and textures vary widely by region, reflecting regional trends. Choose a color and style that complements the style of your home and yard as well as the region in which you live. Colors and styles are often discontinued abruptly, so it's a good idea to buy a few extra units to have on hand for repairs.

Common Brick and Block Projects

A brick barbeque is a sophisticated and satisfying project. This design is built on top of a floating footing, which is designed to shift as a unit when the temperature changes, an important characteristic for a barbeque. Additionally, the interior is built with fire brick and refractory mortar to ensure its heat resistance.

There are many different styles and colors of interlocking block available at most home centers and landscaping stores.

Freestanding pillars create a lovely entrance for a driveway or garden. This design employs a brick cap, which gives the project a touch of elegance and protects it against moisture. The aged appearance of these bricks helps them blend in. Be sure to select bricks that match or complement your home's exterior.

Mortarless block walls, built with a running bond pattern, derive their strength from a coat of surface bonding cement. This bonding cement is strong enough to support even very long walls and it creates an attractive surface wall surface (pages 182 to 183).

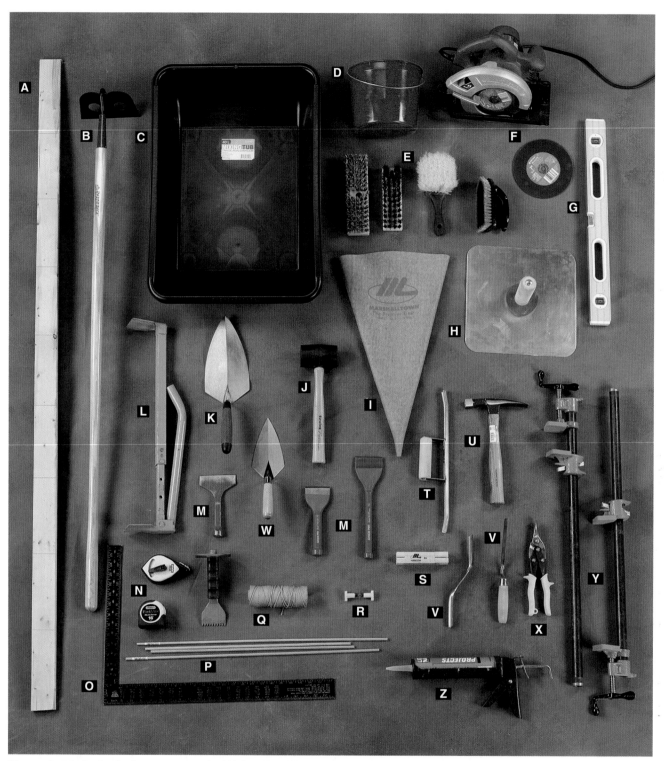

Mason's tools include: a story pole (A) for checking stacked masonry units; masonry hoe (B) and mortar box (C) for mixing mortar; a bucket (D) and stiff bristle brushes (E) for removing stains and loose materials; circular saw and masonry-cutting blades (F) for scoring brick and block; level (G) for checking stacked masonry units; mortar hawk (H) for holding mortar; mortar bag (I) for filling horizontal joints; rubber mallet (J) for setting paver stones; mason's trowel (K) for applying mortar; brick tongs (L) for carrying multiple bricks; masonry chisels (M) for splitting brick, block and stone; a tape measure and chalk line (N) for marking layout lines on footings or slabs; a framing square (O) for setting project outlines; ⅜" dowels (P) for spacers between dry-laid masonry units; mason's string (Q) and line blocks (S) for stacking brick and block; a line level (R) for making layouts and setting slope; sled jointer (T) for finishing long joints; mason's hammer (U) for chipping brick and stone; jointer (V) for finishing mortar joints; pointing trowel (W) for placing mortar on brick and block walls; aviation snips (X) for trimming metal ties and lath; pipe clamps (Y) for aligning brick and block to be scored; caulk gun (Z) for sealing around fasteners and house trim.

Tools & Materials

Laying brick and block is a precise business. Many of the tools necessary for these projects relate to establishing and maintaining true, square and level structures, while others relate to cutting the masonry units and placing the mortar. It makes sense to purchase tools you'll use again, but it's more cost effective to rent specialty items, such as a brick splitter.

Mortar mixes include: Type N, a medium-strength mortar for above grade outdoor use in non-load-bearing (freestanding) walls, barbeques, chimneys, and tuck-pointing; Type S, a high-strength mortar for outdoor use at or below grade, typically used in foundations, retaining walls, driveways, walks, and patios; refractory mortar, a calcium aluminate mortar that is resistant to high temperatures, used for mortaring around firebrick in fireplaces and barbeques; mortar tint for coloring mortar.

Common types of brick and block used for residential construction include: decorative block (A) available colored or plain, decorative concrete pavers (B), fire brick (C), standard 8 × 8 × 16" concrete block (D), half block (E), combination corner block (F), queen-sized brick (G), standard brick pavers (H), standard building bricks (I), and limestone wall cap (J).

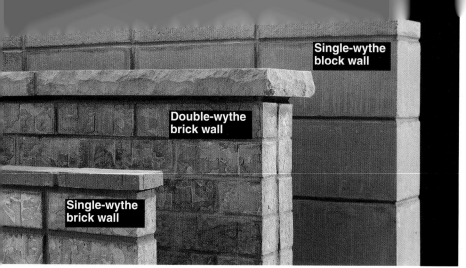

Single-wythe block wall

Double-wythe brick wall

Single-wythe brick wall

Planning Your Brick & Block Project

Like other masonry projects, brick and block projects must start with careful planning. You need to identify the construction techniques and methods that are appropriate for the project, practice any techniques you need to learn, and estimate and order your materials.

Select a construction design that makes sense for your project. There are two basic methods used in stacking brick or block. Structures that are only one unit wide are called *single wythe,* and are typically used for projects like brick barbecues or planters, and for brick veneers. *Double-wythe* walls are two units wide and are used in free-standing applications. Most concrete-block structures are single wythe.

How to Estimate Bricks and Blocks

Standard brick pavers for walks and patios (4 × 8)	surface area (sq. ft. × 5 = number of pavers needed
Standard bricks for walls and pillars (4 × 8)	surface area (sq. ft.) × 7 = number of bricks needed (single brick thickness)
Interlocking Block	area of wall face (sq. ft.) × 1.5 = number of blocks needed
8 × 8 × 16 concrete for freestanding walls	Height of wall (ft.) × length of wall × 1.125 = number of blocks needed

Use this chart to estimate the materials necessary for brick and block projects.

3'

Keep structures as low as you can. Local codes require frost footings and additional reinforcement for permanent walls or structures that exceed maximum height restrictions. You can often simplify your project by designing walls that are below the maximum height.

Add a lattice panel or another decorative element to permanent walls to create greater privacy without having to add structural reinforcement to the masonry structure.

Tips for Planning a Brick or Block Project

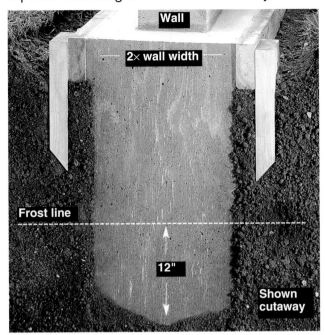

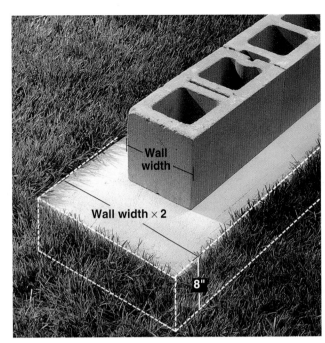

Frost footings are required if a structure will be more than 2 feet tall or if it is tied to another permanent structure. Frost footings should be twice as wide as the structure they support and should extend 8 to 12 inches below the frost line (pages 44 to 47).

Pour a reinforced concrete slab for brick and block structures that are freestanding and under 2 ft. tall. The slab should be twice as wide as the wall, flush with ground level, and at least 8 inches thick. Check with building codes for special requirements. Slabs are poured using the techniques for pouring a sidewalk (pages 48 to 53).

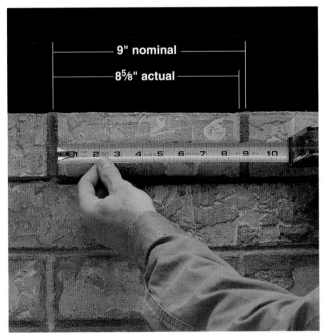

Do not add mortar joint thickness to total project dimensions when planning brick and block projects. The actual sizes of bricks and blocks are $3/8$" smaller than the nominal size to allow for $3/8$"-wide mortar joints. For example, a 9" (nominal) brick has an actual dimension of $8 5/8$", so a wall that is built with four 9" bricks and $3/8$" mortar joints will have a finished length of 36" (4×9").

Test project layouts using $3/8$" spacers between masonry units to make sure the planned dimensions work. If possible, create a plan that uses whole bricks or blocks, reducing the amount of cutting required.

Cut stone is a top-quality material for building walls, pillars and arches. For retaining walls (shown above) cut stone or interlocking block is laid without mortar (except for the top course) so water doesn't become trapped behind the wall. Free-standing structures are often built with mortar (we include both types in this section). Either method can be used to build walls that will last for generations. Both are described in this section.

Basic Techniques

Brick and block projects share some common layout and preparation techniques with poured concrete projects and natural stone projects. But in many regards the actual construction of the projects requires more care and precision than other types (not to mention some heavy lifting). When you're dealing with regular masonry units like brick and block, any wandering of the mortar lines will appear very obvious and detract from the appearance of the structure you're building.

Finished with stucco and topped with lattice panels, this concrete block wall forms an attractive divider between a patio and yard.

How to Lay Out a Wall, Pillar, or Arch

1 To get a sense of the size and impact of a wall or other project before you begin construction, plot the borders of the project, using tall stakes or poles, then tie mason's strings marking the projected top of the structure.

2 Hang landscape fabric or sheets of plastic between the stakes and over the top of the string. View the structure from all sides for an indication of how much it will obstruct views and access, and how it will blend with other elements of the landscape.

Working with a Water Level

Water levels take advantage of the fact that water in an open tube will level itself, no matter how many bends and turns the tube has. This makes a water level ideal for working with long structures, around corners, or on sites where a conventional level won't work. Typical commercially available water levels consist of clear plastic tubes that screw onto the ends of a garden hose (right, top). Mark off 1" increments on each tube. Attach the tubes to the ends of a garden hose, then fill the hose until water is visible in both tubes. Working with a helper, hold the tubes at the ends of the site. Adjust the tubes until the water is at the same mark in each tube (right, bottom). Drive stakes or mark off the level points on your structure. Option: Pricier water levels contain an electronic gauge that's useful when you need precise readings.

How to Plot a Right Angle

1 The 3-4-5 triangle method is the most effective method of plotting right angles for walls, pillars, and other construction. Begin by staking the outside corner of your walls and stringing a mason's string to mark the outside of one wall.

2 Mark a point 3 ft. out along that wall by planting another stake.

3 Position the end of one tape measure at the outside corner and open it past the 4 ft. mark. Have an assistant position the end of another tape measure at the 3 ft. stake and open it past the 5 ft. mark. Lock the tape measures and adjust them so they intersect at the 4 ft. and 5 ft. marks.

4 Plant a stake at the meeting point, then run mason's strings from this stake to the outside corner. The 3 ft. and 4 ft. mason's strings form a right angle. Extend or shorten the mason's strings, as required, and stake out the exact dimensions of your structure.

How to Plot a Curve

1 Start by plotting a right angle, using the 3-4-5 triangle method (opposite page). Mark the end points for the curve by measuring and planting stakes equidistant from the outside corner.

2 Tie a mason's string to those stakes. Extend each string back to the outside corner, then hold them tight at the point where they meet. Pull this point toward the inside of the angle until the strings are taut. The strings will complete a square.

3 Plant a stake at their meeting point, then tie a piece of mason's string to that stake, just long enough to reach the stakes marking the endpoints of the curve.

4 Pull the string taut, then swing it in an arc between the end points, using spray paint to mark the curve on the ground.

Tips for Reinforcing Brick & Block Structures

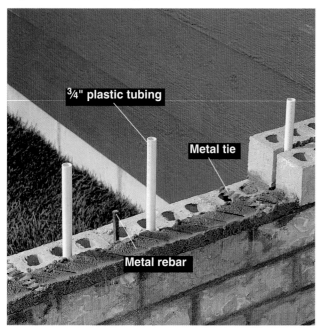

For double-wythe brick projects, use metal ties between wythes for reinforcement. Insert ties directly into the mortar 2 to 3 ft. apart, every third course. Insert metal rebar into the gap between wythes every 4 to 6 ft. (check local building codes). Insert ¾"-diameter plastic tubing between wythes to keep them aligned. Pour a thin mixture of mortar between the wythes to improve the strength of the wall.

For block projects, fill the empty spaces (cores) of the block with thin mortar. Insert sections of metal rebar into the mortar to increase vertical strength. Check with your local building inspector to determine reinforcement requirements, if any.

Provide horizontal reinforcement on brick or block walls by setting metal reinforcing strips into the mortar every third course. Metal reinforcing strips, along with most other reinforcing products, can be purchased from brick and block suppliers. Overlap the ends of metal strips 6" where they meet.

Tips for Working with Brick

Make practice runs on a 2 × 4 to help you perfect your mortar-throwing (pages 114 to 115) and bricklaying techniques. You can clean and reuse the bricks to make many practice runs if you find it helpful, but do not reuse the bricks in your actual project—old mortar can impede bonding.

Test the water absorption rate of bricks to determine their density. Squeeze out 20 drops of water in the same spot on the surface of a brick. If the surface is completely dry after 60 seconds, dampen the bricks with water before you lay them to prevent them from absorbing moisture from the mortar before it has a chance to set.

Use a T-square and pencil to mark several bricks for cutting. Make sure the ends of the bricks are all aligned.

Mark angled cuts by dry-laying the project (as shown with pavers above) and setting the brick or block in position. Allow for ⅜" joints in mortared projects. Pavers have spacing lugs that set the spacing at ⅛". Mark cutting lines with a pencil, using a straightedge where practical to mark straight lines.

How to Score & Cut Brick

Score all four sides of the brick first with a brickset chisel and maul when cuts fall over the web area, and not over the core. Tap the chisel to leave scored cutting marks ⅛" to ¼" deep, then strike a firm final blow to the chisel to split the brick. Properly scored bricks split cleanly with one firm blow.

OPTION: When you need to split a lot of bricks uniformly and quickly, use a circular saw fitted with a masonry blade to score the bricks, then split them individually with a chisel. For quick scoring, clamp them securely at each end with a pipe or bar clamp, making sure the ends are aligned. Remember: wear eye protection when using striking or cutting tools.

How to Angle-cut Brick

1 Mark the final cutting line on the brick. To avoid ruining the brick, you will need to make gradual cuts until you reach this line. Score a straight line for the first cut in the waste area of the brick about ⅛" from the starting point of the final cutting line, perpendicular to the edge of the brick. Make the first cut.

2 Keep the chisel stationary at the point of the first cut, pivot it slightly, then score and cut again. It is important to keep the pivot point of the chisel at the edge of the brick. Repeat until all of the waste area is removed.

How to Cut Brick with a Brick Splitter

1 A brick splitter makes accurate, consistent cuts in bricks and pavers with no scoring required. It is a good idea to rent one if your project requires many cuts. To use the brick splitter, first mark a cutting line on the brick, then set the brick on the table of the splitter, aligning the cutting line with the cutting blade on the tool.

2 Once the brick is in position on the splitter table, pull down sharply on the handle. The cutting blade on the splitter will cleave the brick along the cutting line. TIP: For efficiency, mark cutting lines on several bricks at the same time (see page 111).

How to Cut Concrete Block

1 Mark cutting lines on both faces of the block, then score ⅛" to ¼"-deep cuts along the lines, using a circular saw equipped with a masonry blade.

2 Use a mason's chisel and maul to split one face of the block along the cutting line. Turn the block over and split the other face.

OPTION: Cut half blocks from combination corner blocks. Corner blocks have preformed cores in the center of the web. Score lightly above the core, then rap with a mason's chisel to break off half blocks.

Mixing & Throwing Mortar

A professional bricklayer at work is an impressive sight, even for do-it-yourselfers who have completed numerous masonry projects successfully. The mortar practically flies off the trowel and seems to end up in perfect position to accept the next brick or block.

Although "throwing mortar" is an acquired skill that takes years to perfect, you can use the basic techniques successfully with just a little practice.

The first critical element to handling mortar effectively is the mixture. If it's too thick, it will fall off the trowel in a heap, not in the smooth line that is your goal. Add too much water and the mortar becomes messy and weak. Follow the manufacturer's directions, but keep in mind that the amount of water specified is an approximation. If you've never mixed mortar before, experiment with small amounts until you find a mixture that clings to the trowel just long enough for you to deliver a controlled, even line that holds its shape after settling. Note how much water you use in each batch, and record the best mixture.

Mix mortar for a large project in batches; on a hot, dry day a large batch will harden before you know it. If mortar begins to thicken, add water (called retempering); use retempered mortar within two hours.

Everything You Need:

Tools: Trowel, hoe, shovel.

Materials: Mortar mix, mortar box, plywood blocks.

How to Mix & Throw Mortar

1 Empty mortar mix into a mortar box and form a depression in the center. Add about ¾ of the recommended amount of water into the depression, then mix it in with a masonry hoe. Do not overwork the mortar. Continue adding small amounts of water and mixing until the mortar reaches the proper consistency. Do not mix too much mortar at one time—mortar is much easier to work with when it is fresh.

2 Set a piece of plywood on blocks at a convenient height, and place a shovelful of mortar onto the surface. Slice off a strip of mortar from the pile, using the edge of your mason's trowel. Slip the trowel point-first under the section of mortar and lift up.

3 Snap the trowel gently downward to dislodge excess mortar clinging to the edges. Position the trowel at the starting point, and "throw" a line of mortar onto the building surface. A good amount is enough to set three bricks. Do not get ahead of yourself. If you throw too much mortar, it will set before you are ready.

4 "Furrow" the mortar line by dragging the point of the trowel through the center of the mortar line in a slight back-and-forth motion. Furrowing helps distribute the mortar evenly.

Tips for Special Mortar Treatments

Adding tint to mortar works best if you add the same amount to each batch throughout the project. Once you settle on a recipe, record it so you can mix the same proportions each time.

Use a stiff (dry) mix of mortar for tuck-pointing—it's less likely to shrink and crack. Start by mixing type N mortar mix with half the recommended water. Let the mixture stand for one hour, then add the remaining water and finish mixing.

Laying Brick

Patience, care, and good technique are the key elements to building brick structures that have a professional look. Start with a sturdy, level footing (pages 46 to 47), and don't worry if your initial bricklaying attempts aren't perfect. Survey your work often and stop when you spot a problem. As long as the mortar's still soft, you can remove bricks and try again.

This section features one method of brick wall construction: laying up the ends of the wall first, then filling in the interior bricks. The alternate method, laying one course at a time, is shown with concrete block (pages 120 to 123).

Everything You Need:

Tools: Gloves, trowel, chalk line, level, line blocks, mason's string, jointing tool.

Materials: Mortar, brick, wall ties, rebar (optional).

Buttering is a term used to describe the process of applying mortar to the end of a brick or block before adding it to the structure being built. Apply a heavy layer of mortar to one end of a brick, then cut off the excess with a trowel.

How to Build a Double-wythe Brick Wall

1 Dry-lay the first course by setting down two parallel rows of brick, spaced ¾" to 1" apart. Use a chalk line to outline the location of the wall on the slab. Draw pencil lines on the slab to mark the ends of the bricks. Test-fit the spacing with a ⅜"-diameter dowel, then mark the locations of the joint gaps to use as a reference after the spacers are removed.

2 Dampen the concrete slab or footing with water, and dampen the bricks or blocks if necessary. Mix mortar and throw a layer of mortar on to the footing for the first two bricks of one wythe at one end of the layout. Butter the inside end of the first brick, then press the brick into the mortar, creating a ⅜" mortar bed. Cut away excess mortar.

3 Plumb the face of the end brick, using a level. Tap lightly with the handle of the trowel to correct the brick if it is not plumb. Level the brick end to end. Butter the end of a second brick, then set it into the mortar bed, pushing the dry end toward the first brick to create a joint of ⅜".

4 Butter and place a third brick, using the chalk lines as a general reference, then using a level to check for level and plumb. Adjust any bricks that are not aligned by tapping lightly with the trowel handle.

5 Lay the first three bricks for the other wythe, parallel to the first wythe. Level the wythes, and make sure the end bricks and mortar joints align. Fill the gaps between the wythes at each end with mortar.

Header bricks

6 Cut a half brick, then throw and furrow a mortar bed for a half brick on top of the first course. Butter the end of the half brick, then set the half brick in the mortar bed, creating a ⅜" joint. Cut away excess mortar. Make sure bricks are plumb and level.

7 Add more bricks and half bricks to both wythes at the end until you lay the first bricks in the fourth course. Align bricks with the reference lines. NOTE: To build corners, lay a header brick at the end of two parallel wythes. Position the header brick in each subsequent course perpendicular to the header brick in the previous course (INSET).

(continued next page)

How to Build a Double-wythe Brick Wall (continued)

8 Check the spacing of the end bricks with a straight-edge. Properly spaced bricks will form a straight line when you place the straightedge over the stepped end bricks. If bricks are not in alignment, do not move those bricks already set. Try to compensate for the problem gradually as you fill in the middle (field) bricks (Step 9) by slightly reducing or increasing the spacing between the joints.

9 Every 30 minutes, stop laying bricks and smooth out all the untooled mortar joints with a jointing tool. Do the horizontal joints first, then the vertical joints. Cut away any excess mortar pressed from the joints, using a trowel. When the mortar has set, but is not too hard, brush any excess mortar from the brick faces.

Line block

10 Build the opposite end of the wall with the same methods as the first, using the chalk lines as a reference. Stretch a mason's string between the two ends to establish a flush, level line between ends—use line blocks to secure the string. Tighten the string until it is taut. Begin to fill in the field bricks (the bricks between ends) on the first course, using the mason's string as a guide.

11 Lay the remaining field bricks. The last brick, called the closure brick, should be buttered at both ends. Center the closure brick between the two adjoining bricks, then set in place with the trowel handle. Fill in the first three courses of each wythe, moving the mason's string up one course after completing each course.

Metal wall tie

12 In the fourth course, set metal wall ties into the mortar bed of one wythe and on top of the brick adjacent to it. Space the ties 2 to 3 ft. apart, every three courses. For added strength, set metal rebar into the cavities between the wythes and fill with thin mortar (page 110).

13 Lay the remaining courses, installing metal ties every third course. Check with mason's string frequently for alignment, and use a level to make sure the wall is plumb and level.

14 Lay a furrowed mortar bed on the top course, and place a wall cap on top of the wall to cover empty spaces and provide a finished appearance. Remove any excess mortar. Make sure the cap blocks are aligned and level. Fill the joints between cap blocks with mortar.

Laying Block

Block walls can be built fairly quickly because of the size of the individual blocks. Still, the same patience and attention to detail involved in laying bricks are required. Check your work often, and don't be afraid to back up a step or two to correct your mistakes.

This section features a concrete block wall laid up one course at a time. Make sure you have a sturdy, level footing (page 46 to 47) before you start.

Everything You Need:

Tools: Trowel, chalk line, level, mason's string, line blocks, jointing tool.

Materials: Mortar mix, 8 × 8" concrete blocks, stakes, cap blocks, rebar, wire reinforcing strips.

Buttering a concrete block involves laying narrow slices of mortar on the two flanges at the end of the block. It is not necessary to butter the valley between the flanges unless the project calls for it.

How to Lay Concrete Block

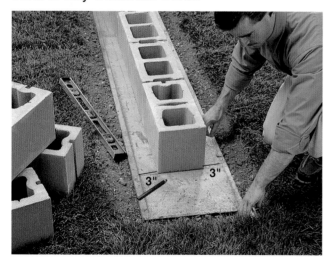

1 Dry-lay the first course, leaving a ⅜" gap between blocks. Draw reference lines on the concrete base to mark the ends of the row, extending the lines well past the edges of the block. Use a chalk line to snap reference lines on each side of the base, 3" from the blocks. These reference lines will serve as a guide when setting the blocks into mortar.

2 Dampen the base slightly, then mix mortar and throw and furrow two mortar lines at one end to create a mortar bed for the combination corner block. Dampen porous blocks before setting them into the mortar beds.

3 Set a combination corner block (page 103) into the mortar bed. Press it into the mortar to create a ⅜"-thick bed joint. Hold the block in place and cut away the excess mortar (save excess mortar for the next section of the mortar bed). Check the block with a level to make sure it is level and plumb. Make any necessary adjustments by rapping on the high side with the handle of a trowel. Be careful not to displace too much mortar.

4 Drive a stake at each end of the project and attach one end of a mason's string to each stake. Thread a line level onto the string and adjust the string until it is level and flush with the top of the corner block. Throw a mortar bed and set a corner block at the other end. Adjust the block so it is plumb and level, making sure it is aligned with the mason's string.

5 Throw a mortar bed for the second block at one end of the project: butter one end of a standard block and set it next to the corner block, pressing the two blocks together so the joint between them is ⅜" thick. Tap the block with the handle of a trowel to set it, and adjust the block until it is even with the mason's string. Be careful to maintain the ⅜" joint.

6 Install all but the last block in the first course, working from the ends toward the middle. Align the blocks with the mason's string. Clean excess mortar from the base before it hardens.

(continued next page)

7 Butter the flanges on both ends of a standard block for use as the closure block in the course. Slide the closure block into the gap between blocks, keeping the mortar joints an even thickness on each side. Align the block with the mason's string.

8 Apply a 1"-thick mortar bed for the half block at one end of the wall, then begin the second course with a half block.

9 Set the half block into the mortar bed with the smooth surfaces facing out. Use the level to make sure the half block is plumb with the first corner block, then check to make sure it is level. Adjust as needed. Install a half block at the other end.

Vertical joints

VARIATION: If your wall has a corner, begin the second course with a full-sized end block that spans the vertical joint formed where the two walls meet. This layout creates and maintains a running bond for the wall.

10 Attach a mason's string for reference, securing it either with line blocks or a nail. If you do not have line blocks, insert a nail into the wet mortar at each end of the wall, then wind the mason's string around and up to the top corner of the second course, as shown above. Connect both ends and draw the mason's string taut. Throw a mortar bed for the next block, then fill out the second course, using the mason's string as a reference line.

11 Every half-hour, tool the fresh mortar joints with a jointing tool and remove any excess mortar. Tool the horizontal joints first, then the vertical joints. Cut off excess mortar, using a trowel blade. When the mortar has set, but is not too hard, brush any excess mortar from the block faces. Continue building the wall until it is complete.

OPTION: When building stack bond walls with vertical joints that are in alignment, use wire reinforcing strips in the mortar beds every third course (or as required by local codes) to increase the strength of the wall. The wire should be completely embedded in the mortar. See page 110 for other block wall reinforcing options.

12 Install a wall cap on top of the wall to cover the empty spaces and create a finished appearance. Set the cap pieces into mortar beds, then butter an end with mortar. Level the cap, then tool to match the joints in the rest of the wall.

A **mortarless concrete block wall** is usually coated with a cement-based veneer that has both a structural function and an aesthetic function. When stacking blocks without mortaring them together, use shims to bring lower locks level with adjacent blocks.

Freestanding Block Walls without Mortar

The project below shows how to lay a block wall without using mortar between blocks. Mortarless walls are built using a running bond pattern, and are simple to construct. They derive their strength from a coating of surface bonding cement on all exposed surfaces. The cement creates a bond between blocks that is strong enough to support even very long walls.

The coating is similar in appearance and workability to stucco, so you can achieve an attractive stucco wall look. For extra strength, you can fill the voids in the concrete blocks with mortar or even concrete. Even a mortarless wall should be set into a bed of mortar on a solid concrete footing.

Everything You Need:

Tools: Aviation snips, mason's trowel, brickset, chisel, maul, mason's string, level, chalk line, line blocks.

Materials: Concrete block, metal ties, wire mesh, type N mortar, surface bonding cement.

How to Lay a Mortarless Block Wall

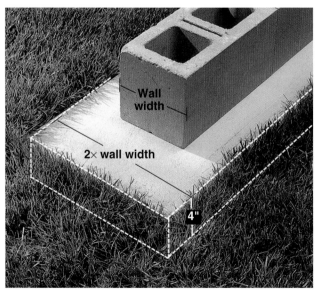

1 Start with a dry layout of the first course on a concrete footing. Where less than half a block is needed, trim two blocks instead. For example, where 3⅓ block lengths are required, use four blocks, and cut two of them to ⅔ their length. You'll end up with a stronger, more durable wall.

2 Mark the corners of the end blocks on the footing with a pencil. Then, remove the blocks and snap chalk lines to indicate where to lay the mortar bed and the initial course of block.

3 Mist the footing with water, then lay a ⅜"-thick bed of mortar on the footing. Take care to cover only the area inside the reference lines.

4 Lay the first course, starting at one end and placing blocks in the mortar bed with no spacing in between blocks. Use solid-faced block on the ends of the wall, and check the course for level.

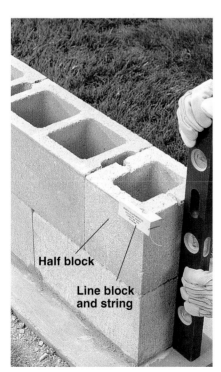

Half block

Line block and string

5 Lay subsequent courses one at a time, using a level to check for plumb and line blocks to check for level. Begin courses with solid-face blocks at each end. Use half blocks, to establish a running bond pattern.

6 Lay wire mesh over the next to last course. Install the top course, then fill block hollows with mortar and trowel the surface smooth. Complete the project by applying surface bonding cement (pages 182 to 183).

7 Complete the block stacking, leveling and testing for plumb as you work. Once the wall is completed, apply concrete veneer to all surfaces, as shown in the project on pages 182 to 183.

Terraced retaining walls work well on steep hillsides. Two or more short retaining walls are easier to install and more stable than a single, tall retaining wall. Construct the terraces so each wall is no higher than 3 ft.

Block Retaining Walls

Retaining walls are often used to level a yard or to prevent erosion on a hillside. In a flat yard, you can build a low retaining wall and fill in behind it to create a raised planting bed.

While retaining walls can be built from many materials such as pressure-treated timbers and natural stone, interlocking blocks are common. Typically made from concrete, interlocking retaining wall blocks are rather inexpensive, very durable, and DIY-friendly. Several styles of interlocking block are available at building centers and landscape materials suppliers. Most types have a natural rock finish that combines the rough texture of cut stone with the uniform shape and size of concrete blocks.

Interlocking block weighs up to 80 lbs. each, so it is a good idea to have helpers when building a retaining wall. Suppliers offer substantial discounts when interlocking block is purchased in large quantities, so you may be able to save money if you coordinate your own project with those of your neighbors.

The retaining walls in this section were built with either interlocking block or cut stone. These

durable materials are easy to work with. No matter what material you use, your wall can be damaged if water saturates the soil behind it, so make sure you include the proper drainage features (pages 127 to 128). You may need to dig a drainage swale (pages 30 to 31) before building in low-lying areas.

Interlocking block is available in several styles at home and garden centers. Many types have a natural rock finish, combining the texture of cut stone with the uniformity of concrete block.

Everything You Need:

Tools: wheelbarrow, shovel, garden rake, line level, hand tamper, tamping machine, small maul, masonry chisel, eye protection, hearing protectors, work gloves, circular saw with masonry cutting blade, level, tap measure, marking pencil, caulk gun.

Materials: stakes, mason's string, landscape fabric, compactible gravel, perforated drain pipe, coarse backfill material, construction adhesive.

Options for Positioning a Retaining Wall

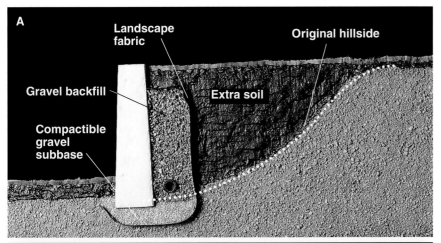

A
Landscape fabric
Original hillside
Gravel backfill
Extra soil
Compactible gravel subbase

B
Soil removed from base of hill
Original hillside
Compactible gravel subbase

(A) Increase the level area above the wall by positioning the wall well forward from the top of the hill. Fill in behind the wall with extra soil, which is available from sand-and-gravel companies.

(B) Keep the basic shape of your yard by positioning the wall near the top of the hillside. Use the soil removed at the base of the hill to fill in near the top of the wall.

Structural features for all retaining walls include: a compactible gravel subbase to make a solid footing for the wall, crushed stone backfill and a perforated drain pipe to improve drainage behind the wall, and landscape fabric to keep the loose soil from washing into and clogging the gravel backfill.

Tips for Building Retaining Walls

Backfill with crushed stone and install a perforated drain pipe about 6" above the bottom of the backfill. Vent the pipe to the side or bottom of the retaining wall, where runoff water can flow away from the hillside without causing erosion.

Make a stepped trench when the ends of a retaining wall must blend into an existing hillside. Retaining walls often are designed so the ends curve or turn back into the slope.

How to Build a Retaining Wall Using Interlocking Block

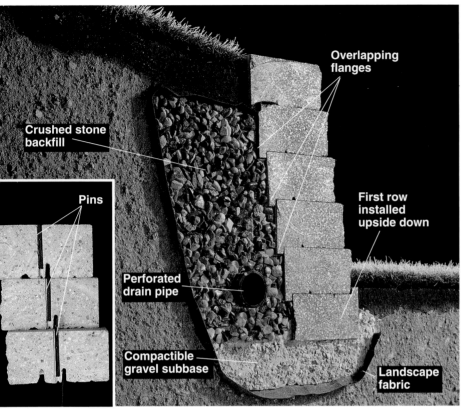

Overlapping flanges

Crushed stone backfill

Pins

First row installed upside down

Perforated drain pipe

Compactible gravel subbase

Landscape fabric

Interlocking wall blocks do not need mortar. Some types are held together with a system of overlapping flanges that automatically set the backward pitch (batter) as the blocks are stacked, as shown in this project. Other types of blocks use a fiberglass pins (INSET).

1 Excavate the hillside, if necessary. Allow 12" of space for crushed stone backfill between the back of the wall and the hillside. Use stakes to mark the front edge of the wall. Connect the stakes with mason's string, and use a line level to check for level.

2 Dig out the bottom of the excavation below ground level, so it is 6" lower than the height of the block. For example, if you use 6"-thick block, dig down 12". Measure down from the string to make sure the bottom base is level.

3 Line the excavation with strips of landscape fabric cut 3 ft. longer than the planned height of the wall. Make sure all seams overlap by at least 6".

4 Spread a 6" layer of compactible gravel over the bottom of the excavation as a subbase and pack it thoroughly. A rented tamping machine, or *jumping jack*, works better than a hand tamper for packing the subbase.

5 Lay the first course of block, aligning the front edges with the mason's string. (When using flanged block, place the first course upside down and backward.) Check frequently with a level, and adjust, if necessary, by adding or removing subbase material below the blocks.

6 Lay the second course of block according to manufacturer's instructions, checking to make sure the blocks are level. (Lay flanged block with the flanges tight against the underlying course.) Add 3 to 4" of gravel behind the block, and pack it with a hand tamper.

7 Make half-blocks for the corners and ends of a wall, and use them to stagger vertical joints between courses. Score full blocks with a circular saw and masonry blade, then break the blocks along the scored line with a maul and chisel.

(continued next page)

How to Build a Retaining Wall Using Interlocking Block (continued)

8 Add and tamp crushed stone, as needed, to create a slight downward pitch (about ¼" of height per foot of pipe) leading to the drain pipe outlet. Place the drain pipe on the crushed stone, 6" behind the wall, with the perforations face down. Make sure the pipe outlet is unobstructed (page 31). Lay courses of block until the wall is about 18" above ground level, staggering the vertical joints.

9 Fill behind the wall with crushed stone, and pack it thoroughly with the hand tamper. Lay the remaining courses of block, except for the cap row, backfilling with crushed stone and packing with the tamper as you go.

10 Before laying the cap block, fold the end of the landscape fabric over the crushed stone backfill. Add a thin layer of topsoil over the fabric, then pack it thoroughly with a hand tamper. Fold any excess landscape fabric back over the tamped soil.

11 Apply construction adhesive to the top course of block, then lay the cap block. Use topsoil to fill in behind the wall and to fill in the base at the front of the wall. Install sod or plants, as desired.

How to Add a Curve to an Interlocking Block Retaining Wall

1 Outline the curve by first driving a stake at each end and then driving another stake at the point where lines extended from the first stakes would form a right angle. Tie a mason's string to the right-angle stake, extended to match the distance to the other two stakes, establishing the radius of the curve. Mark the curve by swinging flour or spray paint at the string end, like a compass.

2 Excavate for the wall section, following the curved layout line. To install the first course of landscape blocks, turn them upside down and backwards and align them with the radius curve. Use a 4-ft. level to ensure the blocks sit level and are properly placed.

3 Install subsequent courses so the overlapping flange sits flush against the back of the blocks in the course below. As you install each course, the radius will change because of the backwards pitch of the wall, affecting the layout of the courses. Where necessary, trim blocks to size. Install using landscape construction adhesive, taking care to maintain the running bond.

4 Use half blocks or cut blocks to create finished ends on open ends of the wall.

Building Brick Pillars

Decorative pillars are easy to design because you don't have to be concerned about the seasonal shifting of attached brick or stone walls. We designed a pair of 12 × 16" pillars using only whole bricks, so you don't need to worry about splitting or cutting. These pillars are refined in appearance, but sturdy enough to last for decades.

Once the last course of bricks is in place, you can add a brick or stone cap for a finished look. Or, build two pillars connected by an arch (pages 136 to 139). If you're planning an arch, consider attaching hardware for an iron gate. It's far easier to place the hardware in fresh mortar, so make a note of the brick courses where the hardware will go. The settings will look cleaner this way, and the hardware will stay secure for a long time.

This 4 foot pillar was built with 18 courses of brick. A brick cap adds a touch of elegance and protects against rain, ice and snow. You can also build pillars with stone caps, or, as shown on the following pages, use cast concrete caps, which are available in many sizes.

Everything You Need:

Tools: Level, bricklayer's trowel, jointing tool, aviation snips, wheelbarrow, shovel, hoe, tape measure, pointing chisel.

Materials: Standard modular bricks (4 × 2⅔ × 8"), dowel, type N mortar mix, ¼" wire mesh, capstone or concrete cap, 2 × 2 lumber, ⅜"-thick wood scraps.

Pour footings (pages 44 to 47) that are 4" longer and wider than the pillars on each side. This project calls for 16 × 20" footings.

Tips for Building Brick Pillars

Use a story pole to maintain consistent mortar joint thickness. Line up a scrap 1 × 2 on a flat tabletop alongside a column of bricks, spaced ⅜" apart. Mark the identical spacing on the 1 × 2. Hold up pole after every few courses to check the mortar joints for consistent thickness.

Cut a straight 2 × 2 to fit tight in the space between the two pillars. As you lay each course for the second pillar, use the 2 × 2 to check the span.

How to Build Brick Pillars

1 Once the footing has cured, dry-lay the first course of five bricks, centered on the footing. Mark reference lines around the bricks.

2 Lay a bed of mortar inside the reference lines and lay the first course.

3 Use a pencil or dowel coated with vegetable oil to create a weep hole in the mortar in the first course of bricks. The hole ensures drainage of any moisture that seeps into the pillar.

4 Lay the second course, rotating the pattern 180°. Lay additional courses, rotating the pattern 180° with each course. Use the story pole and a level to check each face of the pillar after every other course. (It's important to check frequently, since any errors will be exaggerated with each successive course.)

5 After every fourth course, cut a strip of ¼" wire mesh and place it over a thin bed of mortar. Add another thin bed of mortar on top of the mesh, then add the next course of brick.

6 After every five courses, use a jointing tool to smooth the joints that have hardened enough to resist minimal finger pressure.

7 For the final course, lay the bricks over a bed of mortar and wire mesh. After placing the first two bricks, add an extra brick in the center of the course. Lay the remainder of the bricks around it. Fill the remaining joints, and work them with the jointing tool as soon as they become firm.

8 Build the second pillar in the same way as the first. Use the story pole and measuring rod to maintain identical dimensions and spacing.

How to Install a Cap Stone

1 Select a capstone 3" longer and wider than the top of the pillar. Mark reference lines on the bottom for centering the cap. Do not install caps if you are adding an arch to your pillars.

2 Spread a ½"-thick bed of mortar on top of the pillar. Center the cap on the pillar, using the reference lines. Strike the mortar joint under the cap so it's flush with the pillar. NOTE: If mortar squeezes out of the joint, press ⅜"-thick wood scraps into the mortar at each corner to support the cap. Remove the scraps after 24 hours and fill in the gaps with mortar.

135

If you're building an arch over existing pillars, measure the distance between the pillars at several points. The span must be the same at each point in order for the pillars to serve as strong supports for your arch.

Classic Brick Archway

Building an arch over a pair of pillars is a challenging task made easier with a simple, semi-circular plywood form. With the form in place, you can create a symmetrical arch by laying bricks along the form's curved edge. Select bricks equal in length to those used in the pillars.

Brick or concrete archways were very common during the Roman Empire, when clever engineers devised ways to leverage geometry in their favor while constructing baths, aqueducts and many other masonry structures. The principles are so sound and the materials so durable that many ancient archways remain standing today.

Everything You Need:

Tools: Joint chisel, mason's hammer, pry bar, jig saw, circular saw, drill, compass, level, mason's string, trowel, jointing tool, tuck-pointer.

Materials: ¾" plywood, ¼" plywood, wallboard screws (1" and 2"), bricks, type N mortar mix, 2 × 4 and 2 × 8 lumber, shims.

How to Build a Form for an Arch

1 Determine the distance between the inside edges of the tops of your pillars. Divide the distance in half, then subtract ¼". Use this as the radius in Step 2.

2 Mark a point at the center of a sheet of ¾" plywood. Use a pencil and a piece of string to scribe the circle on the plywood, using the radius calculated in Step 1. Cut out the circle with a jigsaw. Mark a line through the center point of the circle and cut the circle in half .

3 Construct the form by bracing the two semicircles, using 2" wallboard screws and 2 × 4s. To calculate the length of the 2 × 4 braces, subtract the combined thickness of the plywood sheets — 1½"—from the width of the pillars, and cut the braces to length. Cover the top of the form with ¼" plywood, attached with 1" wallboard screws.

¼" plywood

2 × 4 brace

¾" plywood

1" wallboard screw

2" wallboard screw

shims

How to Build a Brick Arch

TIP: If your pillars are capped, remove the caps before building an arch. Chip out the old mortar from underneath, using a hammer and joint chisel. With a helper nearby to support the cap, use a pry bar and shims to remove each cap from the pillar.

1 To determine brick spacing, start by centering a brick at the peak and placing a compass point at one edge. With the compass set to the width of one brick plus ¼", mark the form with the pencil.

2 Place the compass point on this new mark and make another mark along the curve. Continue making marks along the curve until less than a brick's width remains.

(continued next page)

3 Divide this remaining width by the number of compass marks, and increase the compass setting by this amount. Using a different color, make final reference marks to either side of the peak. Extend the pencil lines across the curved surface of the form and onto the far edge.

4 Cut two 2 × 8 braces, ½" shorter than pillar height, and prop one against each pillar with 2 × 4 cross braces. Place shims on top of each 2 × 8 to raise the form so its bottom is even with the tops of the pillars. Rest the plywood form on the braces.

5 Mix mortar and trowel a narrow ⅜" layer on top of one pillar. Place one brick, then rap the top with a trowel handle to settle it. Butter the bottom of each subsequent brick, and place it in position.

6 Place five bricks, then tack a string to the center point of the form on each side, and use the strings to check each brick's alignment. Take care not to dislodge other bricks as you tap a brick into position.

7 To balance the weight on the form, switch to the other side. Continue alternating until space for one brick remains. Smooth previous joints with a jointing tool as they become firm.

8 Butter the center, or *keystone*, brick as accurately as possible and ease it into place. Smooth the remaining joints with a jointing tool.

9 Lay a bed of mortar over the first course, then lay the second course halfway up each side, maintaining the same mortar joint thickness as in the first layer. Some of the joints will be staggered, adding strength to the arch.

10 Dry-lay several more bricks on one side—using shims as substitutes for mortar joints—to check the amount of space remaining. Remove the shims and lay the final bricks with mortar, then smooth the joints with a jointing tool.

11 Leave the form in place for a week, misting occasionally. Carefully remove the braces and form. Tuck-point and smooth the joints on the underside of the arch.

139

Brick Barbecue

The barbecue design shown here is constructed with double walls—an inner wall, made of heat-resistant fire brick set on edge, surrounding the cooking area, and an outer wall, made of engineer brick. We chose this brick because its larger dimensions mean you'll have fewer bricks to lay. You'll need to adjust the design if you select another brick size. A 4" air space between the walls helps insulate the cooking area. The walls are capped with thin pieces of cut stone.

Refractory mortar is recommended for use with fire brick. It is heat resistant and the joints will last a long time without cracking. Ask a local brick yard to recommend a refractory mortar for outdoor use.

The foundation combines a 12"-deep footing supporting a reinforced slab. This structure, known as a floating footing, is designed to shift as a unit when temperature changes cause the ground to shift. Ask a building inspector about local Building Code specifications.

Everything You Need:

Tools: Tape measure, hammer, brickset chisel, mason's string, shovel, aviation snips, reciprocating saw or hack saw, mason's string, masonry hoe, shovel, wood float, chalk line, level, wheelbarrow, mason's trowel, jointing tool.

Materials: Garden stakes, 2 × 4 lumber, 18-gauge galvanized metal mesh, #4 rebar, 16-gauge tie wire, bolsters, fire brick ($4\frac{1}{2}$ × $2\frac{1}{2}$ × 9"), engineer brick (4 × $3\frac{1}{5}$ × 8"), type N mortar, refractory mortar, $\frac{3}{8}$"-dia. dowel, metal ties, 4" tee plates, engineer brick (4 × 2 × 12"), brick sealer, stainless steel expanded mesh ($23\frac{3}{4}$ × 30"), cooking grills ($23\frac{5}{8}$ × $15\frac{1}{2}$"), ash pan.

A note about bricks: The brick sizes recommended allow you to build the barbecue without splitting a lot of bricks. If the bricks recommended here are not easy to find in your area, a local brick yard can help you adjust the project dimensions to accommodate different brick sizes.

How to Pour a Floating Footing

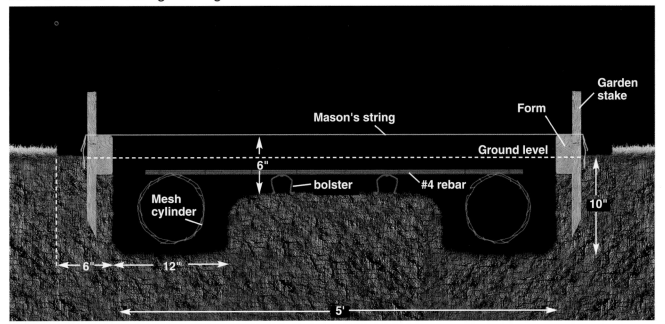

Lay out a 4 × 5 ft. area. Dig a continuous trench, 12" wide × 10" deep, along the perimeter of the area, leaving a rectangular mound in the center. Remove 4" of soil from the top of the mound, and round over the edges. Set a 2 × 4 form (page 28) around the site so that the top is 2" above the ground along the back and 1½" above the ground along the front. This slope will help shed water. Reinforce the footing with metal mesh and five 52"-long pieces of rebar. Use a mason's string and a line level to ensure that the forms are level from side to side. Roll the mesh into 6"-dia. cylinders and cut them to fit into the trench, leaving a 4" gap between the cylinder ends and the trench sides. Tie the rebar to the mesh so the outside pieces are 4" from the front and rear sides of the trench, centered from side to side. Space the remaining three bars evenly in between. Use bolsters where necessary to suspend the bar within the pour. Coat the forms with vegetable oil, and pour the concrete.

How to Build a Brick Barbecue

1 After the footing has cured for one week, use a chalk line to mark the layout for the inner edge of the fire brick wall. Make a line 4" in from the front edge of the footing, and a center line perpendicular to the first line. Make a 24 × 32" rectangle that starts at the 4" line and is centered on the center line.

2 Dry-lay the first course of fire brick around the outside of the rectangle, allowing for ⅛"-thick mortar joints. NOTE: Proper placement of the inner walls is necessary so they can support the grills. Start with a full brick at the 4" line to start the right and left walls. Complete the course with a cut brick in the middle of the short wall.

(continued next page)

3 Dry-lay the outer wall, as shown here, using $4 \times 3\frac{1}{5} \times 8"$ nominal engineer brick. Gap the bricks for $\frac{3}{8}"$ mortar joints. The rear wall should come within $\frac{3}{8}"$ of the last fire brick in the left inner wall. Complete the left wall with a cut brick in the middle of the wall. Mark reference lines for this outer wall.

4 Make a story pole. On one side, mark eight courses of fire brick, leaving a $\frac{3}{8}"$ gap for the bottom mortar joint and $\frac{1}{8}"$ gaps for the remaining joints. The top of the final course should be 36" from the bottom edge. Transfer the top line to the other side of the pole. Lay out 11 courses of engineer brick, spacing them evenly so that the final course is flush with the 36" line. Each horizontal mortar joint will be slightly less than $\frac{1}{2}"$ thick.

5 Lay a bed of refractory mortar for a $\frac{3}{8}"$ joint along the reference lines for the inner wall, then lay the first course of fire brick, using $\frac{1}{8}"$ joints between the bricks.

6 Lay the first course of the outer wall, using type N mortar. Use oiled $\frac{3}{8}"$ dowels to create weep holes behind the front bricks of the left and right walls. Alternate laying the inner and outer walls, checking your work with the story pole and a level after every other course.

7 Start the second course of the outer wall using a half brick butted against each side of the inner wall, then complete the course. Because there is a half brick in the right outer wall, you need to use two three-quarter bricks in the second course to stagger the joints.

8 Place metal ties between the corners of the inner and outer walls, at the second, third, fifth, and seventh courses. Use ties at the front junctions and along the rear walls. Mortar the joint where the left inner wall meets the rear outer wall.

9 Smooth the mortar joints with a jointing tool when the mortar has hardened enough to resist minimal finger pressure. Check the joints in both walls after every few courses. The different mortars may need smoothing at different times.

10 Add tee plates for grill supports above the fifth, sixth, and seventh courses. Use 4"-wide plates with flanges that are no more than $3/32$" thick. Position the plates along the side fire brick walls, centered 3", 12", 18", and 27" from the rear fire brick wall.

11 When both walls are complete, install the capstones. Lay a bed of type N mortar for a $3/8$"-thick joint on top of the inner and outer walls. Lay the capstone flat across the walls, keeping one end flush with the inner face of the fire brick. Make sure the bricks are level, and tool the joints when they are ready. After a week, seal the capstones and the joints between them with brick sealer and install the grills.

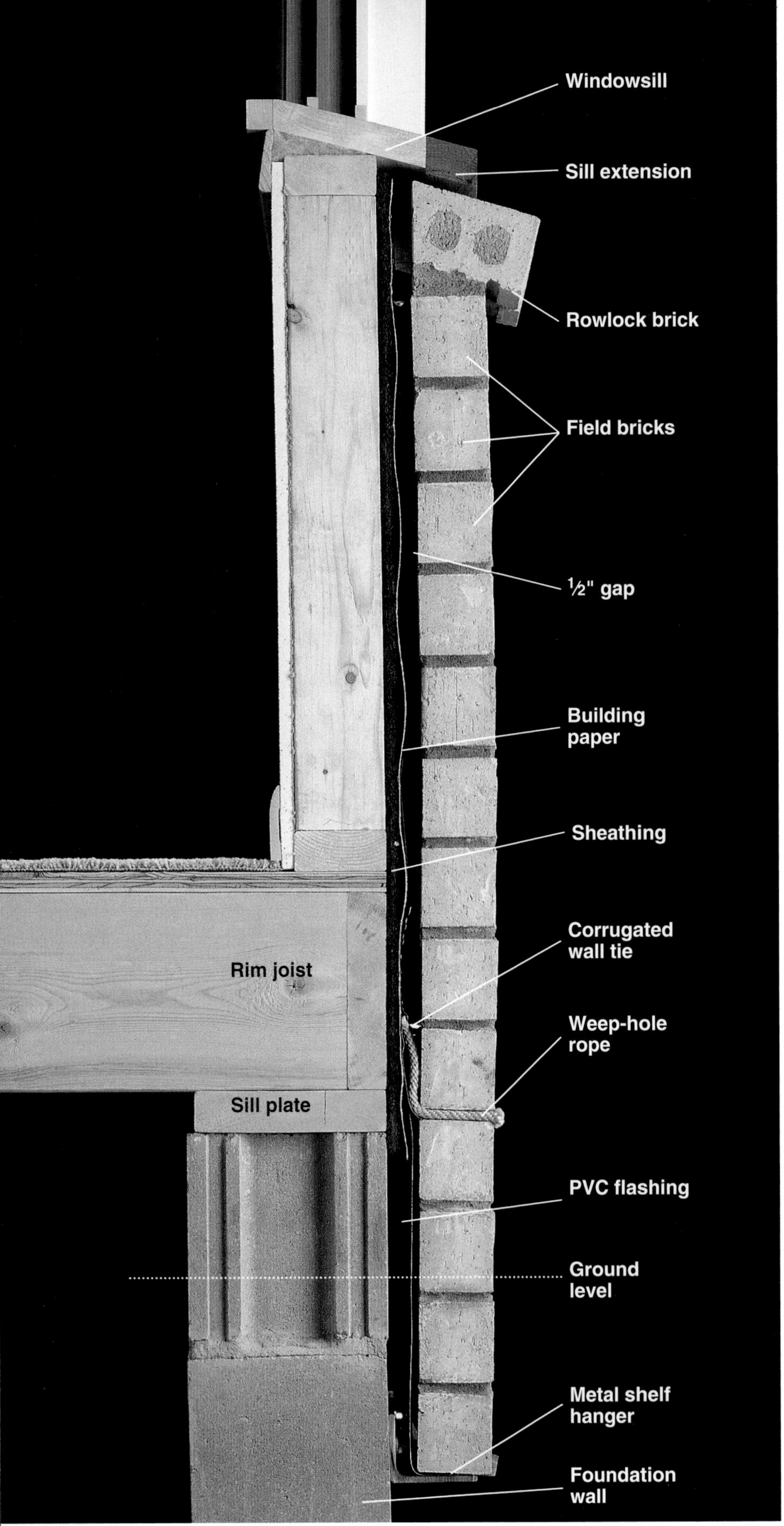

Brick Wall Veneers

Brick veneer is essentially a brick wall built around the exterior walls of a house. It's attached to the house with metal wall ties and supported by a metal shelf hanger on the foundation. It's best to use queen-sized bricks for veneer projects because they're thinner than standard construction bricks. This means less weight for the house walls to support. Even so, brick veneer is quite heavy. Ask your local building inspector about building code rules that apply to your project. In the project shown here, brick veneer is installed over the foundation walls and side walls, up to the bottom of the windowsills on the first floor of the house. The siding materials in these areas are removed before installing the brick.

Construct a story pole before you start laying the brick so you can check your work as you go along to be sure your mortar joints are of a consistent thickness. A standard ⅜" gap is used in the project shown here.

Everything You Need:

Tools: hammer, circular saw, combination square, level, drill with masonry bit, socket wrench set, staple gun, mason's trowel, masonry hoe, mortar box, mason's chisel, maul.

Materials: pressure-treated 2 × 4s, ⅜ × 4" lag screws and washers, 2 × 2, lead sleeve anchors, angle iron for metal shelf supports, 30 mil PVC roll flashing, corrugated metal wall ties, brickmold for sill extensions, sill-nosing trim, Type N mortar, bricks, ⅜-dia. cotton rope.

Anatomy of a brick veneer facade: Queen-sized bricks are stacked onto a metal or concrete shelf and connected to the foundation and walls with metal ties. Rowlock bricks are cut to follow the slope of the windowsills, then laid on edge over the top course of bricks.

Labels (from photo):
- Windowsill
- Sill extension
- Rowlock brick
- Field bricks
- ½" gap
- Building paper
- Sheathing
- Corrugated wall tie
- Weep-hole rope
- Rim joist
- Sill plate
- PVC flashing
- Ground level
- Metal shelf hanger
- Foundation wall

How to Install Brick Veneer

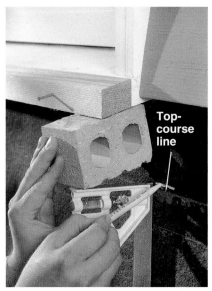

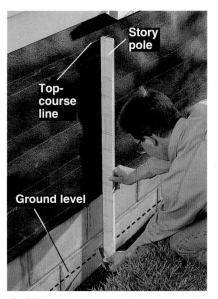

1 Remove all siding materials in the area you plan to finish with brick veneer. Before laying out the project, cut the sill extension from a pressure-treated 2 × 4. Tack the extension to the sill temporarily.

2 Precut the bricks to follow the slope of the sill and overhang the field brick by 2". Position this rowlock brick directly under the sill extension. Use a combination square or level to transfer the lowest point on the brick onto the sheathing (marking the height for the top course of brick in the field). Use a level to extend the line. Remove the sill extensions.

3 Make a story pole long enough to span the project area. Mark the pole with ⅜" joints between bricks. Dig a 12"-wide, 12"-deep trench next to the wall. Position the pole so the top-course line on the sheathing aligns with a top mark for a brick on the pole. Mark a line for the first course on the wall, below ground level.

4 Extend the mark for the first-course height across the foundation wall, using a level as a guide. Measure the thickness of the metal shelf (usually ¼"), and drill pilot holes for 10d nails into the foundation at 16" intervals along the first-course line, far enough below the line to allow for the thickness of the shelf. Slip nails into the pilot holes to create temporary support for the shelf.

5 Set the metal shelf onto the temporary supports. Mark the location of the center web of each block onto the vertical face of the shelf. Remove the shelf and drill ⅜"-diameter holes for lag screws at the web marks. Set the shelf back onto the temporary supports and outline the predrilled holes on the blocks. Remove the shelf and drill holes for the masonry anchors into the foundation, using a masonry bit. Drive masonry anchors into the holes.

(continued next page)

6 Reposition the shelf on the supports so the predrilled holes align with the masonry anchors. Attach the shelf to the foundation wall with ⅜ × 4" lag screws and washers. Allow 1/16" for an expansion joint between shelf sections. Remove the temporary support nails.

7 After all sections of the metal shelf are attached, staple 30 mil PVC flashing above the foundation wall so it overlaps the metal shelf.

8 Test-fit the first course on the shelf. Work in from the ends, using spacers to set the gaps between bricks. You may need to cut the final brick for the course. Or, choose a pattern such as running bond that uses cut bricks.

9 Build up the corners two courses above ground level, then attach line blocks and mason's string to the end bricks. Fill in the field bricks so they align with the strings. Every 30 minutes, smooth mortar joints that are firm.

10 Attach another course of PVC flashing to the wall so it covers the top course of bricks, then staple building paper to the wall so it overlaps the top edge of the PVC flashing by at least 12". Mark wall-stud locations on the building paper.

11 Use the story pole to mark layout lines for the tops of every fifth course of bricks. Attach corrugated metal wall ties to the sheathing where the brick lines meet the marked wall-stud locations.

146

12 Fill in the next course of bricks, applying mortar directly onto the PVC flashing. At every third mortar joint in this course, tack a 10" piece of $\frac{3}{8}$"-dia. cotton rope to the sheathing so it extends all the way through the bottom of the joint, creating a weep hole for drainage. Embed the metal wall ties in the mortar beds applied to this course.

13 Add courses of bricks, building up corners first, then filling in the field. Embed the wall ties into the mortar beds as you reach them. Use corner blocks and a mason's string to verify the alignment, and check frequently with a 4-ft. level to make sure the veneer is plumb.

14 Apply a $\frac{1}{2}$"-thick mortar bed to the top course, and begin laying the rowlock bricks with the cut ends against the wall. Apply a layer of mortar to the bottom of each rowlock brick, then press the brick up against the sheathing, with the top edge following the slope of the windowsills.

Sill-nosing trim

15 Finish-nail the sill extensions to the windowsills. Nail sill-nosing trim to the siding to cover any gaps above the rowlock course. Fill cores of exposed rowlock blocks with mortar, and caulk any gaps around the veneer with silicone caulk.

Brick Planter

Brick is the masonry material of choice for elegant entry planters. It also complements a brick-paver landing. For a foundation for the planter, pour a slab that is separated from adjacent structures, such as a landing or house foundation, by isolation joints. With larger planter projects, a frost footing often is required; check with your local building code.

Everything You Need:

Tools: Mason's string, line level, drill, level, shovel, rake, hoe, wheelbarrow, hand tamper, rubber mallet, jointing tool, tape measure, broom, mason's trowel.

Materials: Type S mortar, bricks, screws, 1 × 4 lumber, stakes, 1 × 4 concrete step forms, pavers, compactible gravel, ⅜"-diameter copper or PVC tubing, sand, isolation board, cap bricks, landscape fabric.

Your planter can capture the rustic beauty of an antique trough or dress up a brick entryway. This brick planter is designed to match the brick-paver landing project (pages 159 to 161).

How to Build a Brick Planter

1 Excavate the building site, install forms and isolation boards, and pour a concrete base for the project. Let the foundation cure for three days before building on it. Remove forms, then trim isolation boards so they are level with the tops of adjoining structures, like the landing shown above. TIP: Cover adjoining surfaces for protection.

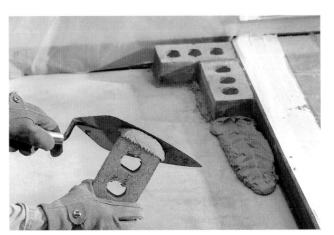

2 Test-fit the first course of the project, then outline the project on the concrete surface. Dampen the surface slightly, then mix mortar and throw a mortar bed in one corner (pages 116 to 119). Begin laying bricks for the project, buttering the exposed end of each brick before setting it.

Corner return
bricks

3 Lay one section of the first course, checking the bricks frequently with a level to make sure the tops are level and even. Lay two corner *return* bricks perpendicular to the end bricks in the first section, and use a level to make sure they are even across the tops.

Weep-hole tubes

4 Install weep holes for drainage in the first course of bricks, on the sides farthest away from permanent structures. Cut ⅜"-diameter copper or PVC tubing about ¼" longer than the width of one brick, and set the pieces into the mortar joints between bricks, pressing them into the mortar bed so they touch the footing. Make sure mortar doesn't block the openings.

5 Finish building all sides of the first course. Lay the second course of bricks, reversing the directions of the corner bricks to create staggered vertical joints if using a running-bond pattern. Fill in brick courses to full height, building up one course at a time. Check frequently to make sure the tops of the bricks are level and sides are plumb.

6 Install cap bricks to keep water from entering the cores of the brick and to enhance the visual effect. Set the cap bricks into a ⅜"-thick mortar bed, buttering one end of each cap brick. Let the mortar cure for one week. Before adding soil, pour a 4" to 6"-thick layer of gravel into the bottom of the planter for drainage, then line the bottom and sides of the planter with landscape fabric to prevent dirt from running into and clogging the drainage tubes.

Paving with Dry-set Brick

Laying a patio with brick pavers and sand is simple and results in a patio that is attractive and functional. A patio functions best when it is as large as a standard room, 100 square feet or more. An array of patio paver types is available to match your home and complement landscape elements (page 103).

How to Build a Brick-paver Patio

1 To find exact patio measurements and reduce the number of cut bricks needed, test-fit perpendicular rows of brick pavers on a flat surface. Lay two rows to reach the rough length and width of your patio, then measure the rows to find the exact size.

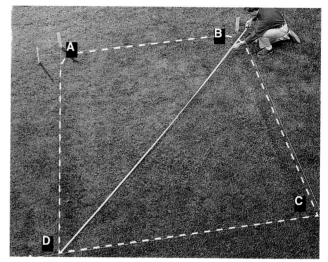

2 With stakes and mason's strings, plot a rectangle that matches the dimensions of your patio, using the 3-4-5 triangle method (page 26). Make sure that the rectangle is square: the diagonals (A to C and B to D) must have the same measurement. If not, adjust the stakes until the diagonals are equal. The strings will serve as a reference for excavating the patio site.

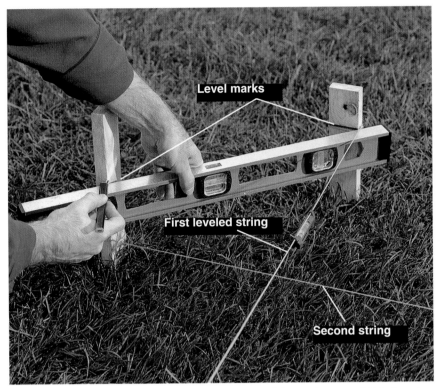

3 Using a line level as a guide, adjust one of the strings until it is level. When the string is level, mark its height on the stakes at each end. To adjust each remaining string so it is level and even with the first string, use a level as a guide for marking adjacent stakes, then adjust the strings to the reference marks. Use a line level to make sure that all strings are level.

4 To ensure proper drainage, a patio should slope ⅛" per foot away from the house. Measure from the high end to the low end (in feet) and multiply the number by ⅛. Measure down from the level marks on the low-end stakes, and mark the drop distance.

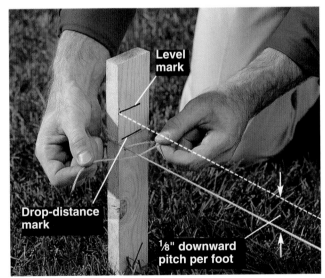

5 Lower the strings at the low-end stakes so the strings are even with the drop distance marks. Keep all strings in place as a guide while excavating and installing edging.

6 Remove all sod inside the strings and 6" beyond the edges of the planned patio. NOTE: If your patio will have rounded corners, use a garden hose or rope to outline the excavation.

(continued next page)

How to Build a Brick-paver Patio (continued)

7 Starting at the outside edge, excavate the patio site so it is at least 5" deeper than the thickness of the pavers. For example, if your pavers are 1¾" thick, excavate to a depth of 6¾". Follow the slope of the side strings, and periodically use a long 2 × 4 to check the bottom of the excavation site for high and low spots.

8 Pour compactible gravel over the patio site, then rake it into a smooth layer at least 4" deep. The thickness of the subbase layer may vary to compensate for unevenness in the excavation. Use a long 2 × 4 to check the surface of the subbase for high and low spots, and add or remove compactible gravel as needed.

9 Pack the subbase, using a power tamper, until the surface is firm and flat. Check the slope of the subbase by measuring down from the side strings (see step 12). The space between the strings and the subbase should be equal at all points.

10 Cut strips of landscape fabric and lay them over the subbase to contain the gravel and prevent weeds from growing up through the patio. Make sure the strips overlap by at least 6".

11 Install rigid plastic edging around the edges of the patio below the reference strings. Anchor the edging by driving galvanized spikes through the predrilled holes and into the subbase. To allow for possible adjustments, drive only enough spikes to keep the edging in place.

12 Check the slope by measuring from the string to the top of the edging at several points. The measurement should be the same at each point. If not, adjust the edging by adding or removing sub-base material under the landscape fabric until the edging follows the slope of the strings.

13 For curves and rounded patio corners, use rigid plastic edging with notches on the outside flange. It may be necessary to anchor each section of edging with spikes to hold curved edging in place.

14 Remove the reference strings, then set 1"-thick pipes or wood strips across the patio area, spaced every 6 ft., to serve as depth spacers for laying the sand base.

(continued next page)

How to Build a Brick-paver Patio (continued)

15 Lay a 1"-thick layer of sand over the landscape fabric and smooth it out with a garden rake. Sand should just cover the tops of the depth spacers.

16 Water the sand thoroughly, and pack it lightly with a hand tamper.

17 Screed the sand to an even layer by resting a long 2 × 4 on the spacers embedded in the sand and drawing the 2 × 4 across the spacers, using a sawing motion. Add extra sand to fill footprints and low areas, then water, tamp, and screed the sand again until it is smooth and firmly packed.

18 Remove the embedded spacers along the sides of the patio base, then fill the grooves with sand and pat them smooth with the hand tamper.

19 Lay the first border paver in one corner of the patio. Make sure the paver rests firmly against the rigid plastic edging.

20 Lay the next border paver so it is roughly ⅛" from the previous paver. Set the pavers by tapping them into the sand with a rubber mallet. Use the depth of the first paver as a guide for setting the remaining pavers.

21 Working outward from the corner, install 2-ft.-wide sections of border pavers and interior pavers, following the desired pattern. Keep the joints between pavers very tight. Set each paver by tapping it with the mallet.

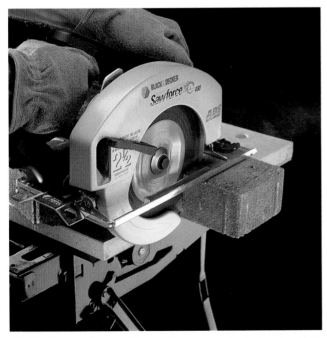

22 Depending on the pattern you choose, you may need to split some pavers. Score the pavers first, using a chisel and maul or a circular saw with a masonry blade (pages 112 to 113). Make the final cuts with a chisel and maul. Wear eye protection and work gloves when using cutting tools.

23 After each section of pavers is set, use a straightedge to make sure the pavers are flat Make adjustments by tapping high pavers deeper into the sand or by removing low pavers and adding a thin layer of extra sand underneath them.

(continued next page)

24 Remove the remaining spacers when the in-stalled surface gets near to them. Fill the gaps left by the spacers with loose sand, and pat the sur-face smooth with a hand tamper (INSET).

25 Continue installing 2-ft.-wide sections of border pavers and interior pavers. As you approach the opposite side of the patio, reposition the rigid plastic edging, if necessary, so full-sized pavers will fit without cutting.

26 At rounded corners and curves, install border pavers in a fan pattern with even gaps between the pavers. Gentle curves may accommodate full-sized border pavers, but for sharper bends you may need to mark and trim wedge-shaped border pavers to make them fit.

27 Lay the remaining interior pavers. Where partial pavers are needed, hold a paver over the gap, and mark the cut with a pencil and straightedge. Cut pavers with a circular saw and masonry blade. After all pavers are installed, drive in the remaining edging spikes and pack soil behind the edging.

28 Use a long, straight 2 × 4 to make sure the entire patio is flat. Adjust high pavers by tapping them deeper into the sand. Remove low pavers and add a thin layer of extra sand underneath. After adjusting uneven pavers, use line blocks and mason's string to check that rows are straight.

29 Spread a ½" layer of sand over the patio. Use a power tamper to compress the entire patio and pack sand into the joints.

30 Sweep up the loose sand, then soak the patio area thoroughly to settle the sand in the joints. Let the surface dry completely. If necessary, repeat step 29 until the gaps between pavers are packed tightly with sand.

Dry-mortar option: For a finished masonry look, install pavers with ⅜" gaps. Fill the gaps with a dry mixture made from 4 parts sand and 1 part dry mortar. After spreading the dry mixture and tamping the patio, sprinkle the surface with water. Finish the wet mortar joints with a jointing tool. After mortar hardens, scrub the pavers with water and a coarse rag.

Variations for Building with Brick Pavers

Consider pattern variations. There are many ways to lay pavers for a more decorative effect. The basketweave and herringbone patterns (above) are two common styles. When considering pattern variations, take into account the amount of cutting that is required by some patterns. Generally, diagonal patterns like the herringbone will require cut pavers all the way around the border.

Stand pavers on end (known as *soldier* style) to create a deep border for paving projects. Using soldier-style border pavers is especially effective when you are laying pavers over an existing concrete slab, because the border will hide the exposed edges of the concrete.

Set pavers into sand for backyard landscaping projects, such as patios and garden walkways. Using sand-set pavers is a quick, easy method for creating masonry projects, but be prepared to re-set pavers occasionally, especially in colder climates, where frost heave may cause a sand-set surface to buckle.

Pour a concrete slab with the surface about 2" below grade to create a solid, permanent foundation for pavers that are bonded together with mortar. Mortared pavers and a sturdy foundation are desirable for paver projects that will experience high traffic, where soil and subsoil below the project are unstable, or in areas where extensive freezing and thawing occur.

Brick or concrete pavers can be set into sand or mortared to a concrete footing or, in some cases, a sidewalk or driveway. Because of freeze/thaw issues, the success rate for mortared paver projects is significantly higher in more temperate climates.

Mortared Pavers

The entry area is the first detail that visitors to your home will notice. Create a memorable impression by building a brick-paver step landing that gives any house a more formal appearance. Add a special touch to the landing by building a permanent planter next to it (page 148 to 149), using matching brick.

In many cases, a paver landing like the one shown here can be built directly over an existing sidewalk. Make sure the sidewalk is structurally sound and free from major cracks. If adding an adjoining structure, like a planter, create a separate building base and be sure to include isolation joints so the structure is not connected to the landing area or to the house.

Using the same techniques, you can turn an old concrete walkway into a dramatic mortared brick path (pages 162 to 163). The mortar applied over the old concrete provides a level foundation for the new brick surface.

Everything You Need:

Tools: Drill, level, masonry hoe, rubber mallet, mortar bag, jointing tool, mason's trowel.

Materials: Isolation board, type S mortar, pavers, plastic sheeting.

How to Build a Brick-paver Step Landing

1 Dry-lay the pavers onto the concrete surface and experiment with the arrangement to create a layout that uses whole bricks, if possible. Mark outlines for the layout onto the concrete. Attach an isolation board to prevent the mortar from bonding with the foundation. Mix a batch of mortar, and dampen the concrete slightly.

2 Lay a bed of mortar for three or four border pavers, starting at one end or corner. Level off the bed to about ½" in depth with the trowel.

3 Begin laying the border pavers, buttering an end of each paver with mortar as you would a brick. Set pavers into the mortar bed, pressing them down so the bed is ⅜" thick. Cut off excess mortar from the tops and sides of the pavers. Use a level to make sure the pavers are even across the tops, and check mortar joints to confirm that they are uniform in thickness.

4 Finish the border section next to the foundation, checking with a level to make sure the row is even in height. Trim off any excess mortar, then fill in the third border section, leaving the front edge of the project open to provide easier access for laying the interior field pavers.

5 Apply a ½"-thick bed of mortar between the border pavers in the work area closest to the foundation. Because mortar is easier to work with when fresh, mix and apply the mortar in small sections (no more than 4 sq. ft.).

6 Begin setting pavers in the field area, without buttering the edges. Check the alignment with a straightedge. Adjust paver height as needed, making sure joints are uniform in width. NOTE: Pavers often are cast with spacing flanges on the sides, but these are for sand-set projects. Use a spacing guide, like a dowel, when setting pavers in mortar.

7 Fill in the rest of the pavers to complete the pattern in the field area, applying mortar beds in small sections. Add the final border section. Every 30 minutes add mortar to joints between pavers until it is even with the tops. TIP: To minimize mess when adding mortar, use a mortar bag to deliver the mortar into the joints.

8 Smooth and shape the mortar joints with a jointing tool. Tool the full-width "running" joints first, then tool the joints at the ends of the pavers. Let the mortar dry for a few hours, then remove any residue by scrubbing the pavers with a coarse rag and water. Cover the walkway with plastic and let the mortar cure for at least two days. Remove plastic, but do not walk on the pavers for at least one week.

How to Install Brick Pavers over Concrete

1 Select a paver pattern. Dig a trench around the concrete, slightly wider than the thickness of one paver. Dig the trench so it is about 3½" below the concrete surface. Soak the pavers with water (dry pavers absorb moisture, weakening the mortar strength).

2 Sweep the old concrete, then hose off the surface and sides with water to clear away dirt and debris. Mix a small batch of mortar according to manufacturer's directions. For convenience, place the mortar on a scrap of plywood.

3 Install edging bricks by applying a 1½" layer of mortar to the side of the concrete slab and to one side of each brick. Set bricks into the trench, against the concrete. Brick edging should be 1½" higher than the thickness of the brick pavers.

4 Finish the joints on the edging bricks with a jointer (step 9), then mix and apply a ½"-thick bed of mortar to one end of the sidewalk, using a trowel. Mortar hardens very quickly, so work in sections no larger than 4 sq. ft.

5 Make a screed for smoothing mortar by notching the ends of a short 2 × 4 to fit between the edging bricks. Depth of the notches should equal the thickness of the pavers. Drag the screed across the mortar bed until the mortar is smooth.

6 Lay the paving bricks one at a time into the mortar, maintaining a ½" gap between pavers. (A piece of scrap plywood works well as a spacing guide.) Set the pavers by tapping them lightly with a rubber mallet.

7 As each section of pavers is completed, check with a level to make sure the tops of the pavers are even.

8 When all the pavers are installed, use a mortar bag to fill the joints between the pavers with fresh mortar. Work in 4-sq.-ft. sections, and avoid getting mortar on the tops of the pavers.

9 Use a jointer to finish the joints as you complete each 4-sq.-ft. section. For best results, finish the longer joints first, then the shorter joints. Use a trowel to remove excess mortar.

10 Let the mortar dry for a few hours, then remove any residue by scrubbing the pavers with a coarse rag and water. Cover the walkway with plastic and let the mortar cure for at least two days. Remove plastic, but do not walk on pavers for at least one week.

Pre-cast concrete step forms make it easy to build a durable outdoor staircase. By overlapping the forms in varying arrangements, you can shape a staircase with curves, angles, and even spirals. Lay two forms side-by-side to create larger steps.

Building Steps with Pre-cast Forms

Pre-cast concrete step forms are ideal for building attractive steps without having to build wood forms and pour the concrete yourself. In a few hours, you can excavate, lay pre-cast forms, and pour in concrete. Or, pour a sand bed inside the forms and fill them with brick pavers (above).

Many manufacturers sell pavers that are sized to fit inside the forms they make. Decide how many forms you'll need for the steps you plan to build and the paver pattern you wish to use, then consult the manufacturer's specifications to determine the number of pavers required.

Everything You Need:

Tools: Mason's string, drill, level, shovel, rake, hand tamper, tape measure, rubber mallet, broom.

Materials: Straight 2 × 4 board, stakes, screws, concrete step forms, pavers, compactible gravel, sand.

How to Build Steps with Pre-cast Forms

1 Mark the outline of your steps with stakes and string, then excavate for the first step. Dig a hole 6" deeper than the height of the step and 4" wider and longer than the step on all sides.

2 Fill the hole with compactible gravel. Rake the gravel to create a slight downward slope ($\frac{1}{8}$" per foot) from back to front, for drainage. Tamp it well with a hand tamper, then set the first form in place. Use a level to make sure the form is level from side to side and has the proper slope from back to front.

3 Add a layer of gravel inside the form and tamp it well. The distance between the gravel and the top of the form should equal the thickness of a paver plus 1". Next, add a 1"-thick layer of sand over the gravel. Use a 2 × 4 set across the form to measure as you go.

4 Lay the pavers in the form in the desired pattern, keeping them level with the top of the form. Adjust as needed, using a rubber mallet or by adding sand underneath. Use a broom to spread sand over the pavers to fill the joints.

5 Excavate for the next step, accounting for the overlap and a 4" space behind and at the sides for gravel. Fill and tamp the gravel so the front is level with the top of the first step. Repeat steps 2 to 4. When all steps are installed, backfill with dirt along the sides.

Stucco & Veneer

Stucco is a mixture of Portland cement, lime, sand and a tinting agent that, once cured, creates an exceptionally durable shell that has a unique warmth and inviting texture.

Working with Stucco & Veneer

Working with stucco is a craft that's been practiced for hundreds of years. Today's stucco is a combination of portland cement, masonry cement, sand, and (in the finish coat) lime, all mixed with water. The dry ingredients are widely available in premixed bags. The mixture is applied to walls and worked with either a trowel or a brush to achieve the desired effect.

Stuccoing an entire house from scratch is a demanding proposition. But repairing or remodeling small sections (pages 278 to 279) is not difficult. Walls that are kept in good condition and "redashed" occasionally with a restorative coat can last for decades.

Stucco can be applied to masonry surfaces, such as concrete block, or over wood or other materials that have been covered with building paper and metal lath. When applying stucco over brick or block, two coats—a $3/8$"-thick base coat and a 1/4"-thick finish coat—are applied. Over building paper and metal lath, three coats are applied—a scratch coat ($3/8$"-1/2" thick), a brown coat ($3/8$" thick), and a finish coat ($1/8$" thick).

Follow manufacturer's instructions regarding drying times between coats.

Veneer stone may consist of thin cuts of quarried stone or tinted concrete blocks that look like natural stone but are lighter and easier to install.

If you want the look of stone on your house without the rigors of cutting and moving heavy materials, stone veneer is ideal. Stone veneer is pieces of natural or manufactured stone, cut or molded for use in non-load-bearing, cosmetic applications, such as facing exterior walls or freestanding concrete block walls. Veneers are growing in popularity because they offer an easy way to add a touch of grandeur to any structure.

While veneer projects may seem less complex than other masonry projects, they add a great deal of weight to a wall and need to be carefully thought out. Begin by checking local building codes for allowable height, reinforcement, use of wall ties, space between the veneer and wall sheathing, drainage, and specifications for the metal support shelves. A building permit may be required.

After you've chosen the veneer stone and decided on the design's dimensions, do a dry run on a flat surface, checking for unexpected challenges and obstacles. If you're adding the veneer to the exterior of a house, examine the area around the foundation. Builders often install a concrete ledge just below grade as a base for veneer. If your house does not have that base, attach a metal support shelf to the foundation (pages 144 to 145).

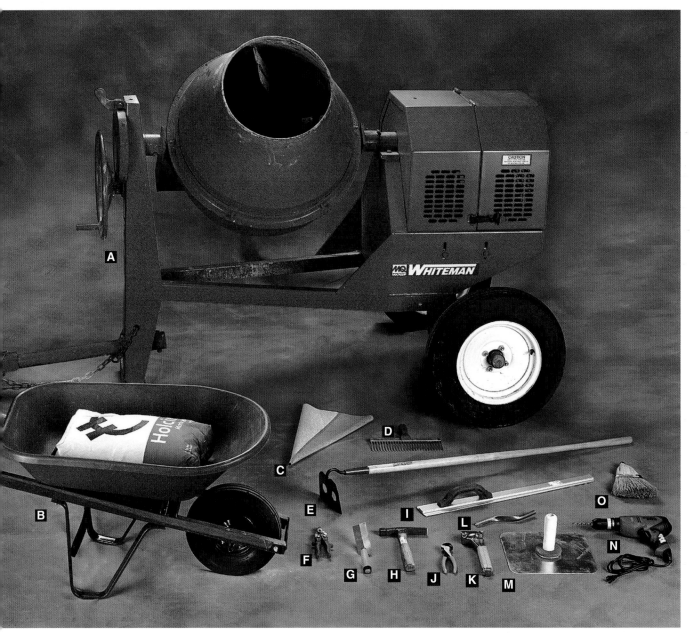

Tools for stucco and veneer projects include: Cement mixer for mixing stucco mixture (A); wheelbarrow (B) and masonry hoe (E) for mixing mortar for the veneer; mortar bag (C) for filling joints between veneer stones; metal rake (D) for creating scratches in interim coats of stucco; aviation snips (F) for cutting expanded metal lath; mason's hammer (H) and wide-mouth nippers (J) for shaping veneer stones; darby (I) for smoothing early coats of stucco; stapler (K) for attaching building paper and expanded metal lath; jointing tool (L) for smoothing mortar joints; mortar hawk (M) for holding the stucco or mortar; drill (N) for installing a level ledge against the foundation; whisk broom (O) for removing excess mortar from veneer stones and for creating texture on stucco; * square end trowel not pictured.

Tools and Materials

The tools necessary for stucco and veneer projects are common to most masonry projects, and experienced do-it-yourselfers probably own most of them. Some of the materials for these projects, however, are quite specialized. Two types of veneer are available. One is natural stone that has been cut into thin pieces designed for finishing walls, hearths, and other surfaces. The other is concrete that has been molded and tinted to look like natural stone, but is lighter and easier to apply to these surfaces.

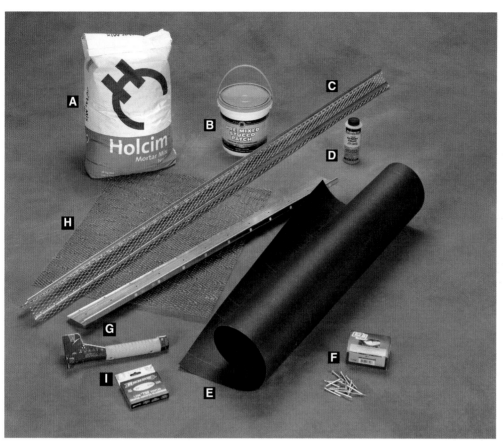

Materials for stucco and veneer projects include: Type M mortar mix (A) and mortar tint (D) (optional) for filling the joints between stones; stucco mix (B) for the coats of stucco material, building paper (E) and self-furring expanded metal lath (H) for the base; 1½" (minimum) galvanized roofing nails (F) for attaching the metal lath, metal edging (G) and drip screed (C) for the corners of the project, heavy-duty staples (I) for attaching the building paper and the metal lath.

Ingredients of scratch (base) coat, and brown coat stucco

3 parts sand
2 parts portland cement
1 part masonry cement
Water

Ingredients of finish coat stucco

1 part lime
3 parts sand
6 parts white cement
Tint (as desired)
Water

To make stucco mix: Combine dry stucco ingredients with water, following the directions for each coat (there are three). For the finish coat, mix a test batch first. Add measured amounts of Portland cement, sand, lime, water and tint until you find the proper combination. Or, you can buy premixed stucco.

Stucco and veneer each has its own individual character and charm. But as the outdoor stucco fireplace surround and brick veneer roof wall demonstrate, they can make a smashing design statement together.

Planning Your Stucco & Veneer Projects

Finishing an entire house with stucco or veneer stone is a demanding job best left to a mason, but finishing partial walls or full walls of a small addition, garage, or shed can be quite satisfying. In order for the finished project to appear to be a natural part of the original architecture, the colors of the new materials and the proportions of the design must complement the existing materials and style of the house.

If the original walls of your house are finished with stucco, you'll probably need to tint your finish coat to match. Even if the original stucco was white, that finish has probably darkened consid-

erably. Tinting the new stucco is the best way to match the new with the old. Follow the manufacturer's instructions for the tint you purchase, and plan to experiment until you find a good match. Let each test batch dry thoroughly before you settle on the proportions. Keep notes as you test so you can reproduce the results for each subsequent batch of stucco.

Planning a stucco project extends to the weather. It's important to work on stucco projects during mild weather (50 to 80 degrees F) and not to work in areas that are exposed to direct sun. Cold or hot weather or direct sun affect the

Tips for Planning a Veneer Project

Choosing a veneer stone that complements your house and landscape is critical to the success of your project. Repeating an existing color or shape of stone from the exterior or landscape usually works very well. If there is no stone to match or complement, try choosing veneer that resembles stone native to the area.

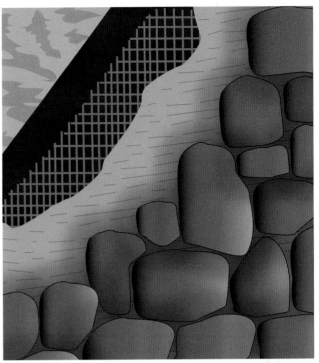

Evaluate your sheathing and determine what steps need to be taken to prepare for the veneer. The project in this chapter illustrates installing veneer over plywood sheathing, which has the strength to support layers of building paper, lath, and veneer. If your walls are covered with fiberboard or any other type of sheathing, ask the veneer manufacturer for recommendations.

stucco's drying process and can lead to cracks and other damage to the stucco material.

The first step in a veneer project is deciding where the veneer will be placed. A sense of proportion is critical to a successful veneer design. Some home designs present logical starting and stopping points for the veneer; others require careful observation and consideration regarding placement of the veneer.

Once you've determined its placement, it's time to estimate the square footage of veneer stone required for your project. Start by multiplying the length by the height of the area, and then subtract the square footage of window and door openings and corner pieces. When these calculations are complete, increase your estimate by 5 to 10 percent to allow for trimming and waste.

Consult the manufacturer's recommendations regarding the direction of work. Installing from the top down makes cleanup easier, since it reduces the amount of splatter on preceding courses. However, some manufacturers recommend working from the bottom to the top.

Most brick veneer is installed during new construction, but it also offers a great opportunity to retrofit some formal appeal to your house facade.

Basic Techniques

Applying a stucco finish to a wall or adding brick or stone veneer require some patience and planning, with an emphasis on the structural. Both types of wall finishes are heavy and require well-secured support mesh that provides tooth for the cement products. It may not be the most glamorous part of the job, but driving the fasteners that hold the lathe or the support brackets to your house is probably number one on the necessary techniques list.

But once the substrate is securely attached, stuccoing is actually a lot like painting–only with extremely heavy paint and a brush that's solid metal. Applying the mortar base for veneer stones and brick also is primarily an exercise in slathering cement into expanded lath.

It's during the application of the second and third coats of stucco that artistry and careful brushwork begin to supplant the more powerful strokes. And it is during the setting of the veneer stones or bricks into the mortar base that your eye for detail and aesthetic sensibility become more important.

Of course, no age-old technique would be balanced without a newfangled "plug-and-play" variation, which you'll see in the mortarless veneer siding project starting on page 188. Here, the ability to secure a metal ledge to a wall is a very important technique to master, but after that stacking the shingle-like chunks of masonry siding is fairly routine.

Finally, setting outdoor tile onto a concrete patio shares a few layout and materials handling requirements with other masonry projects, but it really has more in common with installing a ceramic tile floor. If you've never tiled a floor, find an article on that project for some useful background on how to tile a patio.

Tips for Preparing Surfaces for Stucco

Attach building paper to wood frame construction, using heavy-duty staples or roofing nails. Overlap sheets 4". In some regions, more than one layer of building paper may be required. Ask your local building inspector about code specifications.

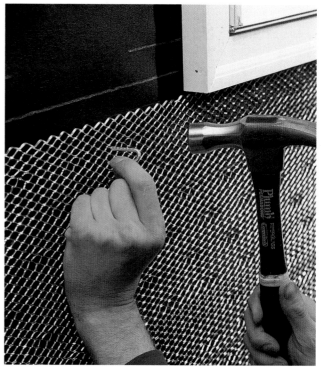

Install self-furring expanded metal lath over the paper with 1½" roofing nails or fencing staples, driven into studs every 6". Sheets of lath should overlap 1" horizontally and 2" vertically. Make sure the lath is installed with the rougher side facing out.

Install metal edging along edges of walls, and drip, or *weep*, screed at the base to achieve clean corners and edges when you apply stucco. Make sure edging is level and plumb, then attach it with roofing nails.

Use aviation snips to trim the excess lath, edging, and drip screed. Wear safety goggles and heavy gloves as protection from sharp edges.

Tips for Applying Stucco

Use a power concrete mixer for large projects. Add water to the mix until it forms a workable paste, following manufacturer's instructions.

Begin at the top or the bottom of the wall. Hold a mortar hawk close to the wall, and press stucco into the lath with a metal trowel. Press firmly to fill voids, and cover the mesh as smoothly as possible.

Tips for Finishing Stucco

Develop a formula that yields a consistent color and texture. Test finish batches first by applying them to a scrap of wood. Let the samples dry for at least an hour, for an indication of their color after the stucco has cured. Record the proper proportions.

Mix the finish batch, so it contains slightly more water than the scratch and brown coats. The mix should still stay on the mortar hawk without running.

Cover a float with carpet to make an ideal tool for achieving a float-finish texture. Experiment on a small area.

Achieve a wet-dash finish by flinging, or *dashing,* stucco onto the surface. Let the stucco cure undisturbed.

For a dash-trowel texture, dash the surface with stucco, using a whisk broom (left), then flatten the stucco by troweling over it.

Tips for Applying Veneer

Parging, or wetting and mortaring a stone, improves the bond between the stone and the wall. To parge a stone, wet the stone and then apply mortar to its back before pressing it onto the mortared wall.

Dry-lay natural stones to devise an attractive layout so that large and small stones, with hues and shapes that alternate pleasingly across the span of the project. Unless you know a trick for defying gravity, arrange the stones on horizontal surface while dry-laying.

Install the corner pieces first, then install flat pieces, working toward the center of the wall. Place the stones so that the joints are ½" wide or less, and as consistent across the wall as possible.

Build a banker if you will need to cut or shape a large number of stones. Construct frames out of 2 × 2s, and sandwich a piece of ½" plywood between the frames. Attach pieces by driving 3½" coarse-threaded wallboard screws through from both sides, and fill it with sand. Set the frame on two columns of concrete blocks if you prefer to stand while working.

Update the exterior of your house with brick, stone or stucco veneer. Whether installed to cover an unattractive foundation or to accent an otherwise ordinary exterior, veneers add color and texture to your house. They also add weight to a wall, so ask an inspector about Building Code rules before you start.

Applying Stucco & Veneer to Walls

Masonry materials are ideal for protecting and enhancing the look of exterior walls, both new and old. If house siding has deteriorated, you can tear it off and install a lightweight brick veneer, using mortar and wall ties (pages 144 to 147). If you build an addition, you can use stucco to match or complement the materials on existing walls (pages 180 to 181). Stucco is also easy to repair or restore. Thin veneers of natural or manufactured stone are growing rapidly in popularity because they are easy to work with and add a touch of grandeur to any structure. These materials all work well on garden walls, too. With brick, stone, or stucco, you can turn an ordinary concrete block wall into an attractive element of your garden. With concrete block and super-strong surface bonding cement (pages 182 to 183), you can build a wall with a stucco-style surface, using no mortar at all.

Tips for Planning:

• Use brick or stone veneer as a decorative accent on the front face or entry area of your house. Installing veneer around an entire house is a demanding project best left to a professional.

• Ask your local building inspector about allowable height, reinforcement, use of wall ties, space between veneer and wall sheathing, drainage, and specifications for metal support shelves. A building permit may be required.

• Cut bricks before you start. With stone, do a dry run on a flat surface before you start.

• Examine the area around your foundation. Builders often install a concrete ledge just below grade as a base for veneer. If your house has no base, attach a metal support shelf to the foundation (pages 144 to 145).

Options for Finishing Exterior Walls

Renew an old foundation by applying brick or stone veneer from ground level up to the sill plate. The foundation must be free from structural damage.

Veneer stone may consist of thin cuts of quarried stone or tinted concrete blocks that look like natural stone but are lighter and easier to install.

Full-wall veneer is applied from the foundation to the roof soffit. Because of the extreme weight of full-wall veneer, extensive reinforcement is required. Installation is not generally recommended for do-it-yourselfers; consult a professional.

Stucco is a durable finish that can be tinted to blend with surroundings. Window trim is removed to apply stucco to house walls. Narrow trowel cuts under the trim serve as control joints, preventing large cracks from appearing later.

Applying Stucco

By adding tint to the mixture, you can produce just about any color stucco you desire, from a subtle off-white to a stately blue.

Good wall preparation is the first step for an attractive, durable finish. If the walls are wood, attach building paper and metal lath to create a tight seal and a gripping surface for the stucco. Concrete block walls are already fairly water-tight and are rough enough that stucco can be applied directly to the block. During new block construction, make the mortar joints flush with the blocks in preparation for a stucco finish.

Once you've prepared the wall surface, plan to spend several days applying the three stucco coats—scratch coat, brown coat, and finish coat—that guarantee a tight seal and a professional appearance.

Everything You Need

Tools: Cement mixer, wheelbarrow, mortar hawk, mason's trowel, square-end trowel, darby or long wood float, hammer, staple gun, level, utility knife, aviation snips, spade, bucket, fine-tined metal rake.

Materials: Building paper, expanded galvanized metal lath (diamond mesh, minimum 2.5 lb.), 1½" galvanized nails, 1½" wire nails, staples, stucco mix, 1½" wire nails, 1 × 2 board.

How to Finish Walls with Stucco

1 Staple building paper to the entire wall, and trim excess with a utility knife. Trim the lath and edging to size, using aviation snips, and nail them to the wall. Rub your hand down the lath—it will feel rough when positioned upright. Check the edging for level.

2 Mix the scratch coat by adding water and kneading it with a trowel to form a workable paste. Beginning at either the top or the bottom of the wall, hold the mortar hawk close to the wall and press mud into the mesh with a square-end trowel. Press firmly to fill any voids. Cover the mesh completely.

3 Wait for the scratch coat to harden enough so an impression remains when you press on it. Rough up the surface by making shallow horizontal scratches the length of the wall.

TIP:

You can make a scratching tool by pounding a row of 1½" wire nails through a 1 × 2.

4 Mist the surface occasionally for 48 hours. Mix and apply the brown coat approximately ⅜" thick, then level the entire surface with a wood darby to provide a roughened gripping surface for the finish coat.

5 Mix the finish coat, adding tint as required, and slightly more water than in previous coats. The mix should still sit on the mortar hawk without running. Apply the finish coat so the edging is fully embedded (about ⅛" thick).

6 Finish the surface by throwing stucco at the wall with a whisk broom, then flattening the stucco with a trowel. Wait 24 hours for the finish coat to set up, then mist 2 to 3 times a day for two days, and once a day for another three days.

Mix small batches of dry surface bonding cement, water, and concrete acrylic fortifier, according to the manufacturer's instructions, until you get a feel for how much coating you can apply before it hardens.

An accelerant in the cement causes the mix to harden quickly—within 30 to 90 minutes, depending on weather conditions. The cement can be tinted before application.

Surface-bonding Cement

Surface bonding cement is a stucco-like compound that you can use to dress up your concrete and cinder block walls. It also adds strength, durability, and water resistance to the walls.

What distinguishes surface bonding cement from stucco is the addition of fiberglass to the blend of portland cement and sand. The dry mixture is combined with water and acrylic fortifier to form a cement plaster that can bond with concrete, brick, or block for an attractive, water-resistant coating.

Before applying the bonding cement, make sure you have a very clean surface, with no crumbling masonry, so the coating can form a durable bond. Because surface bonding cement dries quickly, it's important to mist the brick or block with water before applying the cement so the

cement dries slowly. As with most masonry projects, the need to dampen the wall increases in very dry weather.

The bonding cement can be used on both mortared and mortarless walls, and on both load bearing and non-load bearing walls. However, it is not recommended for walls higher than 15 courses of block.

Everything You Need

Tools: Garden hose with spray attachment, bucket, wheelbarrow, mortar hawk, square-end trowel, groover, caulk gun.

Materials: Surface bonding cement, concrete acrylic fortifier, tint (optional), silicone caulk.

How to Finish Walls with Surface-bonding Cement

1 Starting near the top of the wall, mist a 2 × 5-ft. section on one side of the wall with water to prevent the blocks from absorbing moisture from the cement once the coating is applied.

2 Mix the cement in small batches, according to the manufacturer's instructions, and apply a $\frac{1}{16}$"- to $\frac{1}{8}$"-thick layer to the damp blocks, using a square-end trowel. Spread the cement evenly by angling the trowel slightly and making broad upward strokes.

3 Use a wet trowel to smooth the surface and create the texture of your choice. Rinse the trowel frequently to keep it clean and wet.

4 To prevent random cracking, use a groover to cut control joints from the top to the bottom of the wall, every 4 ft. for a 2-ft.-high wall, and every 8 ft. for a 4-ft.-high wall. Seal hardened joints with silicone caulk.

Whether it covers the whole house, one story only or just a smaller accent area, natural stone veneer has unsurpassed character and gives your house the impression of permanence.

Applying Stone Veneer

Whether you use natural or manufactured veneer, wet each stone, then apply mortar to the back before pressing it onto the mortared wall. Wetting and mortaring a stone (called parging) results in maximum adhesion between the stone and the wall. The challenge is to arrange the stones so that large and small stones and various hues and shapes alternate across the span of the wall.

This project is designed for installing veneer stone over plywood sheathing, which has the strength to support layers of building paper, lath, and veneer. If your walls are covered with fiberboard or any other type of sheathing, ask the veneer manufacturer for recommendations.

Note: Installing from the top down makes cleanup easier since it reduces the amount of splatter on preceding courses. However, manufacturers advise bottom-up installation for some veneers. Read the manufacturer's guidelines carefully before you begin.

Ordering stone veneer:
Find the square footage of veneer stone required for your project by multiplying the length by the height of the area. Subtract the square footage of window and door openings and corner pieces. One linear foot of corner pieces covers approximately ¾ of a square foot of flat area, so you can reduce the square footage of flat stone required by ¾ sq. ft. for each linear foot of inside or outside corner. It's best to increase your estimate by 5 to 10 percent to allow for trimming.

Everything You Need
Tools: Hammer or staple gun, drill, wheelbarrow, hoe, square-end trowel, circular saw, wide-mouth nippers or mason's hammer, dust mask, level, jointing tool, mortar bag, spray bottle, whisk broom.

Materials: Type M mortar mix, mortar tint (optional), 15# building paper, expanded galvanized metal lath (diamond mesh, minimum 2.5#), 1½" (minimum) galvanized roofing nails or heavy-duty staples, 2 × 4 lumber.

How to Finish Walls with Stone Veneer

1 Cover the wall with building paper, overlapping seams by 4". Nail or staple lath every 6" into the wall studs and midway between studs. Nails or staples should penetrate 1" into the studs. Paper and lath must extend at least 16" around corners where veneer is installed.

2 Stake a level 2 × 4 against the foundation as a temporary ledger to keep the bottom edge of the veneer 4" above grade. The gap between the bottom course and the ground will reduce staining of the veneer by plants and soil.

3 Spread out the materials on the ground so you can select pieces of varying size, shape, and color, and create contrast in the overall appearance. Alternate the use of large and small, heavily textured and smooth, and thick and thin pieces.

4 Mix a batch of Type M mortar that's firm, but still moist. Mortar that's too dry or too wet is hard to work with and may fail to bond properly.

(continued next page)

TIP:

Mix in small amounts of water to retemper mortar that has begun to thicken.

5 Use a square-end trowel to press a ½" to ¾" layer of mortar into the lath. To ensure that mortar doesn't set up too quickly, start with a 5 sq. ft. area. Once you determine your pace, you can mortar larger areas.

6 Install corner pieces first, alternating long and short legs. Wet and parge each piece, then press it firmly against the freshly mortared wall so some mortar squeezes out. Joints between stones should be no wider than ½" and should remain as consistent as possible across the wall.

7 Once the corner pieces are in place, install flat pieces, working from the corner toward the center of the wall.

8 If mortar becomes smeared on a stone, remove it with a whisk broom or soft-bristle brush after the mortar has begun to dry. Never use a wire brush or a wet brush of any kind.

9 Use wide-mouth nippers or a mason's hammer to trim and shape pieces to fit. Do your best to limit trimming so each piece retains its natural look.

10 You can hide cut edges that are well above or below eye level simply by rotating a stone. If an edge remains visible, use mortar to cover. Let the mortar cure for 24 hours, then remove the 2 × 4 and stakes, taking care not to dislodge any stones.

11 Once the wall is covered in veneer, fill in the joints, using a mortar bag and tuck-pointing mortar. Take extra care to avoid smearing the mortar. You can tint the tuck-pointing mortar to complement the veneer.

12 Smooth the joints with a jointing tool once the mortar is firm. Once the mortar is dry to the touch, use a dry whisk broom to remove loose mortar—water or chemicals can leave permanent stains.

Brick veneer siding attaches to your house with mechanical fasteners, so you can achieve the appeal of brick without the mess of mortar.

Mortarless Brick Veneer Siding

An interesting new siding product is now available that mimics the appearance and durability of classic brick, but that installs as easily as any other siding material. Mortarless brick veneer systems use stackable bricks to create an appealing façade on wood, steel, or concrete structures. The high-strength concrete bricks are long-lasting—manufacturers offer warranties up to 50 years. And because brick veneer does not require mortar, installation is well within the capabilities of interested homeowners.

Veneer bricks are available in 3" and 4" heights, and are either 8" or 9" long, depending on the producer. Bricks weigh approximately 5 lbs. each and add 3¼" to the face of walls. While veneer brick systems can be used in both new construction and remodel projects, application is restricted due to the added load: up to 30 feet high on standard wood framed walls. Consult with a professional builder or structural engineer for walls taller than 30 ft., as well as sections of wall above roofs.

When planning a brick veneer siding project, it's best to work with the manufacturer or a local dealer to determine material availability in your area. To accurately estimate materials, you'll need to know the total surface area to be covered with veneer brick, the width of each wall and opening for starter strip, and the length of each corner for quantity of corner strip and corner block.

Prior to installation, make sure the framing and wall substrate is sound and the house adequately insulated. Extend all plumbing and electrical pipes, boxes, and meters to accommodate the additional thickness created by the veneer brick and furring strips.

The following pages discuss the installation of brick veneer siding on standard wood framed walls. All openings require extra support in the form of ¾" plywood lintels. Lintel size is determined by the width of the opening and the brick installation method over the opening (soldier coursing shown here). Contact the manufacturer or product producer (see Resources, page 298) for information regarding lintel sizing, as well as installation of veneer brick on other framing styles.

Everything You Need:

Tools: tape measure, chalkline, 4-ft. level, utility knife, circular saw, miter saw with diamond masonry-cutting blade or wet masonry saw, hammer drill with masonry bits, cordless drill with various drivers, rubber mallet, caulk gun, work gloves, safety glasses, dust mask, earplugs.

Materials: ¾" plywood, furring strips, flashing, self-adhesive waterproof membrane (1 × 3, 1 × 4, 1 × 6), scrap 2 × 4, #10 × 2½" and #10 × 4" corrosion-resistant wood screws, outside corner strips, starter strips, veneer bricks, outside corner blocks, inside corner blocks, window sill block, construction adhesive, exterior-grade caulk.

Tips for Installing Brick Veneer Siding

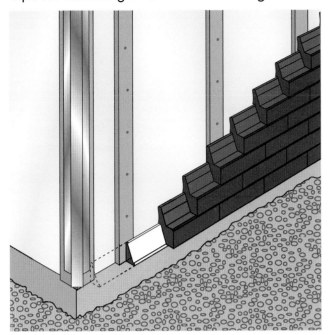

Brick veneer is stacked in courses with staggered joints, much like traditional brick. However, the first course of the mortarless system is installed on a starter strip and fastened with corrosion-resistant screws to 1 × 3 furring strips at each stud location. Bricks are then fastened every fourth course thereafter. At outside corners, a specialty strip is fastened to 1 × 4 furring strips. Corner blocks for both outside and inside corners are secured with screws and construction adhesive.

Before installing brick veneer siding, make sure all openings are properly sealed. For best results, use a self-adhesive waterproof membrane. Install the bottom strip first, then the side strips so they overlap the bottom strip. Place the top strip to overlap the sides. Install drip-edge flashing where appropriate.

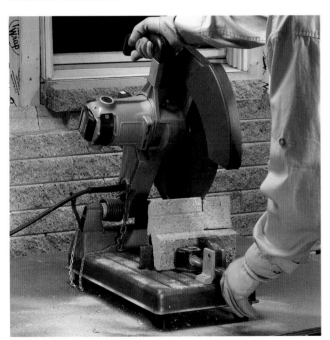

Cut veneer brick using a miter saw with a diamond blade or a wet masonry saw. When cutting brick, protect yourself with heavy work gloves, safety glasses, earplugs, and a dust mask. See pages 112 to 113 for more brick cutting tips.

Pre-drill holes in bricks that require fastening, using a hammer drill with a 3/16" masonry bit. Position the brick face-up on the ground and secure with your foot. Drill through the notch in the top portion of the brick, holding the drill bit at 90° to the ground.

(continued next page)

How to Install Mortarless Brick Veneer Siding

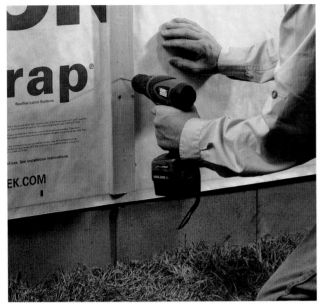

1 Snap a level chalkline ¾" above the foundation on each wall of the house. Align the bottom end of furring strips above the chalkline. Fasten 1 × 3 furring strips at each stud location with #10 × 2½" corrosion-resistant wood screws. Install 1 × 4 furring strips at outside corners and 1 × 6s at inside corners.

2 For each opening, cut ¾" plywood lintels to a size of 15" high × 12" longer than the width of the opening. Center the lintel above the opening so 6" extends beyond each side of the frame, and fasten to framing with #10 screws. Install an aluminum drip-edge above the window frame, then wrap the lintel and flashing with a strip of self-adhesive waterproof membrane.

3 At outside corners, position the first section of corner strip 2" above the chalkline. Plumb the strip using a 4-ft. level, then fasten to the framing with #10 × 4" screws every 10" on alternate sides.

4 Position the starter strip at the chalkline with the flange beneath the ends of the furring strips. Do not overlap corner strips. At inside corners, cut back the starter strip to so it falls 3½" short of adjacent walls. Level the strip, then secure to the framing with #10 × 4" corrosion-resistant wood screw at each furring location.

5 At the notch in each corner block, pre-drill a hole at a 30° angle using a hammer drill and a ³⁄₁₆" masonry bit. Place a veneer brick on the starter strip for reference, then slide the first corner block down the corner strip and position it so the bottom edge falls ½" below the bottom edge of the brick. Fasten the brick to the strip with #10 × 2½" wood screws.

6 Continue to install corner blocks using #10 × 2½" screws and construction adhesive between courses. For the top of the corner, measure the remaining length and cut a piece of corner strip to size. Fasten blocks to this loose length, cutting the final piece to size if necessary (see page 189). Secure one last block to the existing corner using construction adhesive, then fit the new assembly in place and fasten with #10 × 2½" screws.

7 For inside corners, pre-drill holes at 30° angles into inside corner blocks. As with outside corners, position the first block so the bottom edge is ½" below the bottom edge of the first course of veneer brick. Fasten the block to the framing with #10 × 4" wood screws. Continue installing blocks with #10 screws and construction adhesive between each course.

8 To create the best overall appearance, place a row of bricks on the starter strip so they extend past the width of the most prominent opening on each wall. Place a brick on the second course at each end of the opening, so each sit evenly above the joint of two bricks below. Sight down from the edges of the opening's frame and adjust the entire row to find a pattern that yields the least amount of small pieces of brick around the opening.

(continued next page)

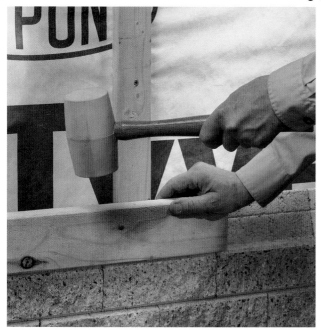

9 Pre-drill holes through veneer bricks for the first course (see page 189). Following the established pattern, install bricks on starter strip. At corners, cut bricks to size (see page 189), so they fit snugly against the blocks. Set bricks using a scrap 2 × 4 and rubber mallet to help maintain consistent course alignment.

10 At each furring strip, hold bricks flat against the wall and secure to the framing with #10 × 2½" screws. Drive screws until the head touches the brick. Do not over tighten.

11 Fill the brick courses, using bricks from different pallets to blend slight variance in color. Set bricks using a scrap of 2 × 4 and a rubber mallet. Check every fourth course for level before fastening bricks to the framing at each furring strip.

12 To install sill blocks below the widow, fasten a horizontal 1 × 3 furring strip under the window frame, extending ⅛" longer than the cumulative width of the sill blocks. Install bricks up to the top of the furring strip, cutting to fit as needed, and fasten each with two #10 × 2½" wood screws. Apply construction adhesive along the top of the furring strip and bricks.

13 Install the sills, angling them downward slightly, and secure with #10 × 4" wood screws, toenailing through the ends or bottom of the sill into the framing. Cut brick filler pieces to bridge the gap between the sill and the last full course of brick; make sure the pieces align with the rest of the course. Install the pieces with construction adhesive. Seal the gap between the window frame and the sill with exterior-grade caulk.

14 Continue installing brick along the openings, to a height no more than the width of one brick. Cut a piece of starter strip to length, align it with the courses on either side of the opening, and secure to the framing with #10 × 2½" screws. Install a course of bricks on the starter strip, fastening them with #10 screws.

15 Cut bricks for the soldier course to length, then install vertically with two #10 × 2½" screws each. For the final brick, cut of the top portion and secure in place with construction adhesive. For a more symmetrical look, place cut bricks in the center of the course.

16 At the tops of walls, install 1 × 3 horizontal furring strips. Secure the second to the last course of bricks to the framing with #10 × 2½" screws, then install the last course with construction adhesive. Notch bricks to fit around joists or cut at an angle for gable walls.

Stone tiles can be laid as veneer over a concrete patio slab—a very easy way to create an elegant looking patio.

Tiling a Patio Slab

Outdoor tile can be made of several different materials and is available in many colors and styles. A popular current trend is to use natural stone tiles with different shapes and complementary colors, as demonstrated in this project. Tile manufacturers may offer brochures giving you ideas for modular patterns that can be created from their tiles. Make sure the tiles you select are intended for outdoor use.

When laying a modular, geometric pattern with tiles of different sizes, it's crucial that you test the layout before you begin and that you place the first tiles very carefully. The first tiles will dictate the placement of all other tiles in your layout.

You can pour a new masonry slab on which to install your tile patio, but another option is to finish an existing slab by veneering it with tile—the scenario demonstrated here.

Outdoor tile must be installed on a clean, flat and stable surface. When tiling an existing concrete pad, the surface must be free of flaking, wide cracks, and other major imperfections. A damaged slab can be repaired by applying a 1- to 2"-thick layer of new concrete over the old surface before laying tile.

NOTE: Wear eye protection when cutting tile and handle cut tiles carefully—the cut edges of some materials may be very sharp.

Everything You Need

Tools: Tape measure, pencil, chalk line, tile cutter or wet saw, tile nippers, square-notched trowel, 2 × 4 padded with carpet, hammer, grout float, grout sponge, caulk gun.

Materials: Tile spacers, buckets, paintbrush and roller, plastic sheeting, thin-set mortar, modular tile, grout, grout additive, grout sealer, tile sealer.

Tile options for landscape installations: Slate and other smooth, natural stone materials are durable and blend well with any landscape but are usually expensive. Quarry tile is less expensive, though only available in limited colors. Exterior-rated porcelain or ceramic tiles are moderately priced and available in a wide range of colors and textures, with many styles imitating the look of natural stone. Terra cotta tile is made from molded clay for use in warmer, drier climates only. Many of these materials require application of a sealer to increase durability and prevent staining and moisture penetration.

Tools for installing exterior tile include: a wet saw for cutting tile quickly and easily (available at rental centers—make certain to rent one that is big enough for the tile size you install), an angle grinder with a diamond-edged cutting blade (also a rental item) for cutting curves or other complex contours, a trowel with square notches (of the size required for your tile size) for spreading the mortar adhesive, spacers for accurate aligning of tiles and setting consistent joint widths, a straight length of 2 x 4 padded along one edge (carpet pad works well) for helping align tile surfaces, a grout float for spreading grout to fill the joints, and a sponge for cleaning excess grout from tile surfaces.

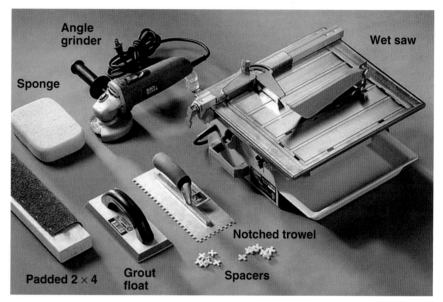

Materials for installing exterior tile include: latex-modified thin-set mortar adhesive that is mixed with water (if you can't find thin-set that is latex modified, buy unmodified thin-set and mix it with a latex additive for mortar, following manufacturer's directions), exterior-rated grout available in a variety of colors to match the tile you use, grout additive to improve durability, grout sealer to help protect grout from moisture and staining, and tile sealer required for some tile materials (follow tile manufacturer's requirements).

Tips for Evaluating Concrete Surfaces

A good surface is free from any major cracks or badly flaking concrete (called spalling). You can apply patio tile directly over a concrete surface that is in good condition if it has control joints (see below).

A fair surface may exhibit minor cracking and spalling but has no major cracks or badly deteriorated spots. Install a new concrete subbase over a surface in fair condition before laying patio tile.

A poor surface contains deep or large cracks, broken, sunken, or heaved concrete, or extensive spalling. If you have this kind of surface, remove the concrete completely and replace it with a new concrete slab before you lay patio tile.

Tips for Cutting Control Joints in a Concrete Patio

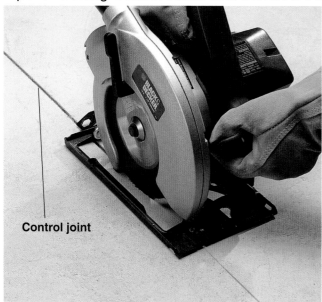

Control joint

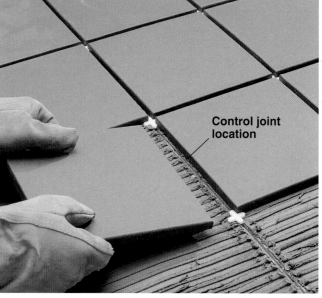

Control joint location

Cut new control joints into existing concrete patios that are in good condition but do not have enough control joints. Control joints allow inevitable cracking to occur in locations that don't weaken the concrete or detract from its appearance. They should be cut every 5 or 6 ft. in a patio. Plan the control joints so they will be below tile joints once the tile layout is established (photo, above right). Use a circular saw with a masonry blade set to 3⁄8" depth to cut control joints. Cover the saw base with duct tape to prevent it from being scratched.

How to Tile a Patio Slab

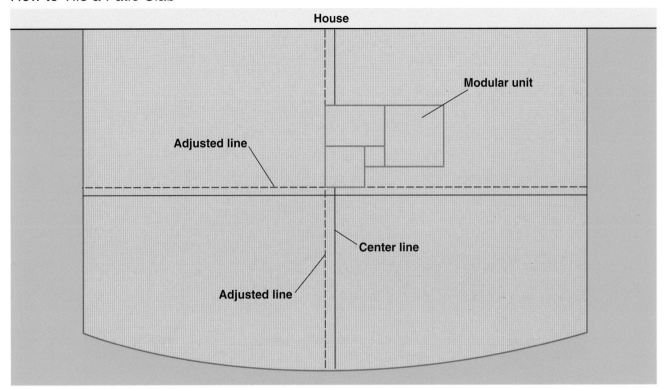

1 To establish a layout for tile with a modular pattern, you must carefully determine the location of the first tile. On the clean and dry concrete surface, measure and mark a centerline down the center of the slab. Test-fit tiles along the line—because of the modular pattern used here, the tiles are staggered. Mark the edge of a tile nearest the center of the pad, then create a second line perpendicular to the first and test-fit tiles along this line.

2 Make adjustments as needed so the modular pattern breaks evenly over the patio surface, and is symmetrical from side to side. You may need to adjust the position of one or both lines. The intersection of the lines is where your tile installation will begin. Outline the position of each group of tiles on the slab.

(continued next page)

How to Tile a Patio Slab (continued)

VARIATION: To establish a traditional grid pattern, test-fit rows of tiles so they run in each direction, intersecting at the center of the patio. Adjust the layout to minimize tile cutting at the sides and ends, then mark the final layout and snap chalklines across the patio to create four quadrants. As you lay tile, work along the chalklines and in one quadrant at a time.

3 Following manufacturer's instructions, mix enough thin-set mortar to work for about 2 hours (start with 4 to 5" deep in a 5-gallon bucket. At the intersection of the two layout lines, use a notched-edge trowel to spread thin-set mortar over an area large enough to accommodate the layout of the first modular group of tiles. Hold the trowel at a 45° angle to rake the mortar to a consistent depth.

4 Set the first tile, twisting it slightly as you push it into the mortar. Align it with both adjusted layout lines, then place a padded 2 × 4 over the center of the tile and give it a light rap with a hammer to set the tile.

5 Position the second tile adjacent to the first with a slight gap between them. Place spacers on end in the joint near each corner and push the second tile against the spacers. Make certain the first tile remains aligned with the layout lines. Set the padded 2 × 4 across both tiles and tap to set. Use a damp cloth to remove any mortar that squeezes out of the joint or gets on tile surfaces. Joints must be at least 1/8"-deep to hold grout.

6 Lay the remaining tiles of the first modular unit, using spacers. Using the trowel, scrape the excess mortar from the concrete pad in areas you will not yet be working to prevent it from hardening and interfering with tile installation.

7 With the first modular unit set, continue laying tile following the pattern established. You can use the chalklines for general reference, but they will not be necessary as layout lines. To prevent squeeze-out between tiles, scrape a heavy accumulation of mortar ½" away from the edge of a set tile before setting the adjacent tile.

Tip: Cutting Contours in Tile

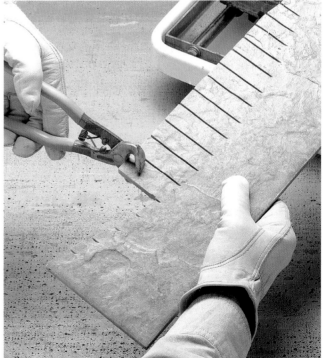

To make convex (above left) or concave (above right) curves, mark the profile of the curve on the tile, then use a wet saw to make parallel straight cuts, each time cutting as close to the marked line as possible. Use a tile nippers to break off small portions of tabs, gradually working down to the curve profile. Finally, use an angle grinder to smooth off the sharp edges of the tabs. Make sure to wear a particle mask when using the tile saw and wear sturdy gloves when using the nippers.

(continued next page)

8 After installing the tile, remove all the spacers, cover the tiled area with plastic, and let the thin-set mortar cure according to the manufacturer's instructions. When tile has fully set, remove the plastic and mix grout, using a grout additive instead of water. Grout additive is especially important in outdoor applications, because it creates joints that are more resilient in changing temperatures.

9 Use a grout float to spread grout over an area that is roughly 10 sq. ft. Push down with the face of the float to force grout into the joints, then hold the float edge at a 45° angle to the tile surfaces and scrape off the excess grout.

10 Once you've grouted this area, wipe off the grout residue, using a damp sponge. Wipe with a light, circular motion—you want to clean tile surfaces but not pull grout out of the joints. Don't try to get the tile perfectly clean the first time. Wipe the area several times, rinsing out the sponge frequently.

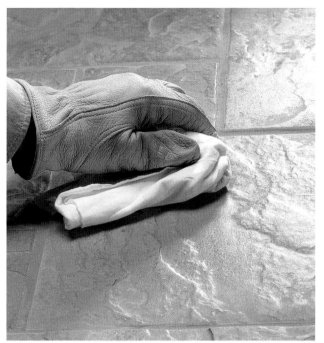

11 Once the grout has begun to set (usually about 1 hour, depending on temperature and humidity), clean the tile surfaces again. You want to thoroughly clean grout residue from tile surfaces because it is difficult to remove once it has hardened. Buff off a light film left after final cleaning with a cloth.

Grouting Porous Tiles

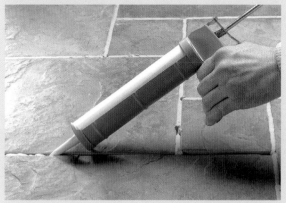

Some tiles, such as slate, have highly porous surfaces that can be badly stained by grout. For these tiles, apply grout by filling an empty caulk tube (available at tile stores and some building centers) with grout, and apply the grout to the joints with a caulk gun. Cut the tip to make an opening just large enough to allow grout to be forced out. Run the tip down the joint between tiles as you squeeze out the grout. Remove the grout that gets on the tile surface with a wet sponge. You may need to use your finger to force grout into the joint—protect your skin by wearing a rubber glove to do this.

12 Cover the patio slab with plastic and let the grout cure according to manufacturer's instructions. Once the grout has cured, use a foam brush to apply grout sealer to only the grout, wiping any spillover off of tile surfaces.

13 Apply tile sealer to the entire surface, using a paint roller. Cover the patio with plastic and allow the sealer to dry completely before exposing the patio to weather or traffic.

Natural Stone

Stone work is a labor-intensive craft. Completing a big stone project on your own can take many days. Assemble a team for your project, rotating the responsibilities to keep everyone involved. With five or more working, you can complete many stone projects in a weekend.

Working with Natural Stone

The greatest challenges to working with natural stone are dealing with its weight and its lack of uniformity when it comes to size and shape. These challenges can be overcome with plenty of helpers, creativity, and determination. If you've never worked with natural stone, take home a few pieces and experiment before undertaking a large project.

Depending on the stone you choose, individual pieces may be quite heavy. The best time to recruit helpers and devise ramps and other lifting and towing devices is before you come across a stone that's too heavy to move into place. Stone supply yards frequently have specialty tools that

you can rent or borrow. Those that don't offer that service undoubtedly will know local sources for such tools.

The unique nature of each piece makes it necessary to cut and sometimes shape or "dress" stones (pages 210 to 213). This often involves removing jagged edges and undesirable bumps, reshaping a stone to improve its stability within the structure, and cutting stones to fit.

Once the stones are cut and ready to put into position, working with them is much like working with any other placed masonry item.

Tips for Working with Stone

Support your back and stomach muscles with a lifting belt and bend at the knees as you lift each stone. If you can't bend your knees while lifting the stone, it is too heavy for you to lift alone. Find a helper or use a ramp or chain to move the stone.

Stone weighs 165 lb./cu. ft., on average. This can make it difficult to place stones precisely. There are many good techniques for moving stone safely and effectively. Use ramps and simple lifting or towing devices, such as chains, to simplify the task any time a stone is too heavy to lift comfortably.

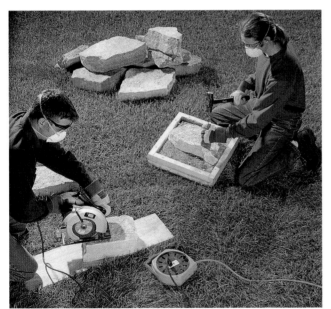

Cutting stones to fit is an important part of working with stone. Keep a circular saw equipped with a silicon-carbide masonry blade on hand, along with a maul and chisel. Some stone masons prefer to do all their cutting with a maul and chisel to avoid unnaturally straight lines, but if there's a lot of splitting to do, you may want one person to take the first pass with a saw (called scoring) while another does the final splitting with a maul and chisel.

Organize stones by size and shape before starting your project. Taking the extra time required at the start of a project will save a lot of effort in the long run. If you're building a wall, stack long stones that will serve as tie stones in one area; filler, or wedge, stones in another area; and the remaining stones in a third.

Home centers carry the materials and tools you will need for most masonry projects. Many brick yards and stone suppliers also carry a wide range of specialty tools that can simplify your projects.

Tools & Materials

Even though most of planet Earth is made of rocks and dirt in various levels of solidity, natural stone can get fantastically expensive. So it pays to use a sharp pencil when you're estimating and sharp tools when you're working the stone to keep expensive waste to a minimum.

If you're doing the work yourself, don't expect to find six tons of premium ashlar at your local building center or gardening outlet. You'll need to do your shopping at a specialty landscape supplier. Where possible (and if you have access to an appropriate vehicle), select and haul the rock yourself to control quality and save delivery fees.

Sand, gravel, topsoil (2" layer)	surface area (sq. ft.) ÷ 100 = tons needed
Flagstone	surface area (sq. ft.) ÷ 100 = tons of stone needed
Ashlar stone for 1-ft.-thick walls	area of wall face (sq. ft.) ÷ 15 = tons of stone needed
Rubble stone for 1-ft.-thick walls	area of wall face (sq. ft.) ÷ 35 = tons of stone needed

Use this chart to estimate the materials you will need. Sizes and weights of materials may vary, so consult your supplier for more detailed information.

How to Estimate Materials

Local brick and stone suppliers will often help you design your project and advise you about estimating materials, local Building Codes, and climate considerations. Many suppliers offer a range of other services as well, such as coordinating landscapers and other contractors to work with you and offering classes in masonry construction.

Tools for Working With Natural Stone

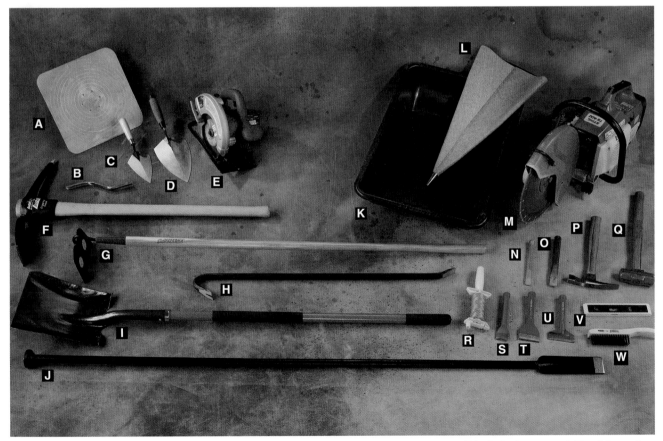

Tools for working with natural stone include: Mortar hawk (A); Jointing tool (B); Pointing trowel (C); Mason's trowel (D); Circular saw with masonry blade (E); Pick-axe (F); Masonry hoe (G); Wrecking bar for prying small to medium stones (H); Square-end spade (I); Heavy-duty spud bar for prying larger stones (J); Mortar box (K); Mortar bag (L); Rental gas-powered masonry saw (M); Cold chisels (N); Mason's hammer (O); Hand maul (P); Masonry chisels (Bricksets) (Q); Level (R); Wire brush (S).

Types & Forms of Stone

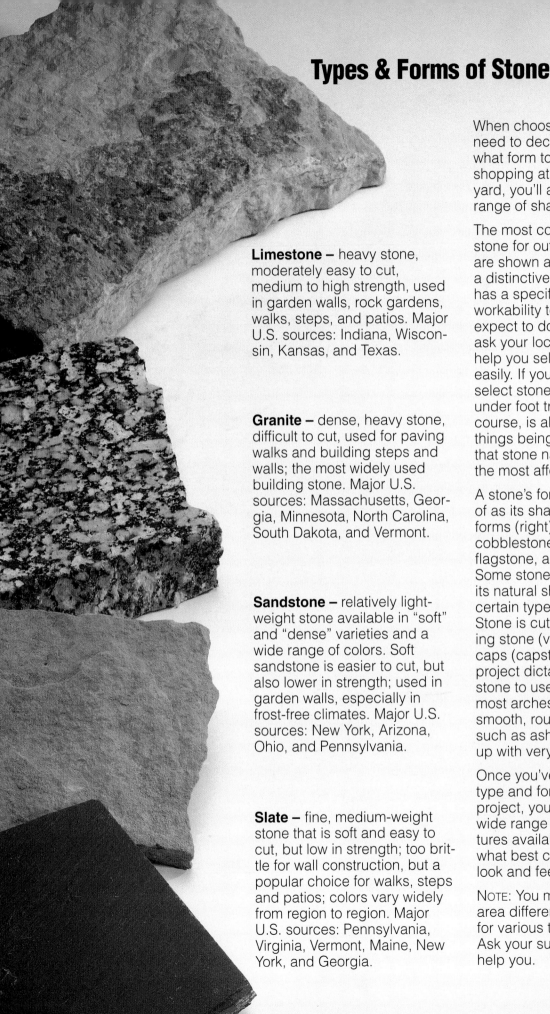

Limestone – heavy stone, moderately easy to cut, medium to high strength, used in garden walls, rock gardens, walks, steps, and patios. Major U.S. sources: Indiana, Wisconsin, Kansas, and Texas.

Granite – dense, heavy stone, difficult to cut, used for paving walks and building steps and walls; the most widely used building stone. Major U.S. sources: Massachusetts, Georgia, Minnesota, North Carolina, South Dakota, and Vermont.

Sandstone – relatively light-weight stone available in "soft" and "dense" varieties and a wide range of colors. Soft sandstone is easier to cut, but also lower in strength; used in garden walls, especially in frost-free climates. Major U.S. sources: New York, Arizona, Ohio, and Pennsylvania.

Slate – fine, medium-weight stone that is soft and easy to cut, but low in strength; too brittle for wall construction, but a popular choice for walks, steps and patios; colors vary widely from region to region. Major U.S. sources: Pennsylvania, Virginia, Vermont, Maine, New York, and Georgia.

When choosing stone, you'll need to decide what type and what form to use. If you're shopping at a stone supply yard, you'll also find a wide range of shades and textures.

The most common types of stone for outdoor construction are shown at left. In addition to a distinctive look, each type has a specific durability and workability to consider. If you expect to do a lot of splitting, ask your local stone supplier to help you select stone that splits easily. If you're laying a walk, select stone that holds up well under foot traffic. Cost, of course, is also a factor. Other things being equal, you will find that stone native to your area is the most affordable.

A stone's form can be thought of as its shape or cut. Common forms (right) include ashlar, cobblestone, rubble, fieldstone, flagstone, and veneer stone. Some stone is uncut because its natural shape lends itself to certain types of construction. Stone is cut thin for use as facing stone (veneer) and wall caps (capstone). Often, the project dictates the form of stone to use. For example, most arches require stone with smooth, roughly square sides, such as ashlar, that can be laid up with very thin mortar joints.

Once you've determined the type and form of stone for your project, you can browse the wide range of shades and textures available and decide what best complements the look and feel of your yard.

NOTE: You may find that in your area different terms are used for various types of stone. Ask your supply yard staff to help you.

Flagstone – large slabs of quarried stone cut into pieces up to 3" thick; used in walks, steps, and patios. Pieces smaller than 16" sq. are often called *steppers.*

Split fieldstone

Fieldstone – stone gathered from fields, dry river beds, and hillsides; used in wall construction. When split into smaller, more manageable shapes, fieldstone is often used in mortared construction. Called *river rock* by some quarries because of the river-bed origin of some fieldstone.

Rubble – irregular pieces of quarried stone, usually with one split or finished face; widely used in wall construction.

Ashlar – quarried stone smooth-cut into large blocks ideal for creating clean lines with thin mortar joints.

Veneer stone – pieces of natural or manufactured stone, cut or molded for use in non-load-bearing, cosmetic applications, such as facing exterior walls or freestanding concrete block walls.

Cobblestone – small cuts of quarried stone or fieldstone; used in walks and paths.

Basic Techniques

You can cut most stone by placing it directly on a bed of flat, soft ground, such as grass or sand, that will absorb some of the shock when the maul strikes the chisel. Use a sandbag for additional support. You can also build a simple cutting platform, called a *banker* to support stones in a bed of sand. Protect yourself by wearing safety glasses and heavy gloves and using the proper tools for the job. A standard brickset chisel and hammer are too light, and a carpenter's framing hammer is too light and is made of brittle material that may chip when striking a chisel. The best tools are a pitching chisel for long, clean cuts, a pointing chisel for removing small bumps, a basic stone chisel, and a maul for tapping the chisels. A mason's hammer—with its pick at one end—is also useful for breaking off small chips.

It is often helpful to mark a stone for cutting while it sits in place on a wall or other structure, but never cut a stone while it is in place, even to remove a small bump. You risk splitting surrounding stones and breaking the mortar bond, if you're using mortar. For splitting, move the stone to soft ground or a banker at the base of the wall.

Everything You Need:

Tools: Maul, stone chisel, pitching chisel, pointing chisel, mason's hammer, circular saw, silicon-carbide masonry blades, GFCI extension cord.

Materials: Stone, sand, 2 × 2s, wallboard.

Tips for Cutting Stone

Laying stones works best when the sides (including the top and bottom) are roughly square. If a side is sharply skewed, score and split it with a pitching chisel, and chip off smaller peaks with a pointing chisel or mason's hammer. REMEMBER: a stone should sit flat on its bottom or top side without much rocking.

"Dress" a stone, using a pointing chisel and maul, to remove jagged edges or undesirable bumps. Position the chisel at a 30 to 45° angle at the base of the piece to be removed. Tap lightly all around the break line, then more forcefully, to chip off the piece. Position the chisel carefully before each blow with the maul.

Build a banker if you plan to do a lot of splitting. This simple sand-bed table provides a sturdy, but shock-absorbent work surface. Place it atop two columns of concrete block if you prefer to stand while splitting. Construct frames out of 2 x 2s, and sandwich a piece of ¾" plywood between the frames. Attach pieces by driving 3½" coarse-threaded wallboard screws through from both sides, and fill it with sand.

Grind the head of a chisel smooth on a grindstone any time the head begins to "mushroom" (curled edges appear). The curling results from repeated blows to the chisel with a maul. Small shards of metal can break free, becoming dangerous projectiles. REMEMBER: Always wear safety goggles when handling cutting tools.

Tips for Cutting Stone with a Circular Saw

A circular saw lets you precut stones with broad surfaces with greater control and accuracy than most people can achieve with a chisel. It's a noisy tool, so wear ear plugs, along with a dust mask and safety goggles. Install a toothless masonry blade on your saw and start out with the blade set to cut ⅛" deep. (Make sure the blade is designed for the material you're cutting. Some masonry blades are designed for hard materials like concrete, marble, and granite. Others are for soft materials, like concrete block, brick, flagstone, and limestone.) Wet the stone before cutting to help control dust, then make three passes, setting the blade ⅛" deeper with each pass. Repeat the process on the other side. A thin piece of wood under the saw protects the saw foot from rough masonry surfaces. REMEMBER: Always use a GFCI outlet or extension cord when using power tools outdoors.

How to Cut Fieldstone

1 Place the stone on a banker, or prop it with sandbags, and mark with chalk or a crayon all the way around the stone, indicating where you want it to split. If possible, use the natural fissures in the stone as cutting lines.

2 Score along the line using moderate blows with a chisel and maul, then strike solidly along the score line with a pitching chisel to split the stone. Dress the stone with a pointing chisel.

How to Cut Flagstone

1 Trying to split a large flagstone in half can lead to many unpredicted breaks. For best results, chip off small sections at a time. Mark the stone on both sides with chalk or a crayon, indicating where you want it to split. If there is a fissure nearby, mark your line there since that is probably where the stone will break naturally.

2 Score along the line on the back side of the stone (the side that won't be exposed) by moving a chisel along the line and striking it with moderate blows with a maul. OPTION: If you have a lot of cutting to do, reduce hammering fatigue by using a circular saw to score the stones, and a maul and chisel to split them. Keep the stone wet during cutting with a circular saw to reduce dust.

3 Turn the stone over, place a pipe or 2 × 4 directly under the chalk line, then strike forcefully with the maul on the end of the portion to be removed.

OPTION: If a paving stone looks too big compared to other stones in your path, simply set the stone in place and strike a heavy blow to the center with a sledge hammer. It should break into several usable pieces.

Thin joints are the strongest. When working with mortar, joints should be ½ to1" thick. Mortar is not intended to create gaps between stones, but to fill the inevitable gaps and strengthen the bonds between stones. Wiggle a stone once it is in place to get it as close as possible to adjoining stones.

Laying Stone

The methods of laying stone are as varied as the stone masons who practice the craft. But all of them would agree on a few general principles:

- Thinner joints are stronger joints. Whether you are using mortar or dry-laying stone, the more contact between stones, the more resistance to any one stone dislodging.

- *Tie stones* are essential in vertical structures, such as walls or pillars. These long stones span at least two-thirds of the width of the structure, tying together the shorter stones around them.

- When working with mortar, most stone masons point their joints deep for aesthetic reasons. The less mortar is visible, the more the stone itself is emphasized.

- Long vertical joints, or *head* joints, are weak spots in a wall. Close the vertical joints by overlapping them with stones in the next course, similar to a running bond pattern in a brick or block wall.

- The sides of a stone wall should have an inward slope (called *batter*) for maximum strength. This is especially important with dry-laid stone. Mortared walls need less batter.

Blend large and small stones in walks or in vertical structures to achieve the most natural appearance. In addition to enhancing visual appeal, long stones in a walk act like the tie stones in a wall, adding strength by bonding with other stones.

Place uneven stone surfaces down and dig out the soil underneath until the stone lies flat. Use the same approach in the bottom course of a dry-laid wall, only make sure stones at the base of a wall slope toward the center of the trench.

Tips for Laying Stone Walls

Tie stones are long stones that span most of the width of a wall, tying together the shorter stones, and increasing the wall's strength. As a guide, figure that 20 percent of the stones in a structure should be tie stones.

A *shiner* is the opposite of a tie stone—a flat stone on the side of a wall that contributes little in terms of strength. A shiner may be necessary when no other stone will fit in a space. Use shiners as seldom as possible, and use tie stones nearby to compensate.

Lay stones in horizontal courses, where possible, a technique called *ashlar* construction. If necessary, stack two to three thin stones to match the thickness of adjoining stones.

With irregular stone, such as untrimmed rubble or field stone, building course by course is difficult. Instead, place stones as needed to fill gaps and to overlap the vertical joints.

Use a batter gauge and level to lay up dry stone structures so the sides angle inward. Angle the sides of a wall 1" for every 2 ft. of height—less for ashlar and free-standing walls, twice as much for round stone and retaining walls.

It is easiest to build a dry stone wall with ashlar—stone that has been split into roughly rectangular blocks. Ashlar stone is stacked in the same running-bond pattern used in brick wall construction; each stone overlaps a joint in the previous course. This technique avoids long vertical joints, resulting in a wall that is attractive and also strong.

Dry Stone Walls

Stone walls are beautiful, long-lasting structures that are surprisingly easy to build provided you plan carefully. A low stone wall can be constructed without mortar, using a centuries-old method known as *dry laying*. With this technique, the wall is actually formed by two separate stacks that lean together slightly. The position and weight of the two stacks support each other, forming a single, sturdy wall. A dry stone wall can be built to any length, but its width must be at least half of its height.

You can purchase stone for this project from a quarry or stone supplier, where different sizes, shapes and colors of stone are sold, priced by the ton. The quarry or stone center can also sell you type M mortar—necessary for bonding the capstones to the top of the wall.

Building dry stone walls requires patience and a

fair amount of physical effort. The stones must be sorted by size and shape. You'll probably also need to shape some of the stones to achieve consistent spacing and a general appearance that appeals to you.

To shape a stone, score it, using a circular saw outfitted with a masonry blade. Place a mason's chisel on the score line and strike with a maul until the stone breaks. Wear safety glasses when using stone-cutting tools.

Everything You Need:

Tools: Mason's string, circular saw with masonry blade, mason's chisel, masonry trowel.

Materials: 12" beveled stakes, crushed stone, cut ashlar stone, capstones, type M mortar.

How to Build a Dry Stone Wall

filler stones

1 Lay out the wall site, using stakes and mason's string. Dig a 6"-deep trench that extends 6" beyond the wall on all sides. Add a 4" crushed stone subbase to the trench, creating a "V" shape by sloping the subbase so the center is about 2" deeper than the edges.

2 Select appropriate stones and lay the first course. Place pairs of stones side by side, flush with the edges of the trench and sloping toward the center. Use stones of similar height; position uneven sides face down. Fill any gaps between the shaping stones with small filler stones.

3 Lay the next course, staggering the joints. Use pairs of stones of varying lengths to offset the center joint. Alternate stone length, and keep the height even, stacking pairs of thin stones if necessary to maintain consistent height. Place filler stones in the gaps.

tie stones

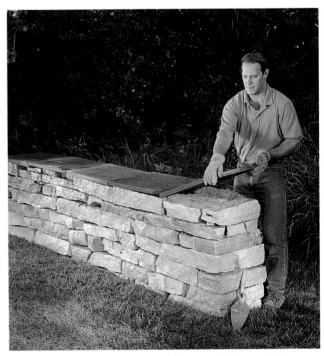

4 Every other course, place a tie stone every 3 ft. You may need to split the tie stones to length. Check the wall periodically for level.

5 Mortar the capstones to the top of the wall, keeping the mortar at least 6" from the edges so it's not visible. Push the capstones together and mortar the cracks in between. Brush off dried excess mortar with a stiff-bristle brush.

Mortared Stone Walls

The mortared stone wall is a classic that brings structure and appeal to any yard or garden. Square-hewn ashlar and bluestone are the easiest to build with, though field stone and rubble also work well and make attractive walls.

Because the mortar turns the wall into a monolithic structure that can crack and heave with the freeze-thaw cycle, a concrete footing is required for a mortared stone wall. To maintain strength in the wall, use the heaviest, thickest stones for the base of the wall and thinner, flatter stones for the cap.

As you plan the wall layout, install tie stones—stones that span the width of the wall (page 215)—about every 3 feet, staggered through the courses both vertically and horizontally through out the wall. Use the squarest, flattest stones to build the "leads," or ends of the wall first, then fill the middle courses. Plan for joints around 1" thick,

and make sure joints in successive courses to not line up. Follow this rule of thumb: cover joints below with a full stone above; locate joints above over a full stone below.

Laying a mortared stone wall is labor-intensive, but satisfying work. Make sure to work safely and enlist friends to help with the heavy lifting.

Everything You Need:

Tools: Tape measure, pencil, chalkline, small whisk broom, tools for mixing mortar (page 114), maul, stone chisel, pitching chisel, trowel, jointing tool, line level, sponge, garden hose.

Materials: concrete materials for foundation (page 44), ashlar stone, Type-N or Type-S mortar, stakes and mason's line, scrap wood, muriatic acid.

How to Build a Mortared Stone Wall

1 Pour a footing for the wall and allow it to cure for one week (pages 44 to 47). Measure and mark the wall location so it is centered on the footing. Snap chalk lines along the length of the footing, for both the front and the back faces of the wall. Lay out corners using the 3-4-5 right angle method as described on page 108.

2 Dry-lay the entire first course. Starting with a tie stone at each end, arrange stones in two rows along the chalklines with joints about 1" thick. Use smaller stones to fill the center of the wall. Use larger, heavier stones in the base and lower courses. Place additional tie stones approximately every 3 feet. Trim stones as needed.

3 Mix a stiff batch of type-N or type-S mortar, following the manufacturer's directions (pages 114 to 115). Starting at an end or corner, set aside some of the stone and brush off the foundation. Spread an even, 2" thick layer of mortar onto the foundation, about ½" from the chalklines—the mortar will squeeze out a little.

4 Firmly press the first tie stone into the mortar, so it is aligned with the chalklines and relatively level. Tap the top of the stone with the handle of the trowel to set it. Continue to lay stones along each chalkline, working to the opposite end of the wall.

(continued next page)

5 After installing the entire first course, fill voids along the center of the wall that are larger than 2" with smaller rubble. Fill the remaining spaces and joints with mortar, using the trowel.

6 As you work, rake the joints using a scrap of wood to a depth of ½"; raking joints highlights the stones rather than the mortared joints. After raking, use a whisk broom to even the mortar in the joints.

VARIATION: You can also tool joints for a cleaner, tighter mortared joint. Tool joints when your thumb can leave an imprint in the mortar without removing any it.

7 Drive stakes at the each end of the wall and align a mason's line with the face of the wall. Use a line level to level the string at the height of the next course. Build up each end of the wall, called the "leads," making sure to stagger the joints between courses. Check the leads with a 4-ft. level on each wall face to make sure it is plumb.

8 If heavy stones push out too much mortar, use wood wedges cut from scrap to hold the stone in place. Once the mortar sets up, remove the wedges and fill the voids with fresh mortar.

TIP: Have a bucket of water and a sponge handy in case mortar oozes or spills onto the face of the stone. Wipe mortar away immediately before it can harden.

9 Fill the middle courses between the leads by first dry laying stones for placement and then mortaring them in place. Install tie stones about every 3 feet, both vertically and horizontally, staggering their position in each course. Make sure joints in successive courses do not fall in alignment.

10 Install cap stones by pressing flat stones that span the width of the wall into a mortar bed. Do not rake the joints, but clean off excess mortar with the trowel and clean excess mortar from the surface of the stones using a damp sponge.

11 Allow the wall to cure for one week, then clean it using a solution of 1 part muriatic acid and 10 parts water. Wet the wall using a garden hose, apply the acid solution, then immediately rinse with plenty of clean, clear water. Always wear goggles, long sleeves and pants, and heavy rubber gloves when using acids.

A well made stone retaining wall will outlast any other retaining wall type, and look beautiful in the process.

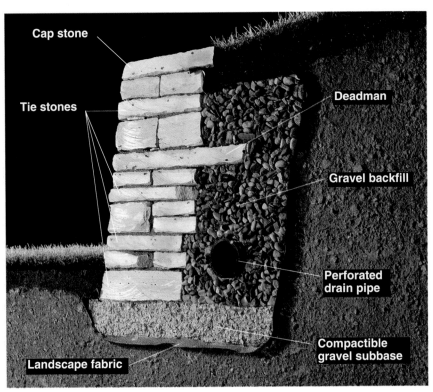

Cut stone has flat, smooth surfaces for easy stacking. For a stable retaining wall, alternate rows of "tie stones" that span the entire width of the wall with rows of smaller stones. Install extra-long stones (called deadmen) that extend back into gravel backfill, spaced every 4 to 6 feet.

Stone Retaining Walls

Retaining walls made from natural cut stone give a traditional, timeless look to a landscape. With its flat surfaces, cut stone is much easier to build with than rubble or field stone. Make sure you have plenty of broad, flat stones to use as tie-stones, capstones, and deadman stones. Dry stone walls require no concrete footings; several inches of compactible gravel are used instead.

Cut-stone retaining walls are built using many of the same techniques as those used for block retaining walls. While cut stone is more expensive and require greater patience in construction, it offers excellent drainage due to the stone spacing in the wall. Before building the retaining wall, prepare the site as directed on pages 128 to 129. Build the wall by placing the largest stones at the bottom and reserving the smoothest, flattest stones for the corners and cap row. Natural stone walls are usually laid out without mortar, although the last two rows can be mortared in place for greater strength.

Everything You Need:

Tools: Wheelbarrow, shovel, garden rake, line level, hand tamper, tamping machine, small maul, masonry chisel, eye protection, hearing protectors, work gloves, level, tape measure, pencil, trowel.

Materials: Stakes, mason's string, landscape fabric, compactible gravel, perforated drain pipe, coarse backfill material, mortar mix.

How to Build a Natural Stone Retaining Wall

1 Spread a 6" layer of compactible gravel subbase into the prepared trench, then sort the stones by size and shape so they can be located easily as you build. Make sure you have enough long stones to serve as tie stones, deadmen, and capstones.

2 Lay rows of stones, following the same techniques for backfilling as for interlocking blocks. Build a backward slant (batter) into the wall by setting each row of stones about 1/2" back from the preceding row. For stability, work tie stones and deadmen into the wall at frequent intervals.

3 Before laying the cap row of stones, mix mortar according to the manufacturer's directions and apply a thick bed along the tops of the installed stones, keeping the mortar 6" from the front face of the wall. Lay the capstones and press them into the mortar. Finish backfilling behind the wall and in the trench at the base of the wall with topsoil. Install sod or other plants as desired.

TIP: Trim irregular stones if needed to make them fit solidly into the wall. Always wear eye protection and hearing protectors when cutting stone. Score the stone first using a masonry blade and circular saw set to 1/8" blade depth, then drive a masonry chisel along the scored line until the stone breaks.

Flagstone walkways combine durability with beauty and work well for casual or formal landscapes.

Flagstone Walkway

Natural flagstone is an ideal material for creating landscape floors. It's attractive and durable and blends well with both formal and informal landscapes. Although flagstone structures are often mortared, they can also be constructed with the sand-set method. Sand-setting flagstones is much faster and easier than setting them with mortar.

There are a variety of flat, thin sedimentary rocks that can be used for this project. Home and garden stores often carry several types of flagstone, but stone supply yards usually have a greater variety. Some varieties of flagstone cost more than others, but there are many affordable options. If you have the opportunity to hand-pick flagstone for your project, select pieces in a variety of sizes from large to small, but all of roughly equal thickness.

The following example demonstrates how to build a straight flagstone walkway with wood edging. If you'd like to build a curved walkway, select another edging material, such as brick or cut stone. Instead of filling gaps between stones with sand, you might want to fill them with topsoil and plant grass or some other ground cover between the stones.

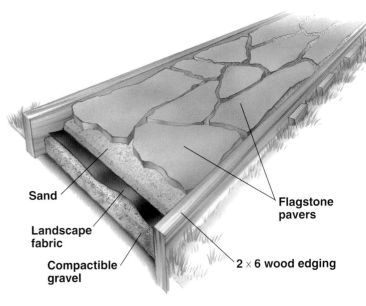

Sand

Landscape fabric

Compactible gravel

Flagstone pavers

2 × 6 wood edging

Everything You Need

Tools: Basic tools, line level, hand tamper, circular saw with masonry blade, power drill, masonry chisel, maul, rubber mallet, sod cutter (optional).

Materials: Landscape fabric, sand, 2 × 6 pressure-treated lumber, galvanized screws, compactible gravel, flagstone pavers, water.

How to Build a Flagstone Walkway

1 Lay out, excavate, and prepare the base for the walkway. Form edging by installing 2 × 6 pressure-treated lumber around the perimeter of the pathway. Drive stakes on the outside of the edging, spaced 12" apart. The tops of the stakes should be below ground level. Drive galvanized screws through the edging and into the stakes.

2 Test-fit the stones over the walkway base, finding an attractive arrangement that limits the number of cuts needed. The gaps between the stones should range between $3/8$" and 2" wide. Use a pencil to mark the stones for cutting, then remove the stones and place them beside the walkway in the same arrangement. Score along the marked lines with a circular saw and masonry blade set to $1/8$" blade depth. Set a piece of wood under the stone, just inside the scored line. Use a masonry chisel and hammer to strike along the scored line until the stone breaks.

3 If you are not planting grass, lay overlapping strips of landscape fabric over the walkway base and spread a 2" layer of sand over it. Make a screed board from a short 2 × 6, notched to fit inside the edging. Pull the screed from one end of the walkway to the other, adding sand as needed to create a level base.

4 Beginning at one corner of the walkway, lay the flagstones onto the sand base. Repeat the arrangement you created in Step 2, with $3/8$"- to 2"-wide gaps between stones. If necessary, add or remove sand to level the stones, then set them by tapping them with a rubber mallet or a length of 2 × 4.

5 Fill the gaps between the stones with sand. (Use topsoil, if you're going to plant grass or ground cover between the stones.) Pack sand into the gaps, then spray the entire walkway with water to help settle the sand. Repeat until the gaps are completely filled and tightly packed with sand.

The flagstone patio is a classic element of modern landscape design. Bluestone (above) is one of the most popular types, but may not be available in all areas since specific types vary by region.

Mortared Flagstone Patio

The stately flagstone patio can be sand-set or mortared using lightly trimmed stone or naturally irregular stone shapes. If you're sandsetting, which is a good idea in colder climates, you'll have the best luck if you cut the stones so they are as large as possible and have straight edges. Small stones don't provide much bearing when they're resting on the sand. But they can be a very effective part of the design if you embed them into mortar, as we do here.

You can install a mortared flagstone patio over an old concrete patio if it is reasonably good repair, or you can pour a new concrete base that's art least 2" thick with 5" of compacted rock below for drainage. If you are sand-setting, you'll want a layer of coarse sand that's at least 1" or 2" thick over a well-compacted base of gravel (see the sand-set paver patio project starting on page 150 for more information).

Everything You Need

Tools: Paint roller with extension pole, pencil, small whisk broom, tools for mixing mortar (page 114), shovel, maul, stone chisel, pitching chisel, 4-ft. level, trowel, straight 2 × 4 stud, grout bag, jointing tool, sponge, garden hose.

Materials: Concrete bonding agent, flagstone stone, Type-N or Type-S mortar.

How to Build a Mortared Flagstone Patio

1 Thoroughly clean the concrete slab. While the slab doesn't need to be in perfect condition, it does need to be sound. Repair large cracks or holes. After repairs have cured, apply a latex bonding agent to the patio surface, following the manufacturer's instructions.

2 Once the bonding agent has set up per the manufacturer's recommendations, dry lay stones on the patio to determine an appealing layout. Work from the center outward and evenly distribute large stones and smaller ones, with ½" to 1" joints between them.

3 Cut stones to size as needed. Mark the cutting line with chalk, then cut the stone, following the techniques on page 213. At the sides of the slab, cut stones even with the edges to accommodate edging treatments.

VARIATION: For a more rustic appearance, allow stones to overhang the edges of the slab. Stones thicker in size can overhang as much as 6", provided that the slab supports no less than two-thirds of the stone. Thinner stones should not overhang more than 3". After stones are mortared in place, fill in beneath the overhanging stones with soil.

(continued next page)

4 Mix a stiff batch of type-N or type-S mortar, following the manufacturer's directions (pages 114 to 115). Starting near the center of the patio, set aside some of the stone, maintaining their layout pattern. Spread a 2" thick layer of mortar onto the slab.

5 Firmly press the first large stone into the mortar, in its same position as in the layout. Tap the stone with a rubber mallet or the handle of the trowel to set it. Use a 4-ft. level and a scrap of 2 × 4 to check for level; make any necessary adjustments.

6 Using the first stone as a reference for the course height, continue to lay stones in mortar, working from the center of the slab to the edges. Maintain ½" to 1" joints.

7 As you work, check for level often, using a straight length of 2 × 4 and the 4-ft. level. Tap stones to make minor adjustments. Once you're done, let the mortar set up for a day or two before walking on it.

8 Use a grout bag to fill the joints with mortar (add acrylic fortifier to the mix to make the mortar more elastic). Do not overfill the joints. Pack loose gravel and small rocks into gaps first to conserve mortar and make stronger joints. Wipe up spilled mortar.

9 Once the mortar is stiff enough that your thumb leaves an impression without mortar sticking to it, rake the joints just enough so the mortar is even with the surface of the stone, so water cannot pool. Use a whisk broom to shape the mortar.

10 Allow the mortar to cure for a few days, then clean the patio with clear water and a stiff bristle brush. After the mortar cures for a week, apply a stone sealer, following the manufacturer's instructions.

A rock garden is an attractive alternative to traditional lawns and garden beds. This garden has been planted with mosses. Small varieties of alpine plants are also good choices.

Roc Garden

Rock gardens offer a good way to landscape difficult sites Sloped areas or sites with sandy soil, for instance, are unfavorable for traditional lawns but are ideal for rock gardens. A rock garden is also a good choice if you're looking for an alternative to traditional groundcovers and garden beds. Rock gardens traditionally feature hardy, alpine plant varieties that typically require only infrequent watering.

Building a rock garden requires excavating the site (preferably a sloping or terraced area) and preparing the soil, placing the rocks, and, finally planting. Moving and positioning large rocks is the most difficult task. If your rock garden site is large, consider hiring a landscape contractor to deliver and place the rocks for you.

Rock gardens will look more natural if they're built with stones that are all the same variety—or at least with stones that are similar in appearance. Using stone like that found in natural outcroppings in your area is a good idea. On the other hand, gardens with a larger variety of stone types have more visual variety and high potential for a very dynamic appearance when arranged with some skill.

Common Rock-Garden Plants (partial list)

Hens-and-Chicks
Snow-in-Summer
Coral bells
Sedum
Dianthus
Rock jasmine
Rockcress
Dwarf juniper
Yarrow

How to Build a Rock Garden

1 The best site for a rock garden is sloping or terraced, ideally with southeast exposure. It should be completely free of deep-rooted weeds. If no such space is available, build up a raised bed with southeast exposure. The alpine plants traditionally used in rock gardens require non-clayey soil, with excellent drainage. If the existing soil is clayey, remove any groundcover and excavate the site to a depth of around 18". Replace the soil with equal parts loam, peat moss, and coarse sand.

2 Begin at the base of the site, placing the most substantial stones first. The idea is to create the impression of a natural subterranean rock formation exposed by weathering. Set the stones in the soil so they are at least half buried and so their most weathered surfaces are exposed. Slightly less than half of the surface of the site should be rock. Avoid even spacing or rows of rocks. Once the rocks are in place, cover the soil with a mulch of complementary pea gravel or rock chips.

3 "New" rocks moved to the site will need to weather before they will look natural. Encourage weathering by promoting moss and lichen growth. In a blender, combine a handful of moss with a cup of buttermilk or yogurt. Paint the mixture on the exposed faces of rocks to promote moss growth.

4 After the rocks are in place for a few days and the soil has settled, begin planting the garden. As with the rocks, focus on native varieties and strive for natural placement, without excessive variety. You can plant several sizes, from small trees or shrubs to delicate alpine flowers. Place plants in crevices and niches between rocks, allowing them to cascade over the surface of the rock.

A moon window is just about the most dramatic garden element you can build. We constructed the wall shown here using cut ashlar mortared around a semicircular form, but using brick is also an option. Once the bottom half of the window has set up, the form is flipped and the top stones are placed. The construction technique for the form is the same one used in building an arch (pages 136 to 139).

Stone Moon Window

You can build circular openings into brick or stone walls, using a single semicircular wood form. Moon windows can be built to any dimension, although lifting and placing stones is more difficult as the project grows larger, while tapering stones to fit is a greater challenge as the circle gets smaller. To minimize the need for cutting and lifting stone, we built this window 2 feet in diameter atop an existing stone wall. Before doing this, you'll need to check with your local building inspector regarding restrictions on wall height, footings, and other design considerations. You may need to modify the dimensions to conform with the local Building Code.

Make sure to have at least one helper on hand. Building with stone is always physically demanding, and steps such as installing the brace and form (opposite page) require a helper.

Everything You Need:

Tools: Jig saw, circular saw, drill, tape measure, level, mortar box, mason's hoe, trowels, jointing tool or tuck-pointer, mortar bag, stone chisel, maul.

Materials: ¾" plywood, ¼" plywood, wallboard screws (1" and 2"), tapered shims, 2 × 4 and 2 × 8 lumber, 4 × 4 posts, type M mortar (stiff mix), ashlar stone.

How to Build a Stone Moon Window

1 Build a plywood form, following the instructions on page 136. Select stones for the top of the circle with sides that are squared off or slightly tapered. Dry-lay the stones around the outside of the form, spacing the stones with shims that are roughly ¼" thick at their narrow end.

2 Number each stone and a corresponding point on the form, using chalk, then set the stones aside. Turn the form around, and label a second set of stones for the bottom of the circle. TIP: to avoid confusion, use letters to label the bottom set of stones instead of numbers.

3 Prepare a stiff mix of type M mortar (pages 114 and 115) and lay a ½"-thick mortar bed on top of the wall for the base of the circle. Center the stone that will be at the base of the circle in the mortar.

4 Set the form on top of the stone, and brace the form by constructing a sturdy 2 × 4 scaffold and secure it by constructing a bracing structure made from 4 × 4 posts and 2 × 4 lumber. We used pairs of 2 × 4s nailed together for lengthwise supports. Check the form for level in both directions, and adjust the braces as required. Screw the braces to the form, so the edges are at least ¼" in from the edges of the form.

(continued next page)

5 Extend the mortar bed along the wall and add stones, buttering one end of each stone, and tapping them into place with a trowel. Keep the joint width consistent with the existing wall, but set the depth of new joints at about 1", to allow for tuck-pointing.

6 Attach mason's string at the center of the front and back of the form and use the strings to check the alignment of each stone.

7 Stagger the joints as you build upward and outward. Alternate large and small stones for maximum strength and a natural look. Stop occasionally to smooth joints that have hardened enough to resist minimal finger pressure.

8 If large bumps or curves interfere as you lay stones around the circle, dress those stones (page 211), as necessary, so the sides are roughly squared off.

9 Once you've laid stones about ½" beyond the top edge of the form, disassemble the bracing.

10 Invert the form on top of the wall in preparation for laying the top half of the circle. The bottom edge of the form should be set roughly ½" higher than the top of the lower half of the circle. Check the braces for level (both lengthwise and widthwise), and adjust them as necessary and reattach them to the posts.

11 Lay stones around the circle, working from the bottom up, so the top, or keystone, is laid last. If mortar oozes from the joints, insert temporary shims. Remove the shims after 2 hours, and pack the voids with mortar.

12 Once the keystone is in place, smooth the remaining joints. Remove the form. Let the wall set up over-night, then mist it several times a day for a week.

13 Remove any excess mortar from the joints inside the circle. Mist lightly, then tuck-point all joints with stiff mortar so they are of equal depth.

14 Once the joints reach a putty-like consistency, tool them with a jointing tool. Let the mortar harden overnight. Mist the wall for five more days.

Repair & Maintenance

Before

After

Good repairs restore both the appearance and the function to failing concrete structures and surfaces. Careful work can produce a well-blended, successful repair like the one shown above.

Maintaining & Repairing Concrete

Concrete is one of the most durable building materials, but it still requires occasional repair and maintenance. Freezing and thawing, improper finishing techniques, a poor subbase, or lack of reinforcement all can cause problems with concrete. By addressing problems as soon as you discover them, you can prevent further damage that may be difficult or impossible to fix.

Concrete repairs fall into a wide range, from simple cleaning and sealing, to removing and replacing whole sections. Filling cracks and repairing surface damage are the most common concrete repairs.

Another effective repair is resurfacing—covering an old concrete surface with a layer of fresh concrete. It's a good solution to spalling, crazing, or popouts—minor problems that affect the appearance more than the structure. These problems often result from inadequate preparation or incorrect finishing techniques.

As with any kind of repair, the success of the

project depends largely on good preparation and the use of the best repair products for the job. Specially formulated repair products are manufactured for just about every type of concrete repair. Be sure to read the product-use information before purchasing any products; some products need to be used in combination with others.

A good repair can outlast the rest of the structure in some cases, but if structural damage has occurred, repairing the concrete is only a temporary solution. By using the right products and techniques, however, you can make cosmetic repairs that improve the appearance of the surface and keep damage from becoming worse.

Probably the most important point to remember when repairing concrete is that curing makes repairs last longer. That means covering repaired surfaces with plastic sheeting and keeping them damp for at least a week. In dry, hot weather, lift the plastic occasionally, and mist with water.

Concrete Repair Products

Concrete repair products include: vinyl-reinforced concrete patch (A) for filling holes, popouts, and larger cracks; hydraulic cement (B) for repairing foundations, retaining walls, and other damp areas; quick-setting cement (C) for repairing vertical surfaces and unusual shapes; anchoring cement (D) for setting hardware in concrete; concrete sealing products (E); masonry paint (F) concrete recoating product (G) for creating a fresh surface on old concrete; joint-filler caulk (H); pour-in crack sealer (I); concrete cleaner (J); concrete fortifier (K) to strengthen concrete; bonding adhesive (L) to prepare the repair area; and concrete sand mix (M) for general repairs and resurfacing.

Tips for Disguising Repairs

Add concrete pigment or liquid cement color to concrete patching compound to create a color that matches the original concrete. Experiment with different mixtures until you find a matching color. Samples should be dry to show the actual colors.

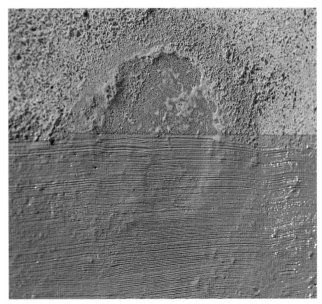

Use masonry paint to cover concrete repairs. Paint can be used on vertical or horizontal surfaces, but high-traffic surfaces will require more frequent touch-up or repainting.

Identifying Problems with Concrete

There are two general types of concrete failure: structural failure, usually resulting from outside forces like freezing water; and surface damage, most often caused by improper finishing techniques or concrete mixtures that do not have the right ratio of water to cement. Surface problems sometimes can be permanently repaired if the correct products and techniques are used. More significant damage can be patched for cosmetic purposes and to resist further damage, but the structure will eventually need to be replaced.

Common Concrete Problems

Sunken concrete is usually caused by erosion of the subbase. Some structures, like sidewalks, can be raised to repair the subbase, then relaid. A more common (and more reliable) solution is to hire a mudjacking contractor to raise the surface by injecting fresh concrete below the surface.

Frost heave is common in colder climates. Frozen ground forces concrete slabs upward, and sections of the slab can pop up. The best solution is to break off and remove the affected section or sections, repair the subbase, and pour new sections that are set off by isolation joints.

Moisture buildup occurs in concrete structures, like foundations and retaining walls, that are in constant ground contact. To identify the moisture source, tape a piece of foil to the wall. If moisture collects on the outer surface of the foil, the source likely is condensation, which can be corrected by installing a dehumidifier. If moisture is not visible on the foil, it is likely seeping through the wall. Consult a professional mason.

Staining can ruin the appearance of a concrete surface or structure. Stains can be removed with commercial-grade concrete cleaner or a variety of other chemicals. For protection against staining, seal masonry surfaces with clear sealant.

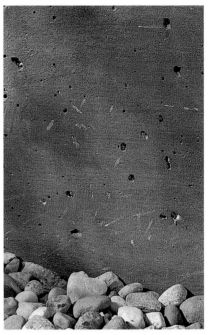

Widespread cracks all the way through the surface, and other forms of substantial damage, are very difficult to repair effectively. If the damage to the concrete is extensive, remove and replace the structure.

Isolated cracks occur on many concrete building projects. Fill small cracks with concrete caulk or crack-filler, and patch large cracks with vinyl-reinforced patching material.

Popouts can be caused by freezing moisture or stress, but very often they occur because the concrete surface was improperly floated or cured, causing the aggregate near the surface of the concrete to loosen. A few scattered popouts do not require attention, but if they are very large or widespread, you can repair them as you would repair holes.

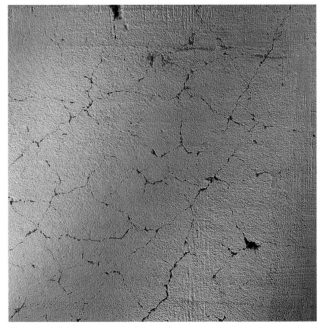

Spalling is surface deterioration of concrete. Spalling is caused by overfloating, which draws too much water to the surface, causing it to weaken and peel off over time. When spalling occurs, it is usually widespread, and the structure may need resurfacing.

Crazing is widespread hairline cracks, usually caused by overfloating or too much portland cement in the concrete. Clean and seal the surface to help prevent further crazing. For a long-term solution, resurface.

Use hydraulic cement or quick-setting cement for repairing holes and chip-outs in vertical surfaces. Because they set up in just a few minutes, these products can be shaped to fill holes without the need for forms. If the structure is exposed constantly to moisture, use hydraulic cement.

Patching Holes

Large and small holes are treated differently when repairing concrete. The best product for filling in smaller holes (less than ½" deep) is vinyl-reinforced concrete patcher. Reinforced repair products should be applied only in layers that are ½" thick or less. For deeper holes, use sand-mix concrete with an acrylic or latex fortifier, which can be applied in layers up to 2" thick.

Patches in concrete will be more effective if you create clean, backward-angled cuts (page 246) around the damaged area, to create a stronger bond. For extensive cutting of damaged concrete, it's best to score the concrete first with a circular saw equipped with a masonry blade. Use a chisel and maul to complete the job.

Everything You Need:

Tools: Trowels, drill with masonry-grinding disc, circular saw with masonry-cutting blade, cold chisel, hand maul, paint brush, screed board, float.

Materials: Scrap lumber, vegetable oil or commercial release agent, hydraulic cement, latex bonding agent, vinyl-reinforced patching compound, sand-mix, concrete fortifier, plastic sheeting.

TIP: You can enhance the appearance of repaired vertical surfaces by painting with waterproof concrete paint once the surface has cured for at least a week. Concrete paint is formulated to resist chalking and efflorescence.

How to Patch Large Areas

1 Mark straight cutting lines around the damaged area, then cut with a circular saw equipped with a masonry-cutting blade. Set the foot of the saw so the cut bevels away from the damage at a 15° angle. Chisel out any remaining concrete within the repair area. TIP: Set the foot of the saw on a thin board to protect it from the concrete.

2 Mix sand-mix concrete with concrete acrylic fortifier, and fill the damaged area slightly above the surrounding surface.

3 Smooth and feather the repair with a float until the repair is even with the surrounding surface. Recreate any surface finish, like brooming, used on the original surface. Cover the repair with plastic and protect from traffic for at least one week.

Caulking Gaps around Masonry

Cracks between a concrete walk and foundation may result in seepage, leading to a wet basement. Repair cracks with caulk-type concrete patcher.

Caulk around the mud sill, the horizontal wooden plate where the house rests on the foundation. This area should be recaulked periodically to prevent heat loss.

How to Patch Small Holes

1 Cut out around the damaged area with a masonry-grinding disc mounted on a portable drill (or use a hammer and stone chisel). The cuts should bevel about 15° away from the center of the damaged area. Chisel out any loose concrete within the repair area. Always wear gloves and eye protection.

2 Apply a thin layer of latex bonding agent. The adhesive will bond with the damaged surface and create a strong bonding surface for the patching compound. Wait until the latex bonding agent is tacky (no more than 30 minutes) before proceeding to the next step.

3 Fill the damaged area with vinyl-reinforced patching compound, applied in ¼ to ½" layers. Wait about 30 minutes between applications. Add layers of the mixture until the compound is packed to just above surface level. Feather the edges smooth, cover the repair with plastic, and protect from traffic for at least one week.

How to Patch Concrete Floors

1 Clean the floor with a vacuum, and remove any loose or flaking concrete with a masonry chisel and hammer. Mix a batch of vinyl floor patching compound following manufacturer's directions. Apply the compound using a smooth trowel, slightly overfilling the cavity. Smooth the patch flush with the surface.

2 After the compound has cured fully, use a floor scraper to scrape the patched areas smooth.

How to Apply Floor Leveler

1 Remove any loose material and clean the concrete thoroughly; the surface must be free of dust, dirt, oils, and paint. Apply an even layer of concrete primer to the entire surface, using a long-nap paint roller. Let the primer dry completely.

2 Following the manufacturer's instructions, mix the floor leveler with water. The batch should be large enough to cover the entire floor area to the desired thickness (up to 1"). Pour the leveler over the floor.

3 Distribute the leveler evenly using a gage rake or spreader. Work quickly: the leveler begins to harden in 15 minutes. You can use a trowel to feather the edges and create a smooth transition with an uncovered area. Let the leveler dry for 24 hours.

Use concrete repair caulk for quick-fix repairs to minor cracks. Although convenient, repair caulk should be viewed only as a short-term solution to improve appearance and help prevent further damage from water penetration.

Filling Cracks

The materials and methods you should use for repairing cracks in concrete depend on the location and size of the crack. For small cracks (less than ¼" wide), you can use gray-tinted concrete caulk for a quick fix. For more permanent solutions, use pourable crack filler or fortified patching cements. The patching cements are polymer compounds that significantly increase the bonding properties of cement, and also allow some flexibility. For larger cracks on horizontal surfaces, use fortified sand-mix concrete; for cracks on vertical surfaces, use hydraulic or quick-setting cement. Thorough preparation of the cracked surface is essential for creating a good bonding surface.

Everything You Need:

Tools: Wire brush, drill with wire wheel attachment, stone chisel, hand maul, paint brush, trowel.

Materials: Latex bonding agent, vinyl-reinforced patching compound, concrete caulk, sand-mix concrete, plastic sheeting.

Tips for Preparing Cracked Concrete for Repair

Clean loose material from the crack using a wire brush, or a portable drill with a wire wheel attachment. Loose material or debris left in the crack will result in a poor bond and an ineffective repair.

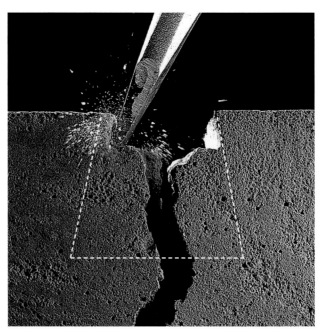

Chisel out the crack to create a backward-angled cut (wider at the base than at the surface), using a stone chisel and hammer. The angled cutout shape prevents the repair material from pushing out of the crack.

How to Repair Small Cracks

1 Prepare the crack for the repair (opposite page), then apply a thin layer of latex bonding agent to the entire repair area, using a paint brush. The latex bonding agent helps keep the repair material from loosening or popping out of the crack.

2 Mix vinyl-reinforced patching compound, and trowel it into the crack. Feather the repair with a trowel, so it is even with the surrounding surface. Cover the surface with plastic and protect it from traffic for at least a week.

Variations for Repairing Large Cracks

Sand

Shown cut away

Horizontal surfaces: Prepare the crack (opposite page), then pour sand into the crack to within ½" of the surface. Prepare sand-mix concrete, adding a concrete fortifier, then trowel the mixture into the crack. Feather until even with the surface, using a trowel.

Vertical surfaces: Prepare the crack (opposite page). Mix vinyl-reinforced concrete or hydraulic cement, then trowel a ¼"- to ½"-thick layer into the crack until the crack is slightly overfilled. Feather the material even with the surrounding surface, then let it dry. If the crack is over ½" deep, trowel in consecutive layers. Let each layer dry before applying another.

(continued next page)

How to Seal Cracks in Concrete Foundation Walls

1 To determine if a foundation crack is stable, you need to monitor it over the course of several months, particularly over the fall and spring seasons. Draw marks across the crack at various points, noting the length as well as its width at the widest gaps. If the crack moves more than $1/16$", consult a building engineer or foundation specialist.

2 To repair a stable crack, use a chisel to cut a keyhole cut that's wider at the base then at the surface, and no more than $1/2$" deep. Clean out the crack with a wire brush.

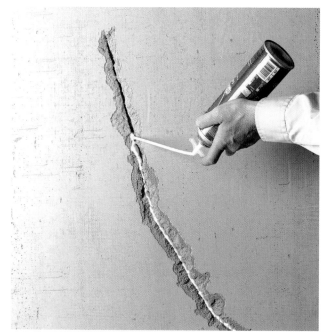

3 To help seal against moisture, fill the crack with expanding insulating foam, working from bottom to top.

4 Mix hydraulic cement according to the manufacturer's instructions, then trowel it into the crack, working from the bottom to top. Apply cement in layers no more than $1/2$" thick, until the patch is slightly higher than the surrounding area. Feather cement with the trowel until it's even with the surface and allow to dry thoroughly.

Damaged concrete steps are an unsightly and unsafe way to welcome visitors to your home. Repairing cracks as they develop not only keeps the steps in a safer and better looking condition, it prolongs their life.

Repairing Steps

Isolated damage to step surfaces, like the deep popout being repaired above, can be fixed to renew your steps. If damage is extensive, you may need to replace the steps.

Steps require more maintenance and repair than other concrete structures around the house because heavy use makes them more susceptible to damage. Horizontal surfaces on steps can be treated using the same products and techniques used on other masonry surfaces. For vertical surfaces, use quick-setting cement, and shape it to fit.

Everything You Need:

Tools: Trowel, wire brush, paint brush, circular saw with masonry-cutting blade, chisel, float, edger.

Materials: Scrap lumber, vegetable oil or commercial release agent, latex bonding agent, vinyl-reinforced patching compound, quick-setting cement, plastic sheeting.

How to Replace a Step Corner

1 Retrieve the broken corner, then clean it and the mating surface with a wire brush. Apply latex bonding agent to both surfaces. If you do not have the broken piece, you can rebuild the corner with patching compound (below).

2 Spread a heavy layer of fortified patching compound on the surfaces to be joined, then press the broken piece into position. Lean a heavy brick or block against the repair until the patching compound sets (about 30 minutes). Cover the repair with plastic and protect it from traffic for at least one week.

How to Patch a Step Corner

1 Clean chipped concrete with a wire brush. Brush the patch area with latex bonding agent.

2 Mix patching compound with latex bonding agent, as directed by the manufacturer. Apply the mixture to the patch area, then smooth the surfaces and round the edges, as necessary, using a flexible knife or trowel.

3 Tape scrap lumber pieces around the patch as a form. Coat the insides with vegetable oil or commercial release agent so the patch won't adhere to the wood. Remove the wood when the patch is firm. Cover with plastic and protect from traffic for at least one week.

How to Patch Step Treads

1 Make a cut in the stair tread just outside the damaged area, using a circular saw with a masonry-cutting blade. Make the cut so it angles toward the back of the step. Make a horizontal cut on the riser below the damaged area, then chisel out the area in between the two cuts.

2 Cut a form board the same height as the step riser. Coat one side of the board with vegetable oil or commercial release agent to prevent it from bonding with the repair, then press it against the riser of the damaged step, and brace it in position with heavy blocks. Make sure the top of the form is flush with the top of the step tread.

3 Apply latex bonding agent to the repair area with a clean paint brush, wait until the bonding agent is tacky (no more than 30 minutes), then press a stiff mixture of quick-setting cement into the damaged area with a trowel.

4 Smooth the concrete with a float, and let it set for a few minutes. Round over the front edge of the nose with an edger. Use a trowel to slice off the sides of the patch, so it is flush with the side of the steps. Cover the repair with plastic and wait a week before allowing traffic on the repaired section.

Concrete slabs that slant toward the house can lead to foundation damage and a wet basement. Even a level slab near the foundation can cause problems. Consider asking a concrete contractor to fix it by mud-jacking, forcing wet concrete underneath the slab to lift the edge near the foundation.

Miscellaneous Concrete Repairs

There are plenty of concrete problems you may encounter around your house that are not specifically addressed in many repair manuals. These miscellaneous repairs include such tasks as patching contoured objects that have been damaged and repairing masonry veneer around the foundation of your house. You can adapt basic techniques to make just about any type of concrete repair. Remember to dampen concrete surfaces before patching so that the moisture from concrete and other patching compounds is not absorbed into the existing surface. Be sure to follow the manufacturer's directions for the repair products you use.

Everything You Need:

Tools: Putty knife, trowel, hand maul, chisel, wire brush, aviation snips, drill, soft-bristle brush.

Materials: Quick-setting cement, emery paper, wire lath, masonry anchors, concrete acrylic fortifier, sand-mix.

How to Repair Shaped Concrete

1 Scrape all loose material and debris from the damaged area, then wipe down with water. Mix quick-setting cement and trowel it into the area. Work quickly—you only have a few minutes before concrete sets up.

2 Use the trowel or a putty knife to mold the concrete to follow the form of the object being repaired. Smooth the concrete as soon as it sets up. Buff with emery paper to smooth out any ridges after the repair dries.

How to Repair Masonry Veneer

1 Chip off the crumbled, loose, or deteriorated veneer from the wall, using a cold chisel and maul. Chisel away damaged veneer until you have only good, solid surface remaining. Use care to avoid damaging the wall behind the veneer. Clean the repair area with a wire brush.

2 Clean up any metal lath in the repair area if it is in good condition. If not, cut it out with aviation snips. Add new lath where needed, using masonry anchors to hold it to the wall.

3 Mix fortified sand-mix concrete (or specialty concrete blends for wall repair), and trowel it over the lath until it is even with the surrounding surfaces.

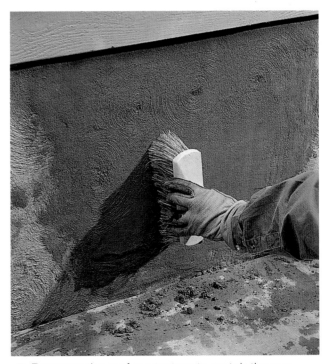

4 Recreate the surface texture to match the surrounding area. For our project, we used a soft-bristled brush to stipple the surface. To blend in the repair, add pigment to the sand mixture or paint the repair area after it dries.

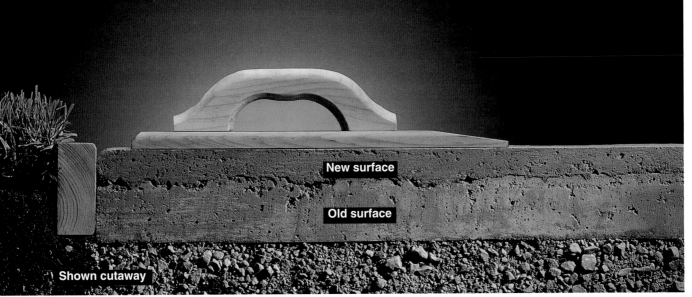

New surface

Old surface

Shown cutaway

Resurface concrete that has surface damage, such as spalling or popouts. Because the new surface will be thin (1" to 2"), use sand-mix concrete. If you are having ready-mix concrete delivered by a concrete contractor, make sure they do not use aggregate larger than ½" in the mixture.

Resurfacing a Concrete Walkway

Concrete that has surface damage but is still structurally sound can be preserved by resurfacing—applying a thin layer of new concrete over the old surface. If the old surface has deep cracks or extensive damage, resurfacing will only solve the problem temporarily. Because new concrete will bond better if it is packed down, use a dry, stiff concrete mixture that can be compacted with a shovel.

Everything You Need:

Tools: Shovel, wood float, broom, circular saw, maul, drill, paint brush, paint roller and tray, wheelbarrow, screed board, groover, edger, hose, bricklayer's trowel, jointer, rubber mallet, level, mortar bag.

Materials: Stakes, 2 × 4 lumber, vegetable oil or commercial release agent, 4" wall-board screws, sand-mix concrete, bonding adhesive, plastic sheets, brick pavers, Type N mortar.

How to Resurface Using Fresh Concrete

1 Clean the surface thoroughly. If the surface is flaking or spalled, scrape it with a spade to dislodge as much loose concrete as you can, then sweep the surface clean.

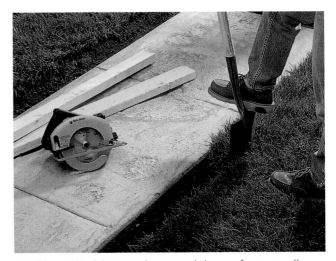

2 Dig a 6"-wide trench around the surface on all sides to create room for 2 × 4 forms.

3 Stake 2 × 4 forms flush against the sides of the concrete slabs, 1" to 2" above the surface (make sure height is even). Drive stakes every 3 ft. and at every joint in forms. Mark control joint locations onto the outside of the forms directly above existing control joints. Coat the inside edges of the forms with vegetable oil or commercial release agent.

4 Apply a thin layer of bonding adhesive over the entire surface. Follow the directions on the bonding adhesive product carefully. Instructions for similar products may differ slightly.

5 Mix concrete, using sand-mix concrete. Make the mixture slightly stiffer (drier) than normal concrete. Spread the concrete, then press down on the concrete with a shovel or 2 × 4 to pack the mixture into the forms. Smooth the surface with a screed board.

6 Float the concrete with a wood float, then tool with an edger, and cut control joints (page 52) in the original locations. Recreate any surface treatment, such as brooming, used on the original surface. Let the surface cure for one week, covered with plastic. Seal the concrete.

Sealing Interior Concrete Floors

Concrete is a versatile building material. Most people are accustomed to thinking of concrete primarily as a utilitarian substance, but it can also mimic a variety of flooring types and be a colorful and beautiful addition to any room.

Whether your concrete floor is a practical surface for the garage or an artistic statement of personal style in your dining room, it should be sealed. Concrete is a hard and durable building material, but it is also porous. Consequently, concrete floors are susceptible to staining. Many stains can be removed with the proper cleaner, but sealing and painting prevents oil, grease, and other stains from penetrating the surface in the first place; thus, cleanup is considerably easier.

Prepare the concrete for sealer application by acid etching. Etching opens the pores in concrete surfaces, allowing sealers to bond with it. All smooth or dense concrete surfaces, such as garage floors, should be etched before applying stain. The surface should feel gritty, like 120-grit sandpaper, and allow water to penetrate it. If you're not sure whether your floor needs to be etched or not, it's better to etch. If you don't etch when it is needed, you will have to remove the sealer residue before trying again.

Everything You Need

Tools: Garden hose or pressure washer (for outdoors and garages only), stiff bristle broom, acid-tolerant bucket, sprinkling can or acid-tolerant pump spray, 4-in.-wide synthetic bristle paint brush, paint tray, soft-woven roller cover with ½" nap, long-handle paint roller, wet/dry shop vacuum.

Materials: Long pants and long-sleeve shirt, rubber boots, rubber gloves, safety goggles, chlorine respirator, acid etcher, alkaline-base neutralizer (ammonia, gardener's lime, baking soda, or Simple Green cleaning solution), concrete sealer.

Tips for Acid Etching Concrete Floors

A variety of acid etching products is available:
Citric acid is a biodegradable acid that does not produce chlorine fumes. It is the safest etcher and the easiest to use, but it may not be strong enough for some very smooth concretes. Sulfamic acid is less aggressive than phosphoric acid or muriatic acid, and it is perhaps the best compromise between strength of solution and safety. Phosphoric acid is a stronger and more noxious acid than the previous two, but it is considerably less dangerous than muriatic acid. It is currently the most popular etching choice. Muriatic acid (hydrochloric acid) is an extremely dangerous acid that quickly reacts and creates very strong fumes. This is an etching solution of last resort. It should only be used by professionals or by the most serious DIYers. Never add water to acid—only add acid to water.

Acids of any kind are dangerous. Use caution when working with acid etches; it is critical that there be adequate ventilation and that you wear protective clothing, including: safety goggles, rubber gloves, rubber boots, long pants and a long-sleeve shirt. In addition, wear a chlorine respirator—the reaction of any base and acid can release chlorine or hydrogen gas.

Even after degreasing a concrete floor, residual grease or oils can create serious adhesion problems for coatings of sealant or paint. To check whether your floor has been adequately cleaned, pour a glass of water on to the floor. If it is ready for sealing, the water will soak into the surface quickly and evenly. If the water beads, clean the floor again.

How to Acid Etch a Concrete Floor

1 Clean and prepare the surface by first sweeping up all debris. Next, remove all surface muck: mud, wax, and grease. Finally, remove existing paints or coatings.

2 Saturate the surface with clean water. The surface needs to be wet before acid etching. Use this opportunity to check for any areas where water beads up. If water beads on the surface, contaminants still need to be cleaned off with a suitable cleaner or chemical stripper.

3 Test your acid-tolerant pump sprayer with water to make sure it releases a wide, even mist. Once you have the spray nozzle set, check the manufacturer's instructions for the etching solution and fill the pump sprayer with the recommended amount of water.

4 Add the acid etching contents to the water in the acid-tolerant pump sprayer (or sprinkling can). Follow the directions (and mixing proportions) specified by the manufacturer. Use caution.

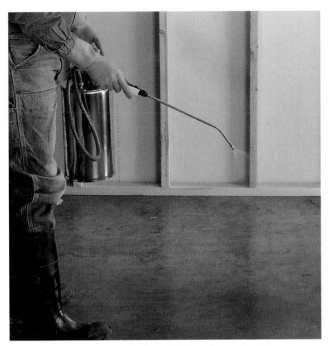

5 Apply the acid solution. Using the sprinkling can or acid-tolerant pump spray unit, evenly apply the diluted acid solution over the concrete floor. Do not allow acid solution to dry at any time during the etching and cleaning process. Etch small areas at a time, 10 × 10 ft. or smaller. If there is a slope, begin on the low side of the slope and work upward.

6 Use a stiff bristle broom or scrubber to work the acid solution into the concrete. Let the acid sit for 5–10 minutes, or as indicated by the manufacturer's directions. A mild foaming action indicates that the product is working. If no bubbling or fizzing occurs, stop the process and re-clean the surface thoroughly.

7 When the fizzing stops, the acid has finished reacting with the alkaline concrete surface. Neutralize any remaining acid by adding a gallon of water to a 5-gallon bucket and then stirring in an alkaline-base neutralizer (options include 1 cup ammonia, 4 cups gardener's lime, a full box of baking soda, or 4 oz. of "Simple Green" cleaning solution).

8 Use a stiff bristle broom to distribute the neutralizing solution over the entire floor area. Sweep the water around until the fizzing stops and then spray the surface with a hose to rinse it.

(continued next page)

9 Use a wet-dry shop vacuum to clean up the rinse water. Although the acid is neutralized, it's a good idea to check your local regulations regarding proper disposal of the neutralized spent acid.

10 When the floor dries, check for residue by rubbing a dark cloth over a small area of concrete. If any white residue appears, continue the rinsing process. Check for residue again. An inadequate acid rinse is even worse than not acid etching at all when it's time to add the sealant.

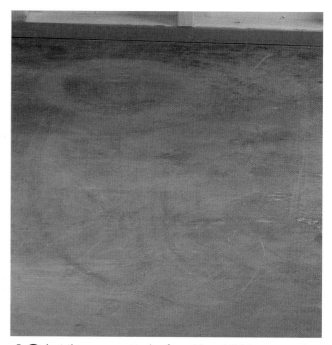

11 If you have any leftover acid you can make it safe for your disposal system by mixing more alkaline solution in the 5-gallon bucket and carefully pouring the acid from the spray unit into the bucket until all of the fizzing stops.

12 Let the concrete dry for at least 24 hours and sweep it thoroughly. The concrete should now have the texture of 120-grit sandpaper and be able to accept concrete sealant. Mask any exposed sill plates or base trim before sealing.

How to Seal a Concrete Floor

 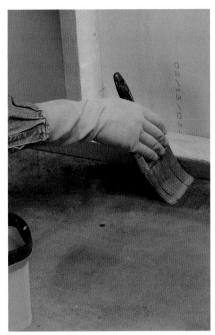 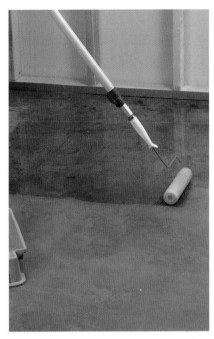

1 Etch, clean, and dry concrete. Mix the sealer in a bucket with a stir stick. Lay painter's tape down for a testing patch. Apply sealer to this area and allow to dry to ensure desired appearance. NOTE: Because concrete sealers tend to make the surface slick when wet, add an anti-skid additive to aid with traction, especially on stairs.

2 Use wide painter's tape to protect walls and then, using a good quality 4"-wide synthetic bristle paintbrush, coat the perimeter with sealer.

3 Use a long-handled paint roller with a ½" nap to apply an even coat to the rest of the surface. Do small sections at a time (about 2 × 3 feet). Work in one orientation. Avoid lap marks by always maintaining a wet edge. Do not work the area once the coating has partially dried; this could cause it to lift from the surface. Allow surface to dry according to the manufacturer's instructions, usually 8 to 12 hours.

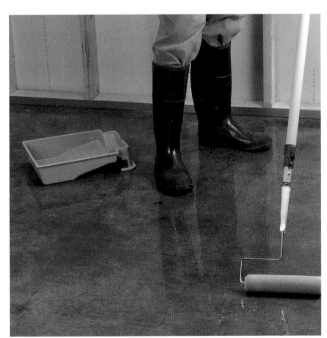 

4 After the first coat has dried, apply the second coat at an orientation 90° from the first coat.

5 Clean tools according to manufacturer's directions.

Epoxy Coatings

An epoxy coating applied to a concrete floor creates an attractive, durable surface that helps protect against chipping and abrasion, staining from gasoline, oil, and water, and also makes cleanup easier. Epoxy coatings are available in limited colors, though most kits contain paint flakes to create a decorative finish.

Surface preparation is critical for epoxy adhesion. Repair any holes, cracks or spalling (pages 238 to 253), and then thoroughly clean using the concrete cleaner provided in the kit, or following the cleaning instructions on page 254. NOTE: Acid etching is not necessary for epoxy coatings.

Do not apply epoxy if concrete already contains a sealer (see "water-bead test" on page 257), or if the moisture content is high (see "moisture test" on page 277). If the floor is painted, test the bond by cutting an "X" through the coat down to the concrete, applying a strip of duct tape over the "X", then quickly ripping away the tape. If more than 25-percent of the paint is removed, you must sand and strip before applying the epoxy. Otherwise, simply scuff the paint coat with sandpaper to ensure a strong bond with the epoxy. New concrete surfaces must cure for a minimum of 30 days. Refer to the manufacturer's instructions for additional installation recommendations.

Everything You Need:

Tools: Razor blade, duct tape, 4" synthetic bristle brush, paint tray, paint roller cover with ½" nap, long-handle paint roller, long pants and long-sleeve shirt, safety goggles.

Materials: Concrete cleaner, epoxy concrete floor coating kit (containing two-part epoxy and paint flakes).

How to Apply an Epoxy Coating

1 After thoroughly cleaning the floor, mix the epoxy by pouring all of part A into part B, then stirring for a few minutes. Allow the mixture to stand for 30 minutes under normal conditions (60°-70°F). See manufacturer's recommendations for other conditions. NOTE: Do not add decorative paint flakes to mixture.

2 After 30 minutes, begin painting along the perimeter using a 4" synthetic bristle brush. Work quickly, the epoxy must be applied in accordance with the manufacturer's pot time, typically two hours under normal conditions.

3 After perimeter painting, begin applying an even coat of epoxy to the floor surface, using a paint roller with $\frac{1}{2}$" nap and an extension pole. Work in manageable 4 foot × 4 foot sections. Maintain a wet edge around each section to prevent lap marks.

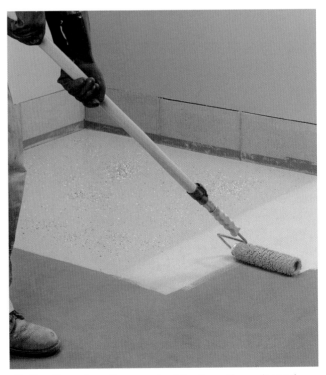

4 After the section is completed, broadcast, or toss, the decorative paint flakes onto the wet epoxy surface in an even, random pattern. Epoxy can be rolled over loose flakes that fall outside of the wet section.

5 Continue to roll epoxy in 4 foot sections, broadcasting the paint flakes as you work. Once the entire surface is covered, allow epoxy to dry at least 24 hours before walking on it, and a minimum of seven days before driving on it. Clean all tools using warm water and mild detergent.

Choose the best materials and techniques for repairing problems with brick and block structures. A simple chip or popout, like the one shown above, can be fixed easily by packing the damaged area with latex-fortified mortar. More extensive problems require more complicated solutions.

Repairing Brick & Block

Brick, block, and mortar are very durable building materials. But when they are combined in a permanent structure, stress and the forces of nature can lead to damage that requires attention. Common examples of brick and block structural problems include walls with failing mortar joints, cracked or crumbling bricks or blocks, and worn or discolored surfaces.

Many common brick and block problems can be corrected with simple repairs. These require just a few basic masonry tools (opposite page) and a minimal investment of time and money. The completed repair job will result in a dramatic im-

provement in the appearance and strength of the structure. With regular maintenance and cleaning, repaired structures will provide many years of productive use.

Brick and block are used frequently in the construction of foundation walls, retaining walls, and other load-bearing structures. Simple repairs, like filling cracks, can be done with little risk. Always get a professional evaluation from a masonry contractor before attempting major repairs to brick and block structures. Review the basic techniques for working with brick and block before starting your project.

Tools for Repairing Brick & Block Structures

Basic tools for repairing brick and block include: a masonry chisel (A) for cutting new brick or block, stone chisel (B) for breaking up and repairing masonry structures, raking tool (C) for cleaning mortar out of joints, mason's trowel (D) for applying mortar to concrete block, pointing trowel (E) for applying mortar to brick or block and for smoothing out fresh repairs, mason's hammer (F), ½"-wide (G) and ⅜"-wide (H) jointing tools for packing fresh mortar into joints, and jointer (I) for finishing mortar joints.

Tips for Working with Mortar

Add concrete fortifier to mortar for making repairs. Fortifier, usually acrylic or latex based, increases the mortar's strength and its ability to bond.

Add mortar tint to plain mortar so repairs blend in. Compare tint samples, available from concrete products suppliers, to match mortar colors.

Identifying Brick & Block Problems

Inspect damaged brick and block structures closely before you begin any repair work. Accurately identifying the nature and cause of the damage is an important step before choosing the best solution for the problem.

Look for obvious clues, like overgrown tree roots, or damaged gutters that let water drain onto masonry surfaces. Also check the slope of the adjacent landscape; it may need to be regraded to direct water away from a brick or block wall.

Repairs fail when the original source of the problem is not eliminated prior to making the repair. When a concrete patch separates, for example, it means that the opposing stresses causing the crack are still at work on the structure. Find and correct the cause (often a failing subbase or stress from water or freezing and thawing), then redo the repair.

Types of Brick & Block Problems

Deteriorated mortar joints are common problems in brick and block structures—mortar is softer than most bricks or blocks and is more prone to damage. Deterioration is not always visible, so probe surrounding joints with a screwdriver to see if they are sound.

Major structural damage, like the damage to this brick porch, usually requires removal of the existing structure, improvements to the subbase, and reconstruction of the structure. Projects of this nature should only be attempted by professional masons.

Damage to concrete blocks often results from repeated freezing and thawing of moisture trapped in the wall or in the blocks themselves. Instead of replacing the whole block, chip out the face of the block and replacing it with a concrete paver with the same dimensions as the face of the block (pages 272 to 273).

Spalling occurs when freezing water or other forces cause enough directional pressure to fracture a brick. The best solution is to replace the entire brick (pages 270 to 271) while eliminating the source of the pressure, if possible. TIP: Chip off a piece of the damaged brick to use as a color reference when looking for a replacement.

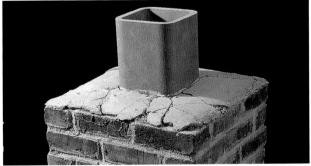

Damaged mortar caps on chimneys allow water into the flue area, where it can damage the chimney and even the roof or interior walls. Small-scale damage (top photo) can be patched with fire-rated silicone caulk. If damage is extensive (bottom photo), repair or replace the mortar cap (page 278).

Stains and discoloration can be caused by external sources or by minerals leeching to the surface from within the brick or block (called efflorescence). If the stain does not wash away easily with water, use a cleaning solution.

Before

After

Make timely repairs to brick and block structures. Tuck-pointing deteriorated mortar joints is a common repair that, like other types of repair, improves the appearance of the structure or surface and helps prevent further damage.

Repairing Brick & Block Walls

The most common brick and block wall repair is tuck-pointing, the process of replacing failed mortar joints with fresh mortar. Tuck-pointing is a highly useful repair technique for any home-owner. It can be used to repair walls, chimneys, brick veneer, or any other structure where the bricks or blocks are bonded with mortar.

Minor cosmetic repairs can be attempted on any type of wall, from free-standing garden walls to block foundations. Filling minor cracks with caulk or repair compound, and patching popouts or chips are good examples of minor repairs. Consult a professional before attempting any major repairs, like replacing brick or blocks, or rebuilding a structure—especially if you are dealing with a load-bearing structure.

Basement walls are a frequent trouble area for homeowners. Constant moisture and stress created by ground contact can cause leaks, bowing, and paint failure. Small leaks and cracks can be patched with hydraulic cement.

Masonry-based waterproofing products can be applied to give deteriorated walls a fresh ap-pearance. Persistent moisture problems are most often caused by improper grading of soil around the foundation or a malfunctioning down-spout and gutter system.

NOTE: The repairs shown in this section feature brick and block walls. The same techniques may be used for other brick and block structures.

Everything You Need:

Tools: Raking tool, mortar hawk, tuck-pointer, jointing tool, bricklayer's hammer, mason's trowel, mason's or stone chisel, pointing trowel, drill with masonry disc and bit, stiff-bristle brush.

Materials: Mortar, gravel, scrap of metal flash-ing, concrete fortifier, replacement bricks or blocks.

How to Tuck-point Mortar Joints

1 Clean out loose or deteriorated mortar to a depth of ¼" to ¾". Use a mortar raking tool (top) first, then switch to a masonry chisel and a hammer (bottom) if the mortar is stubborn. Clear away all loose debris, and dampen the surface with water before applying fresh mortar.

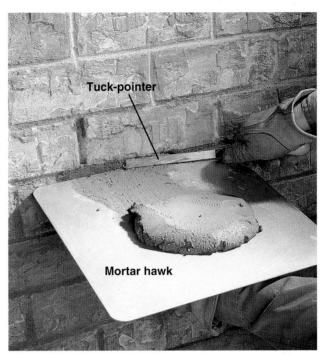

Tuck-pointer

Mortar hawk

2 Mix the mortar, adding concrete fortifier; add tint if necessary. Load mortar onto a mortar hawk, then push it into the horizontal joints with a tuck-pointer. Apply mortar in ¼"-thick layers, and let each layer dry for 30 minutes before applying another. Fill the joints until the mortar is flush with the face of the brick or block.

3 Apply the first layer of mortar into the vertical joints by scooping mortar onto the back of a tuck-pointer, and pressing it into the joint. Work from the top downward.

4 After the final layer of mortar is applied, smooth the joints with a jointing tool that matches the profile of the old mortar joints. Tool the horizontal joints first. Let the mortar dry until it is crumbly, then brush off the excess mortar with a stiff-bristle brush.

How to Replace a Damaged Brick

1 Score the damaged brick so it will break apart more easily for removal: use a drill with a masonry-cutting disc to score lines along the surface of the brick and in the mortar joints surrounding the brick.

2 Use a mason's chisel and hammer to break apart the damaged brick along the scored lines. Rap sharply on the chisel with the hammer, being careful not to damage surrounding bricks. TIP: Save fragments to use as a color reference when you shop for replacement bricks.

3 Chisel out any remaining mortar in the cavity, then brush out debris with a stiff-bristle or wire brush to create a clean surface for the new mortar. Rinse the surface of the repair area with water.

4 Mix the mortar for the repair, adding concrete fortifier to the mixture, and tint if needed to match old mortar. Use a pointing trowel to apply a 1"-thick layer of mortar at the bottom and sides of the cavity.

5 Dampen the replacement brick slightly, then apply mortar to the ends and top of the brick. Fit the brick into the cavity and rap it with the handle of the trowel until the face is flush with the surrounding bricks. If needed, press additional mortar into the joints with a pointing trowel.

6 Scrape away excess mortar with a masonry trowel, then smooth the joints with a jointing tool that matches the profile of the surrounding mortar joints. Let the mortar set until crumbly, then brush the joints to remove excess mortar.

Tips for Removing & Replacing Several Bricks

For walls with extensive damage, remove bricks from the top down, one row at a time, until the entire damaged area is removed. Replace bricks using the techniques shown above and in the section on building with brick and block. CAUTION: Do not dismantle load-bearing brick structures like foundation walls—consult a professional mason for these repairs.

For walls with internal damaged areas, remove only the damaged section, keeping the upper layers intact if they are in good condition. Do not remove more than four adjacent bricks in one area—if the damaged area is larger, it will require temporary support, which is a job for a professional mason.

How to Reface a Damaged Concrete Block

1 Drill several holes into the face of the deteriorated block at the cores (hollow spots) of the block using a drill and masonry bit. Wear protective eye covering when drilling or breaking apart concrete.

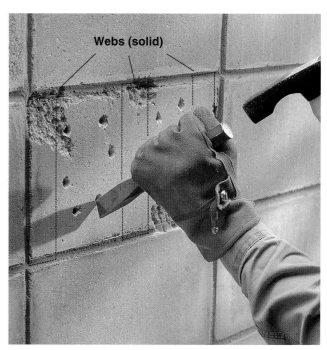

2 Using the holes as starting points, chip away the face of the block over the core areas, using a chisel and hammer. Be careful not to damage surrounding blocks and try to leave the block face intact in front of the solid web areas.

3 Use a stone chisel to carefully chip out a 2"-deep recess in the web areas. Mark and score cutting lines 2" back from the block face, then chisel away the block in the recess area. Avoid deepening the recess more than 2" because the remaining web sections provide a bonding surface for the concrete paver that will be installed to replace the face of the concrete block.

4 Mix mortar (page 114), then apply a 1"-thick layer to the sides and bottom of the opening, to the webs, and to the top edge and web locations on the paver (use an 8 × 16" paver to fit standard blocks). Press the paver into the cavity, flush with the surrounding blocks. Add mortar to the joints if needed, then prop a 2 × 4 against the paver until the mortar sets. Finish the joints with a jointing tool.

How to Reinforce a Section of Refaced Blocks

1 Reinforce repair areas spanning two or more adjacent block faces. Start by drilling a few holes in a small area over a core in the block located directly above the repair area. Chip out the block face between the holes with a cold chisel.

2 Prepare a thin mortar mix made from 1 part gravel and 2 parts dry mortar, then add water. The mixture should be thin enough to pour easily, but not soupy. NOTE: Adding small amounts of gravel increases the strength of the mortar and increases the yield of the batch.

3 Pour the mortar/gravel mixture into the hole above the repair area, using a piece of metal flashing as a funnel. Continue mixing and filling the hole until it will not accept any more mortar. The mortar will dry to form a reinforcing column that is bonded to the backs of the pavers used to reface the blocks.

4 Patch the hole above the repair area by using a pointing trowel to fill the hole with plain mortar mix. Smooth the surface with the pointing trowel. When the mortar resists finger pressure, finish the joint below the patch with a jointing tool.

Cleaning & Painting Brick & Block

Use a pressure washer to clean large brick and block structures. Pressure washers can be rented from most rental centers. Be sure to obtain detailed operating and safety instructions from the rental agent.

Solvent Solutions for Common Brick & Block Blemishes

• **Egg splatter:** Dissolve oxalic acid crystals in water, following manufacturer's instructions, in a nonmetallic container. Brush onto the surface.

• **Efflorescence:** Scrub surface with a stiff-bristled brush. Use a household cleaning solution for surfaces with heavy accumulation.

• **Iron stains:** Spray or brush a solution of oxalic acid crystals dissolved in water, following manufacturer's instructions. Apply directly to the stain.

• **Ivy:** Cut vines away from the surface (do not pull them off). Let remaining stems dry up, then scrub them off with a stiff-bristled brush and household cleaning solution.

• **Oil:** Apply a paste made of mineral spirits and an inert material like sawdust.

• **Paint stains:** Remove new paint with a solution of tri-sodium phosphate (TSP) and water, following manufacturer's mixing instructions. Old paint can usually be removed with heavy scrubbing or sandblasting.

• **Plant growth:** Use weed killer according to manufacturer's directions.

• **Smoke stains:** Scrub surface with household cleanser containing bleach, or use a mixture of ammonia and water.

Check brick and block surfaces annually and remove stains or discoloration. Most problems are easy to correct if they are treated in a timely fashion. Regular maintenance will help brick and block structures remain attractive and durable for a long time. Refer to the information below for cleaning tips that address specific staining problems.

Painted brick and block structures can be spruced up by applying a fresh coat of paint. As with any other painting job, thorough surface preparation and a quality primer are critical to a successful outcome.

Many stains can be removed easily, using a commercial brick and block detergent, available at home centers, but remember:

• Always test cleaning solutions on a small inconspicuous part of the surface and evaluate the results.

• Some chemicals and their fumes may be harmful. Be sure to follow manufacturer's safety and use recommendations. Wear protective clothing.

• Soak the surface to be cleaned with water before you apply any solutions. This keeps solutions from soaking in too quickly. Rinse the surface thoroughly after cleaning to wash off any remaining cleaning solution.

Tips for Cleaning Brick & Block Surfaces

Mix a paste made from cleaning solvents (chart, opposite page) and talcum or flour. Apply paste directly to stain, let it dry, then scrape it off with a vinyl or plastic scraper.

Use a nylon scraper or a thin block of wood to remove spilled mortar that has hardened. Avoid using metal scrapers, which can damage masonry surfaces.

Mask off windows, siding, decorative millwork, and other exposed nonmasonry surfaces before cleaning brick and block. Careful masking is essential if you are using harsh cleaning chemicals, such as muriatic acid.

Tips for Painting Masonry

Clean mortar joints, using a drill with a wire wheel attachment before applying paint. Scrub off loose paint, dirt, mildew, and mineral deposits so the paint will bond better.

Apply masonry primer before repainting brick or block walls. Primer helps eliminate stains and prevent problems such as efflorescence.

Ninety-five percent of wet basement problems occur because water pools near the foundation. The cause is usually failing roof gutters and downspouts or an improperly graded yard. The soil around your house should slope away from the foundation at a rate of ¾" per foot. Before tackling symptoms such as wet basement walls, it's important to repair moisture problems at their source.

Protecting Basement Walls

Failing gutters, broken or leaking pipes, condensation, and seepage are the most common causes of basement moisture. If allowed to persist, dampness can cause major damage to concrete basement walls. There are several effective ways to seal and protect the walls. If condensation is the source of the problem, check first that your clothes dryer is properly vented, and install a dehumidifier. If water is seeping in through small cracks or holes in the walls, repair damaged gutters and leaky pipes, and check the grade of the soil around your foundation. Once you've addressed the problem at its source, create a water-proof seal over openings in the basement walls. To stop occasional seepage, coat the walls with masonry sealer. For more frequent seepage, seal the openings and resurface the walls with a water-resistant masonry coating. Heavy-duty coatings, such as surface bonding cement (opposite page) are best for very damp conditions. Thinner brush-on coatings are also available. For chronic seepage, ask a contractor to install a baseboard gutter and drain system. REMEMBER: To prevent long-term damage, it's necessary to identify the source of the moisture and make repairs both inside and outside your home, so moisture no longer penetrates foundation walls.

Everything You Need:

Tools: Wire brush, heavy-duty stirrer, stiff-bristle paintbrush, sponge, square-end trowel, scratching tool.

Materials: Household cleaner, waterproof masonry sealer, water-resistant masonry coating, aluminum foil, duct tape.

Tips for Inspecting & Sealing Basement Walls

Paint that is peeling off basement walls usually indicates water seepage from outside that is trapped between the walls and the paint.

Tape a square of aluminum foil to a masonry wall to identify high moisture levels. Check the foil after 24 hours. Beads of water on top of the foil indicate high humidity in the room. Beads of water underneath suggest water seepage through the wall from outside.

To control minor seepage through porous masonry, seal walls with a masonry sealer. Clean the walls and prepare the sealer, according to manufacturer's instructions. Apply sealer to the walls, including all masonry joints.

How to Damp-proof Masonry Walls

1 Resurface heavily cracked masonry walls with a water-resistant masonry coating, such as surface bonding cement. Clean and dampen the walls, according to the coating manufacturer's instructions, then fill large cracks and holes with the coating. Finally, plaster a ¼" layer of the coating on the walls, using a square-end trowel. Specially formulated heavy-duty masonry coatings are available for very damp conditions.

2 Let the coating set up for several hours, then scratch the surface with a paint brush cleaner or a homemade scratching too. After 24 hours, apply a second, smooth coat. Mist the wall twice a day for three days as the coating cures.

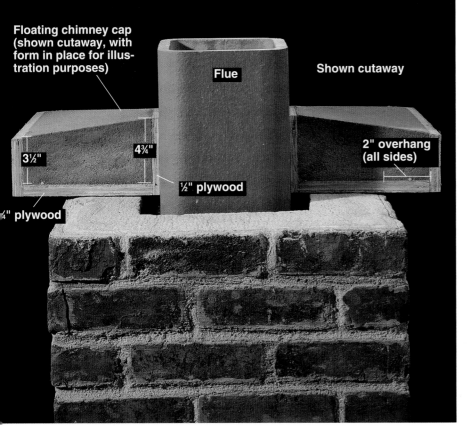

Floating chimney cap (shown cutaway, with form in place for illustration purposes)

Flue

Shown cutaway

3½"

4¾"

½" plywood

¾" plywood

2" overhang (all sides)

A chimney cap expands and shrinks as temperatures change inside and outside the chimney. This often results in cracking and annual treks up to the roof for repairs. A floating chimney cap (above) is cast in a form, using mortar or sand-mix concrete, then placed on the top of the chimney (opposite page). You can repair a damaged cap by chipping off the deteriorated sections and adding fresh mortar (below).

Repairing & Replacing Chimney Caps

Chimney caps undergo stress because the temperatures of the cap and chimney flue fluctuate dramatically. Use fire-rated silicone caulk to patch minor cracks. For more extensive repairs, reapply fresh mortar over the cap, or replace the old cap for a permanent solution.

Everything You Need:

Tools: Hammer, stone chisel, wire brush, drill, float, pointing trowel, tape measure, caulk gun.

Materials: Mortar, concrete fortifier, ½" and ¾" plywood, ¼" dowel, 1½" wood screws, vegetable oil or a commercial release agent, fire-rated silicone caulk, fire-rated rope or mineral wool.

How to Repair a Chimney Cap

1 Carefully break apart and remove the deteriorated sections of the chimney cap, using a stone chisel and hammer. Be very careful when chiseling around the flue.

2 Mix a batch of latex-fortified mortar. Trowel an even layer of mortar all the way around the chimney cap, following the slope of the existing cap. Mortar should cover the chimney from the outside edges of the chimney bricks to the flue. Smooth out the mortar with a wood float, trying to recreate the original slope of the chimney cap. Inspect mortar annually.

How to Cast & Install a Replacement Chimney Cap

1 Measure the chimney and the chimney flue and build a form from ½" and ¾" plywood (form dimensions on opposite page, top). Attach the form to a plywood base, using 1½" wood screws to connect all form parts. Glue ⅜" dowels to the base, 1" inside the form. The dowels will cast a drip edge into the cap. Coat the inside of the form with vegetable oil or a commercial release agent.

2 Prepare a stiff (dry) mixture of mortar to cast the cap—for average-sized chimneys, two 60-lb. bags of dry mix should yield enough mortar. Fill the form with mortar. Rest a wood float across the edges of the form, and smooth the mortar. Keep angles sharp at the corners. Let the cap cure for at least a week, then carefully disassemble the form.

3 Chip off the old mortar cap completely, and clean the top of the chimney with a wire brush. With a helper, transport the chimney cap onto the roof and set it directly onto the chimney, centered so the overhang is equal on all sides. For the new cap to function properly, do not bond it to the chimney or the flue.

4 Shift the cap so the gap next to the flue is even on all sides, then fill in the gap with fire-rated rope or mineral wool. Caulk over the fill material with a very heavy bead of fire-rated silicone caulk. Also caulk the joint at the underside of the cap. Inspect caulk every other year, and refresh as needed.

A masonry fireplace is a treasured feature in many homes. Most fireplaces are constructed with several different materials, including two or more types of brick and mortar, concrete, concrete block, metal, and fireclay. Routine maintenance is essential to the efficiency and longevity of your fireplace, as well as to the safety of your home.

Repairing a Firebox

Masonry fireplaces are built according to strict specifications designed to maximize heating efficiency, smoke exhaustion, and above all, safety. The internal chamber where the fire burns, known as the *firebox*, is made with heat-resistant firebrick and a special mortar that can withstand extremely high temperatures. For added heat resistance, mortar joints in firebrick construction are smaller than with other types of brick, usually $\frac{1}{16}$" to $\frac{1}{4}$" thick.

The firebox reflects the fire's heat into the room, and it insulates the surrounding structure from the high temperatures that can cause damage. Therefore, in addition to having your fireplace and chimney inspected and cleaned regularly, it's a good idea to check the firebox for crumbling mortar joints and loose, cracked, or chipped bricks.

Signs of severe damage or wear in the firebox may indicate serious problems elsewhere in the fireplace or chimney and should be reported to a professional. But you can fix most minor problems yourself, provided you use only materials rated for fireplaces. Some refractory mortars are sold premixed so it is not necessary to add water. Whichever product you select, make sure it is rated for use with fire brick.

Everything You Need:

Tools: Shop light, mirror, flashlight, stiff-bristle brush, sponge, screwdriver, masonry or stone chisel, mason's trowel, jointing tool.

Materials: Fireplace cleaner, firebrick, refractory mortar.

How to Inspect & Repair a Firebox

1 Begin your inspection by cleaning the fireplace thoroughly. If the bricks and mortar joints are not clearly visible, use a fireplace cleaner and a stiff-bristle brush to remove the soot and creosote buildup. Use a shop light and mirror to view the upper areas of the firebox and the damper opening.

2 Using a flashlight, inspect the bricks and mortar in the firebox. Check for loose mortar by lightly scraping the joints with a screwdriver. Look for cracks and feel around for any loose bricks.

3 Remove any loose or damaged bricks, and scrape off the old mortar, using a masonry or stone chisel. Clean the edges of the surrounding brick with a stiff-bristle brush. If you need replacement bricks, bring an original one to a fireplace or brick supplier to be sure you get a perfect match.

4 Apply refractory mortar to the new bricks, following the mortar manufacturer's directions. Gently slide the bricks into place until they are flush with the surrounding bricks. Scrape off excess mortar with a trowel. Use a jointing tool to tool the mortar joints.

Repairing Sand-set Pavers

Successive cycles of freezing and thawing can cause the ground to shift, heaving the bricks in your patio. If this happens, you'll need to remove the displaced bricks and create a level surface underneath. These steps can also be used to repair a brick walkway or replace damaged brick pavers.

Once the bricks are set, fill the joints with sand. Spread a thin layer of sand over the repair area, working it into the joints between the bricks. Sweep up the loose sand, then spray the repair area with water to settle the sand in the joints. If necessary, spread and pack sand over the repair area again, until all of the joints are tightly packed.

Everything You Need:

Tools: Pry bar, garden rake, hand tamper, rubber mallet, 4-ft. level, broom.

Materials: Replacement brick pavers (if necessary), sand.

How to Replace a Paver

1 Remove any pavers that are dislodged, uneven or broken, using a pry bar.

2 Add or remove sand as necessary so the base is level with the surrounding sand. Smooth the sand with a garden rake. Water the sand thoroughly, then pack it down with a hand tamper. Reinstall the bricks, laying them tight against each other.

3 To set the bricks, tap them with a rubber mallet. Use a long level to ensure the bricks are flat and flush with adjoining bricks. Make any necessary changes by adding and removing sand, or tapping high bricks deeper into the sand. Finally, pack the joints tightly with sand.

Maintaining Patio Tile

Much like interior tile floors, tiled patios are extremely durable, but they do require periodic maintenance. Accidents happen and although it takes quite an impact to break an outdoor tile, it is possible. Broken tiles or failed grout can expose the subbase to moisture, which will destroy the floor in time.

Major cracks in grout joints indicate that movement of the subbase has caused the adhesive layer beneath the tile to deteriorate. The adhesive layer must be replaced along with the grout in order to create a permanent repair.

Perhaps the biggest challenge with tile repair is matching the grout color. If you're regrouting an entire patio, just select the color that complements the tile; if you're replacing a tile, you have to blend the new grout with the old. A good tile dealer can help you get the best color match.

Any time you remove tile, check the subbase. If it's no longer smooth, solid, and level, repair, re-place, or resurface it before repairing the tile. If the subbase contains cracks, install a liquid-based isolation membrane system—simply apply the liquid adhesive, lay the membrane over the crack, then apply the final coat over the top and allow to dry thoroughly.

Protect unglazed tile from staining and water spots by periodically applying a coat of tile sealer. Keep dirt from getting trapped in grout lines by sealing them every year or two.

> **Everything You Need:**
>
> Tools: Rotary tool, utility knife, or grout saw; hammer; cold chisel; eye protection; small screwdriver; putty knife; sponge; brush; stiff-bristle brush; bucket; rubber grout float
>
> Materials: Grout, rubber gloves, soft cloth, grout sealer, replacement tile (if necessary)

How to Regrout a Tile Patio

1 Completely remove the old grout, using a rotary tool or a grout saw. Spread the new grout over the tiles, using rubber grout float. Force grout into the joints, holding the float almost flat, then drag the float across the joints diagonally, tilting the face at a 45° angle. TIP: Add latex-fortified grout additive so excess grout is easier to remove.

2 Use the grout float to scrape off excess grout from the surface of the tile. Scrape diagonally across the joints, holding the float in a near-vertical position. Patio tile will absorb grout quickly and permanently, so it is important to remove all excess grout from the surface before it sets. NOTE: It's a good idea to have helpers when working on large areas.

3 After grout has dried for about four hours, use a nail to make sure it has hardened. Use a cloth to buff the surface until any remaining grout film is gone. If buffing does not remove all the film, try using a coarser cloth, such as burlap, or even an abrasive pad to remove stubborn stains. Seal the grout after it cures completely.

How to Replace a Patio Tile

1 Remove the grout from around the damaged tile, using a rotary tool, utility knife (and several blades), or a grout saw. Then, carefully break apart the tile, using a cold chisel and hammer.

2 Scrape away the old mortar with a putty knife. Make sure the subbase is smooth and flat.

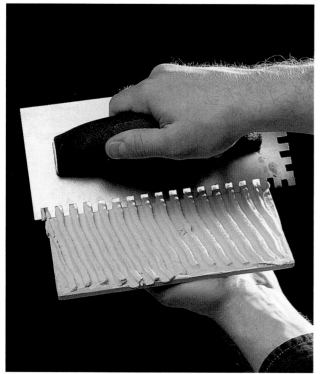

3 Use a notched trowel to cover the entire back of the replacement tile with an even layer of dry-set mortar.

4 Set the tile in place, and press down firmly to create a good bond. If necessary, use a carpet-covered 2 × 4 and a rubber mallet to tap the tile flush with the neighboring tiles.

5 Use a small screwdriver to remove excess mortar that has oozed into the grout joints, then wipe up any mortar from the tile surface. When the mortar has dried completely, grout around the tile.

6 Mix matching grout according to the manufacturer's directions and fill the grout lines, applying the grout with a grout float. Carefully wipe of excess before it dries.

Grout Sealer

Like the tile inside your house, exterior patio tile must be watertight. All the grout lines must be solid, fully packed and free of cracks or chips. Neglecting problems can result in damage to the subbase, and possibly the entire tile job.

Apply grout sealer to grout joints every one to two years to protect against water, wear, and stains. Use a sponge brush to spread the sealer and keep it off the tiles. If you do spill on the tiles, wipe it up immediately. Allow new grout to cure fully before sealing it.

Repairing Stucco

Although stucco siding is very durable, it can be damaged, and over time it can crumble or crack. The directions given below work well for patching small areas less than two sq. ft. For more extensive damage, the repair is done in layers, as shown on the opposite page.

Everything You Need:

Tools: Caulk gun, disposable paintbrush, putty knife, mason's trowel, square-end trowel, hammer, whisk broom, wire brush, masonry chisel, aviation snips, pry bar, drill with masonry bit, scratching tool.

Materials: Metal primer, stucco patching compound, bonding adhesive, denatured alcohol, metal primer, stucco mix, masonry paint, $1\frac{1}{2}$" roofing nails, 15# building paper, self-furring metal lath, masonry caulk, tint, metal stop bead.

Fill thin cracks in stucco walls with masonry caulk. Overfill the crack with caulk, and feather until it's flush with the stucco. Allow the caulk to set, then paint it to match the stucco. Masonry caulk stays semiflexible, preventing further cracking.

How to Patch Small Areas

1 Remove loose material from the repair area, using a wire brush. Use the brush to clean away rust from any exposed metal lath, then apply a coat of metal primer to the lath.

2 Apply premixed stucco repair compound to the repair area, slightly overfilling the hole, using a putty knife or trowel. Read manufacturer's directions, as drying times vary.

3 Smooth the repair with a putty knife or trowel, feathering the edges to blend into the surrounding surface. Use a whisk broom or trowel to duplicate the original texture. Let the patch dry for several days, then touch it up with masonry paint.

How to Repair Large Areas

1 Make a starter hole with a drill and masonry bit, then use a masonry chisel and hammer to chip away stucco in the repair area. NOTE: Wear safety glasses and a particle mask or respirator when cutting stucco. Cut self-furring metal lath to size and attach it to the sheathing, using roofing nails. Overlap pieces by 2". If the patch extends to the base of the wall, attach a metal stop bead at the bottom.

TIP: Premixed stucco works well for small jobs, but for large ones, it's more economical to mix your own.

2 To mix your own stucco, combine three parts sand, two parts portland cement, and one part masonry cement. Add just enough water so the mixture holds its shape when squeezed (INSET). Mix only as much as you can use in one hour.

3 Apply a ⅜"-thick layer of stucco directly to the metal lath. Push the stucco into the mesh until it fills the gap between the mesh and the sheathing. Score horizontal grooves into the wet surface, using a scratching tool. Let the stucco dry for two days, misting it with water every two to four hours.

4 Apply a second, smooth layer of stucco. Build up the stucco to within ¼" of the original surface. Let the patch dry for two days, misting every two to four hours.

5 Combine finish-coat stucco mix with just enough water for the mixture to hold its shape. Dampen the patch area, then apply the finish coat to match the original surface. Dampen the patch periodically for a week. Let it dry for several more days before painting.

Repairing Stonework

Damage to stonework is typically caused by frost heave, erosion or deterioration of mortar, or by stones that have worked out of place. Dry-stone walls are more susceptible to erosion and popping, while mortared walls develop cracks that admit water, which can freeze and cause further damage.

Inspect stone structures once a year for signs of damage and deterioration. Replacing a stone or repointing crumbling mortar now will save you work in the long run.

A leaning stone column or wall probably suffers from erosion or foundation problems, and can be dangerous if neglected. If you have the time, you can tear down and rebuild dry-laid structures, but mortared structures with excessive lean need professional help.

Everything You Need:

Tools: Maul, chisel, camera, shovel, hand tamper, level, batter gauge, stiff-bristle brush, trowels for mixing and pointing, mortar bag, masonry chisels.

Materials: Wood shims, carpet-covered 2 × 4, chalk, compactible gravel, replacement stones, type M mortar, mortar tint.

Stones in a wall can become dislodged due to soil settling, erosion, or seasonal freeze-thaw cycles. Make the necessary repairs before the problem migrates to other areas.

Tips for Replacing Popped Stones

Return a popped stone to its original position. If other stones have settled in its place, drive shims between neighboring stones to make room for the popped stone. Be careful not to wedge too far.

Use a 2 × 4 covered with carpet to avoid damaging the stone when hammering it into place. After hammering, make sure a replacement stone hasn't damaged or dislodged the adjoining stones.

How to Rebuild a Dry-stone Wall Section

1 Before you start, study the wall and determine how much of it needs to be rebuilt. Plan to dismantle the wall in a "V" shape, centered on the damaged section. Number each stone and mark its orientation with chalk so you can rebuild it following the original design. TIP: Photograph the wall, making sure the markings are visible.

2 Capstones are often set in a mortar bed atop the last course of stone. You may need to chip out the mortar with a maul and chisel to remove the capstones. Remove the marked stones, taking care to check the overall stability of the wall as you work.

3 Rebuild the wall, one course at a time, using replacement stones only when necessary. Start each course at the ends and work toward the center. On thick walls, set the face stones first, then fill in the center with smaller stones. Check your work with a level, and use a batter gauge to maintain the batter of the wall. If your capstones were mortared, re-lay them in fresh mortar. Wash off the chalk with water and a stiff-bristle brush.

TIP: If you're rebuilding because of erosion, dig a trench at least 6" deep under the damaged area, and fill it with compactible gravel. Tamp the gravel with a hand tamper. This will improve drainage and prevent water from washing soil out from beneath the wall.

Tips for Repairing Mortared Stone Walls

Tint mortar for repair work so it blends with the existing mortar. Mix several samples of mortar, adding a different amount of tint to each, and allow them to dry thoroughly. Compare each sample to the old mortar, and choose the closest match.

Use a mortar bag to restore weathered and damaged mortar joints over an entire structure. Remove loose mortar (see below) and clean all surfaces with a stiff-bristle brush and water. Dampen the joints before tuck-pointing, and cover all of the joints, smoothing and brushing as necessary.

How to Repoint Mortar Joints

1 Carefully rake out cracked and crumbling mortar, stopping when you reach solid mortar. Remove loose mortar and debris with a stiff-bristle brush. TIP: Rake the joints with a chisel and maul, or make your own raking tool by placing an old screwdriver in a vice and bending the shaft about 45°.

2 Mix type M mortar, then dampen the repair surfaces with clean water. Working from the top down, pack mortar into the crevices, using a pointing trowel. Smooth the mortar when it has set up enough to resist light finger pressure. Remove excess mortar with a stiff-bristle brush.

How to Replace a Stone in a Mortared Wall

1 Remove the damaged stone by chiseling out the surrounding mortar, using a masonry chisel or a modified screwdriver (opposite page). Drive the chisel toward the damaged stone to avoid harming neighboring stones. Once the stone is out, chisel the surfaces inside the cavity as smooth as possible.

2 Brush out the cavity to remove loose mortar and debris. Test the surrounding mortar, and chisel or scrape out any mortar that isn't firmly bonded.

3 Dry-fit the replacement stone. The stone should be stable in the cavity and blend with the rest of the wall. You can mark the stone with chalk and cut it to fit (page 211), but excessive cutting will result in a conspicuous repair.

4 Mist the stone and cavity lightly, then apply type M mortar around the inside of the cavity, using a trowel. Butter all mating sides of the replacement stone. Insert the stone and wiggle it forcefully to remove any air pockets. Use a pointing trowel to pack the mortar solidly around the stone. Smooth the mortar when it has set up.

Pressure Washing Masonry & Stonework

To clean the masonry and stonework surfaces around the outside of your home, there is nothing that works faster or more effectively than a pressure washer. A typical residential-grade unit can be as much as 50 times more powerful than a standard garden hose, while using up to 80% less water.

A pressure washer comprises an engine to generate power, a pump to force water supplied from a garden hose through a high-pressure hose, and a nozzle to accelerate the water stream leaving the system. This results in a high-pressure water jet ranging from 500 to 4000 PSI (pounds per square inch).

But PSI only does not account for a pressure washers cleaning power. Gallons per minute (GPM) dictates the spray's ability to rinse away loosened dirt and grime from the area; a pressure washer with a higher GPM cleans faster than a lower-flow unit. For general cleaning around your outdoor home, a pressure washer around 2500 PSI and 2.5 GPM is more than sufficient.

Pressure washing is quite simple: firmly grasp the spray wand with both hands, depress the trigger and move the nozzle across the surface to be cleaned. Although different surfaces require different spray patterns and pressure settings, it is not difficult to determine the appropriate cleaning approach for each project. The nozzle is adjustable—from a low-pressure, wide-fan spray for general cleaning and rinsing, to a narrow, intense stream for stubborn stains. But the easiest way to control the cleaning is to simply adjust the distance between the nozzle and the surface—move the nozzle back to reduce the pressure; move the nozzle closer to intensify it.

To successfully clean any masonry or stone surface using a pressure washer, follow these tips:

- When cleaning a new surface, start in an inconspicuous area, with a wide spray pattern and the nozzle 4- to 5-ft. from the surface. Move closer to the surface until the desired effect is achieved.

- Keep the nozzle in constant motion, spraying at a steady speed with long, even strokes to ensure consistent results.

- Maintain a consistent distance between the nozzle and the cleaning surface.

- When cleaning heavily soiled or stained surfaces, use cleaning detergents formulated for pressure washers. Always rinse the surface before applying the detergent. On vertical surfaces, apply detergent from bottom to top, and rinse from top to bottom. Always follow the detergent manufacturer's directions.

- After pressure washing, always seal the surface with an appropriate surface sealer (e.g., concrete sealer for cement driveways), following the product manufacturer's instructions.

Pressure Washer Safety

- Always wear eye protection.
- Do not wear open-toed shoes.
- Make sure the unit is on a stable surface and the cleaning area has adequate slopes and drainage to prevent puddles.
- Assume a solid stance, and firmly grasp the spray gun with both hands to avoid injury if the gun kicks back.
- Always keep the high-pressure hose connected to both the pump and the spray gun while the system is pressurized.
- Never aim the nozzle at people or animals—the high-pressure stream of water can cause serious injury.

Tips for Pressure Washing Masonry & Stonework

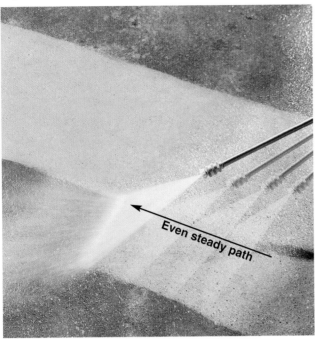

Always keep the nozzle in motion, spraying at a steady speed and using long, even strokes. Take multiple passes over heavily soiled areas. Take care not to dwell on one spot for too long, especially when using narrow, high-pressure spray patterns.

Hold the spray wand so that the nozzle distributes the spray pattern across the surface evenly. Holding the nozzle at too low an angle can cause an uneven spray pattern, resulting in "zebra striping." Also, maintain a consistent distance between the nozzle and the cleaning surface to ensure consistent results and help flush dirt and debris from the area.

Work in identifiable sections, such as the area between the expansion joints in concrete. If there is a slope, work downhill to promote drainage and help flush away dirt and debris. Wet entire surface to prevent streaking.

To prevent streaks on vertical surfaces, always begin pressure washing or applying cleaning detergent at the bottom of the surface, then work upward. When rinsing, start at the top and work downward—gravity will help the clean water flush away dirt, debris, and detergent residue.

Glossary

Adobe — sun-dried clay bricks commonly used in the southwestern United States.

Aggregate — materials such as sand, gravel, and crushed stone used to add strength to concrete and mortar, or to add traction to concrete surfaces.

Air entrainment — the addition of ingredients that cause bubbles to form in wet concrete and mortar, improving workability and frost resistance.

Ashlar — symmetrical stones typically used to lay up walls, pillars, and other vertical structures; also used to refer to patterns that rely on the use of ashlar stone.

Backfill — soil or rubble used as fill behind masonry construction.

Batter — a receding upward slope of the outer face of a wall or other structure; also called batter rate.

Batter gauge — a wooden device (typically homemade) used for gauging the slope of the sides of a vertical structure (see also *Batter).

Bed joint — a horizontal joint in a masonry structure.

Bituminous felt — fiber strips saturated with asphalt; used to form expansion joints in a concrete slab for a patio, sidewalk, or driveway.

Bleed water — a thin layer of water that appears on some concrete mixtures after placement and must be permitted to dry before the concrete is worked.

Bonding agent — a coating designed to facilitate bonding between mortar and an existing surface.

Building paper — asphalt-impregnated paper used as a vapor barrier between wood or other sheathing and an outer surface, such as brick or stone veneer.

Bull float — a large, flat tool made of aluminum, magnesium, or wood; used for smoothing large slabs of freshly poured concrete.

Buttering — the process of using a trowel to place a contoured layer of mortar on a brick or other masonry unit before placement.

Capstone — the top stone or row of stones on a wall, pillar, or other vertical structure.

Cement — (see *Portland cement).

Cobblestone — small cuts of quarried stone or fieldstone; often used in walks and paths.

Concrete — a combination of sand and gravel or crushed stone, held together by cement and water.

Construction joint — a contoured edge added to a portion of a concrete slab, designed to facilitate bonding when a pour must be interrupted.

Control joint — a joint in a concrete slab created by a control jointer or similar tool; designed to regulate cracking.

Darby — a long tool used for leveling and smoothing freshly poured concrete.

Dressing — the process of removing sharp points or protuberances on the exposed face of a stone, using a stone chisel and maul.

Dry mix — any packaged mix (typically sold in bags) that can be combined with water to form concrete, mortar, stucco, or masonry repair material.

Edger — a hand tool used for producing smooth edges on concrete slabs.

Efflorescence — deposits of salts that form after rising to the surface on masonry surfaces.

Expansion joint — also known as an isolation joint; a strip of bituminous felt separating sections of a concrete slab, or between new and old concrete; designed to allow for independent movement during freeze-thaw cycles.

Face — the exposed surface of a stone in masonry construction.

Field brick — one of multiple bricks that form the interior area of a wall, patio, driveway, or other surface.

Fieldstone — a type of stone typically collected from fields, riverbeds, or hillsides, often weather-worn in appearance; used with minor trimming in masonry construction; often used to refer to cobblestones or boulders with a similar appearance.

Finishing — the final texturing steps in masonry work, including leveling, edging, and smoothing joints.

Fire brick — a brick made with heat-resistant *fire clay* for use in fireplaces, chimneys, barbecues, and other high heat applications.

Fireclay mortar — any mortar to which fireclay has been added; now widely substituted with *refractory mortar,* which is less apt to disintegrate when exposed to high temperatures.

Flagstone — quarried stone cut into slabs usually less than 3 in. thick; used in walks, steps, and patios. Pieces smaller than 16" sq. are often called steppers.

Float — a metal or wood tool used on freshly poured concrete to produce a smooth and level surface (known as *floating).

Floating — the technique of using a *float* to smooth and level freshly poured concrete.

Footing — a below-grade poured-concrete structure designed to support masonry and resist shifting.

Form — a wood or metal frame used for establishing the borders of a masonry project (usually poured concrete) and for containing the concrete as it is poured.

Freeze-thaw cycles — seasonal temperature changes that result in shifting of masonry and other structures.

Frost heave — damage to concrete and other paving materials due to ground temperature changes (see also *Freeze-thaw cycles*).

Groover — a tool used for cutting control joints in concrete and other masonry surfaces.

Kerf — one of a series of narrow cuts in a piece of lumber, allowing it to be bent to create a curved construction form.

Key — a concave or contoured surface in freshly poured concrete designed to create a mechanical bond with subsequent layers or batches of concrete.

Landscape fabric — fabric used to contain soil and other loose materials, while allowing water to penetrate; also a barrier to plant growth.

Load-bearing — supporting substantial weight or resisting pressures from *backfill.*

Masonry unit — a brick, paver, block, or stone designed for use in masonry construction.

Mortar — a masonry mixture, usually containing *portland cement* and sand, that is applied with a trowel and hardens to form a bond between masonry units.

Mortar box — a wooden or plastic box used for mixing mortar for masonry projects.

Mortar hawk — a hand-held board used to hold small quantities of mortar during brick or block construction projects.

Mudjacking — the process of pumping fresh concrete under a slab or other structure that has shifted due to frost heave, soil set-tling, erosion, or other factors.

Parging — the technique of applying a layer of mortar to the backs of stones or other veneer materials to maximize contact with the bonding surface.

Plumb — standing perfectly vertical.

Plumb bob — a device, typically consisting of a pointed weight on the end of a string, used for determining that a surface is *plumb.*

Pointing (see *Tuck-pointing*).

Polyethylene — a type of plastic used in rolled sheeting (typically 4 to 6 mils thick) and used as a vapor barrier under slabs and in other masonry applications.

Portland cement — a combination of silica, lime, iron, and alumina that has been heated, cooled, and pulverized to form a fine powder from which concrete, mortar, and other masonry products are made.

PVC — rigid plastic (polyvinyl chloride) material that is highly resistant to heat and chemicals. PVC pipes are sometimes used to maintain spacing between masonry units.

Refractory mortar — a masonry mortar capable of withstanding exposure to high temperatures; used in high heat areas, such as fireplaces, chimneys, and barbecues.

Release agent — a substance applied to forms to prevent poured concrete from bonding with forms as the concrete hardens.

Rowlock — a header brick or other masonry unit laid on edge.

Rubble — irregular pieces of quarried stone, usually with one split or finished face, that are widely used in wall construction; called *rip-rap* when used as irregular fill.

Screed board — also known as a screed; a tool used for *screeding.*

Screeding — the technique of spreading soil, sand, crushed stone, fresh concrete, or other materials evenly across a project site to form a smooth, level surface.

Story pole — a pole or board marked at equal intervals to indicate the positioning of individual masonry units and to gauge mortar joint thickness.

Stucco — a smooth masonry mortar, also called *portland cement plaster;* used to create a weather-resistant barrier over metal lath or masonry surfaces.

Surface bonding cement — a smooth water-resistant masonry mortar designed for use as a coating over brick or concrete block walls for cosmetic, structural, or damp-proofing purposes.

Tie stone — a long stone in a wall or other structure, used to add strength by spanning the width of the structure.

Tuck-pointing — Also called *pointing;* the technique of finishing or repairing mortar joints by adding stiff mortar once the initial batch has dried. In repair projects, loose mortar is first removed to provide a solid surface to which fresh mortar can bond.

Veneer — a material, such as brick or natural or manufactured stone, that is applied to exterior or freestanding walls for cosmetic purposes.

Wall tie — a corrugated metal tie used to link adjacent masonry units or wythes in a structure; also used to secure veneer materials to walls.

Weep-hole — a hole, usually located at the base of a masonry structure to provide drainage for water behind the structure.

Wythe — A section of a wall that is the width of one masonry unit.

Converting Measurements

To Convert:	To:	Multiply by:
Inches	Millimeters	25.4
Inches	Centimeters	2.54
Feet	Meters	0.305
Yards	Meters	0.914
Square inches	Square centimeters	6.45
Square feet	Square meters	0.093
Square yards	Square meters	0.836
Cubic inches	Cubic centimeters	16.4
Cubic feet	Cubic meters	0.0283
Cubic yards	Cubic meters	0.765
Ounces	Milliliters	30.0
Pints (U.S.)	Liters	0.473 (Imp. 0.568)
Quarts (U.S.)	Liters	0.946 (Imp. 1.136)
Gallons (U.S.)	Liters	3.785 (Imp. 4.546)
Ounces	Grams	28.4
Pounds	Kilograms	0.454

To Convert:	To:	Multiply by:
Millimeters	Inches	0.039
Centimeters	Inches	0.394
Meters	Feet	3.28
Meters	Yards	1.09
Square centimeters	Square inches	0.155
Square meters	Square feet	10.8
Square meters	Square yards	1.2
Cubic centimeters	Cubic inches	0.061
Cubic meters	Cubic feet	35.3
Cubic meters	Cubic yards	1.31
Milliliters	Ounces	.033
Liters	Pints (U.S.)	2.114 (Imp. 1.76)
Liters	Quarts (U.S.)	1.057 (Imp. 0.88)
Liters	Gallons (U.S.)	0.264 (Imp. 0.22)
Grams	Ounces	0.035
Kilograms	Pounds	2.2

Lumber Dimensions

Nominal - U.S.	Actual - U.S.	METRIC
1 × 2	¾ × 1½"	19 × 38 mm
1 × 3	¾ × 2½"	19 × 64 mm
1 × 4	¾ × 3½"	19 × 89 mm
1 × 5	¾ × 4½"	19 × 114 mm
1 × 6	¾ × 5½"	19 × 140 mm
1 × 7	¾ × 6¼"	19 × 159 mm
1 × 8	¾ × 7¼"	19 × 184 mm
1 × 10	¾ × 9¼"	19 × 235 mm
1 × 12	¾ × 11¼"	19 × 286 mm
1¼ × 4	1 × 3½"	25 × 89 mm
1¼ × 6	1 × 5½"	25 × 140 mm
1¼ × 8	1 × 7¼"	25 × 184 mm
1¼ × 10	1 × 9¼"	25 × 235 mm
1¼ × 12	1 × 11¼"	25 × 286 mm
1½ × 4	1¼ × 3½"	32 × 89 mm
1½ × 6	1¼ × 5½"	32 × 140 mm
1½ × 8	1¼ × 7¼"	32 × 184 mm
1½ × 10	1¼ × 9¼"	32 × 235 mm
1½ × 12	1¼ × 11¼"	32 × 286 mm
2 × 4	1½ × 3½"	38 × 89 mm
2 × 6	1½ × 5½"	38 × 140 mm
2 × 8	1½ × 7¼"	38 × 184 mm
2 × 10	1½ × 9¼"	38 × 235 mm
2 × 12	1½ × 11¼"	38 × 286 mm
3 × 6	2½ × 5½"	64 × 140 mm
4 × 4	3½ × 3½"	89 × 89 mm
4 × 6	3½ × 5½"	89 × 140 mm

Liquid Measurement Equivalents

1 Pint	= 16 Fluid Ounces	= 2 Cups
1 Quart	= 32 Fluid Ounces	= 2 Pints
1 Gallon	= 128 Fluid Ounces	= 4 Quarts

Converting Temperatures

Convert degrees Fahrenheit (F) to degrees Celsius (C) by following this simple formula: Subtract 32 from the Fahrenheit temperature reading. Then, multiply that number by 5/9. For example, 77°F - 32 = 45. 45 × 5/9 = 25°C.

To convert degrees Celsius to degrees Fahrenheit, multiply the Celsius temperature reading by 9/5. Then, add 32. For example, 25°C × 9/5 = 45. 45 + 32 = 77°F.

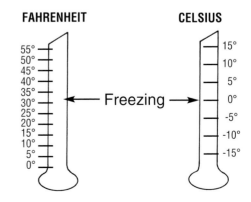

Contributors

Anchor Wall Systems pages 6 (bottom), 222
877-295-5415
www.anchorwall.com

Belgard Pavers pages 9 (top), 10 (both), 173 (both)
800-899-8455
www.belgardpavers.com

Cultured Stone Corporation pages 169, 179 (top right), 184
800-255-1727
www.culturedstone.com

Kemiko Concrete Floor Stain pages 73 (top), 154
903-587-3708
www.kemiko.com

La Habra Stucco pages 6 (top), 168
877-547-8822
www.lahabrastucco.com

NovaBrik page 188
866-678-BRIK (2745)
www.novabrik.com

Vermont Castings page 172
800-525-1898
www.vermontcastings.com

Photographers

Derek Fell's Horticultural Library: p. 6 (bottom).

John Gregor/ColdSnap Photography: p. 4.

Karen Melvin: p. 8 (top).

Jerry Pavia: p. 7 (top).

The Photolibrary Group, Ltd./The Garden Picture Library-Botanica: pp. 7 (center), 8 (bottom), 9 (bottom right), 11 (bottom).

The Photolibrary Group, Ltd./The Garden Picture Library-Andrew Lord: p. 9 (bottom left)

The Photolibrary Group, Ltd./The Garden Picture Library-Allan Pollok-Morris: p. 11 (top left)

The Photolibrary Group, Ltd./The Garden Picture Library-Brigitte & Philippe Perdereau: p. 11 (top right)

The Photolibrary Group, Ltd./The Garden Picture Library-Janet Seaton: p. 14.

The Photolibrary Group, Ltd./The Garden Picture Library-Juliette Wade: p. 100.

Index

(continued next page)

(continued next page)

CREATIVE PUBLISHING
INTERNATIONAL

Complete Guide to Bathrooms
Complete Guide to Ceramic & Stone Tile
Complete Guide to Creative Landscapes
Complete Guide to Decks
Complete Guide to Easy Woodworking Projects
Complete Guide to Finishing Walls & Ceilings
Complete Guide to Flooring
Complete Guide to Home Carpentry
Complete Guide to Home Plumbing
Complete Guide to Home Wiring
Complete Guide to Kitchens
Complete Guide to Landscape Construction
Complete Guide to Masonry & Stonework
Complete Guide to Outdoor Wood Projects
Complete Guide to Painting & Decorating
Complete Guide to Roofing & Siding
Complete Guide to Trim & Finish Carpentry
Complete Guide to Windows & Doors
Complete Guide to Wood Storage Projects
Complete Guide to Yard & Garden Features
Complete Outdoor Builder
Complete Photo Guide to Home Repair
Complete Photo Guide to Home Improvement

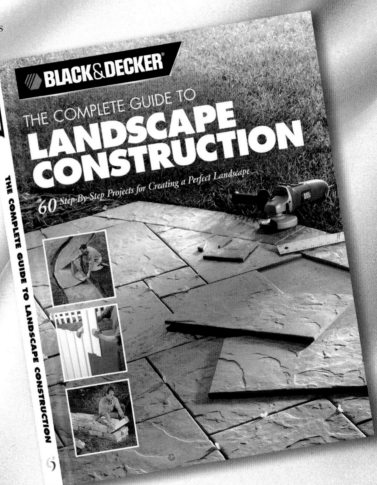

ISBN 1-58923-245-3

CREATIVE PUBLISHING INTERNATIONAL

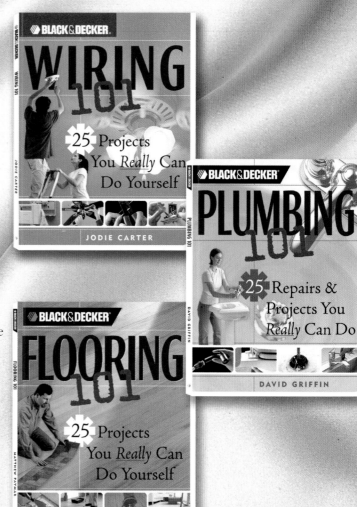